1-20

D1392394

Collins New Advanced History Series

The Economy 1815-1914

Trevor May

Collins London and Glasgow

General Editors
K H Randell. J W Hunt

© Trevor May 1972

Printed in Great Britain
Collins Clear-Type Press
Set in Monotype Plantin

ISBN 0 00 327214 1

Cover illustration:

Contents

Editors' foreword

The series of which this book is a part is designed to meet the needs of students in Six Forms and those taking courses in further and higher education. In assessing these needs two factors especially have been taken into account: the limits on the students' time which preclude the reading of all the important scholarly works, and the importance of providing stimulus to thought and imagination. Therefore the series, which has considerably more space available than even the larger single-volume textbooks on the period, presents the interpretations which have altered or increased our understanding of the age, as well as including sufficient detail to illustrate and enliven the subject. Most important of all, emphasis has been placed on discussion. Instead of outlining supposedly established facts, problems are posed as they were faced by the people of the time and as they confront the historian today in his task of interpretation. The student is thus enabled to approach the subject in an attitude of inquiry, and is encouraged to exercise his own mind on the arguments, never closed, of historiography. In so doing he will gain some knowledge of the methods of historians and of the kinds of evidence they use. He should also find enjoyment by the way.

The arrangement of the series, with several volumes covering particular aspects over a long period, and others with more strict chronological limits, has enabled each author to concentrate on an area of special interest, and should make for flexibility in use by the reader.

K.H.R.
J.W.H.

Full details of historical works referred to in the text will be found in the list of Further Reading on page 213. Only where the work is not included is a full reference given in the text.

Chapter I

The Industrial Revolution to 1815

1 The visible signs of progress Four months before the Battle of Waterloo a Prussian factory commissioner, Johann Georg May, reported to his superiors in Berlin. He had just returned from an official visit to Britain, charged with investigating the state of manufactures, but had found three months too short a time to do justice to his task. 'Anyone who wishes to make proper use of a journey to England', he said, 'should be prepared to stay there for a few years. In this land of efficiency there is a superfluity of interesting things to be seen. There is something new to catch the eye in every step that one takes. Even somebody who lives permanently in England would hardly be in a position to see and describe everything of note.'

Johann May was by no means the only foreign traveller in England eager to discover some of the secrets of her industrial advance, for the collapse of Napoleon's Empire in 1814 opened up Britain to visitors for the first time in twelve years. In the same months that May was here Hans Casper Escher, a Swiss industrialist, was also touring the industrial towns and was equally amazed by what he saw. He marvelled that in a single street in Manchester were more cotton spindles than in the whole of Switzerland. In a fifteen-minute walk he counted over sixty spinning mills, and he felt that he might have arrived in Egypt, 'since so many factory chimneys—required because steam engines are used—stretch upwards towards the sky like great obelisks'.

The accounts which these travellers kept are full of descriptions of colliery railways, iron-framed buildings, gas lighting, steam-heated factories and powered machinery. Steam engines were everywhere to be seen and were, thought May, evidence of England's inventive powers, great wealth and high level of culture. The travellers noted that they were even used for minor purposes; in London some of the pharmacists used steam engines, while a butcher had one for making sausages. Escher expressed shock upon seeing a mechanical crane used to load bales of cotton on to a cart and observed that 'human beings and animals . . . are not made to work as hard as they might be'.

Steam engines need coal—and coal, Escher felt, was the key to our industrial progress. 'Next to its constitution', he wrote, 'England owes its prosperity very largely to its coal deposits. Without its coal England would not have one thousandth of the factories that she now possesses.' Yet in 1787, less than thirty years before, a Frenchman, composing a guide-book for visitors to England, could still say: 'What are the sources of England's power? Maritime commerce and farming; the latter in particular is better understood there than elsewhere, and in general practised upon different principles.' Now, Dr Hobsbawm has warned that 'what the contemporary observer sees is not necessarily the truth, but the historian neglects it at his peril'. Of course, what the contemporary observer sees is dependent upon where he happens to be. The French writer concentrated his attention on the south of England while Escher and May spent more time in the Midlands and the North—in towns like Manchester, the smoke from whose chimneys formed 'a great cloud' which May said could be seen for miles around. It was here that the changes were to be seen; in the last thirty years of the eighteenth century Manchester appears to have grown faster than any other English town, with a population estimated to have more than trebled between 1773 and 1801.

The period was clearly one of rapid advance, with progress fast catching up on prophecy. In 1792 Erasmus Darwin made his oft-quoted prediction:

Soon shall thy arm, UNCONQUERED STEAM! afar

Drag the slow barge, or drive the rapid car . . .

Steam was sufficiently conquered by 1814 for Escher and May

to report the fulfilment of both of these prophecies. Indeed, the steamboats which Escher saw on the Clyde were far from slow, for their paddles propelled them forwards at 'a rapid pace' and they plied 'as regularly as stage coaches on the roads'.

Amongst the many changes at this time those in the field of technology have perhaps received more attention than others. Such technical and mechanical advances caught the imagination of contemporaries and have a similar appeal to us; the tendency is therefore understandable. To the historian, however, it may be misleading. The whole fabric of the economy and society was in progress of transformation, and more than technology—or even industry—was revolutionised by the 'Industrial Revolution'. No examination of the nineteenth-century economy could be complete without an understanding of the forces which were at work to produce this change.

2 The historian's changing interest So complex is the Industrial Revolution that it is helpful to trace the development of the concept and the historian's interest in it. The term itself appears to have been coined by the French economist, Blanqui, who in 1837 claimed that since the late eighteenth century, Britain had experienced economic changes affecting her national life as fundamental as the political changes which had changed the face of France in 1789. The idea was developed by Marx, although the term came into general use only after the publication of Toynbee's *Lectures on the Industrial Revolution* in 1884. Together with other early writers on the subject he was conscious of the social injustice which existed in his own day, and consequently concentrated on the 'social costs' of the Industrial Revolution. This emphasis is to be seen particularly in the works of J.L. and Barbara Hammond—*The Village Labourer* (1912), *The Town Labourer* (1918), and *The Skilled Labourer* (1919). The questions to which these authors drew attention remain important and controversial and are considered in the next chapter.

The changes were seen by the early historians in a dramatic light and were boldly painted in black and white. This is forcefully illustrated by Beard, who in 1901 wrote:

England of the first part of the eighteenth century was virtually a mediae-
val England, quiet, primeval, and undisturbed by the roar of trade and
commerce. Suddenly, almost like a thunderbolt from a clear sky were
ushered in the storm and stress of the Industrial Revolution. (Quoted in
Flinn, 1966, page 3.)

Yet shortly afterwards Paul Mantoux, in his book *The Industrial Revolution in the Eighteenth Century*, began to place the revolutionary changes of the second half of the eighteenth century in their evolutionary background—a synthesis which was pushed further by T. S. Ashton in 1948 when he published *The Industrial Revolution, 1760-1830*. Ashton began to show key factors in the mechanism of economic growth, placing great emphasis on the role of the industrialist as well as the inventor, and showing the significance of non-economic developments such as the part played by Dissenters.

There was an increasingly close relationship between the work of historians and economists, for although it had long been seen that economic theory could help in the understanding of history, it now became apparent that the historian might have a contribution to make to the solution of economic problems. Of these, a major one facing the nations of the world after the Second World War was that of economic development. With only a small minority of the world's population having experienced an industrial revolution, economists were in eager pursuit of a formula for rapid economic development which would enable them to construct a 'growth model', and might act as a blueprint for positive action. The study of the first industrial revolution—that of Britain—therefore became of immediate relevance, and emphasis shifted away from social costs to an examination of origins.

In 1956 the American economist, W. W. Rostow, introduced a theory which has stimulated much thought and not a little criticism. He coined the phrase 'the take-off into self-sustained growth', pursuing the analogy of an aircraft taking off from the ground. He implied that a certain rate of growth would sustain itself, just as an aircraft, having gained sufficient speed to leave the ground can, so long as it maintains that speed, keep flying. This 'take-off' required certain conditions, two major ones being a rise in the rate of productive investment from, say, 5 per cent or less to over 10 per cent of the national income, and the development of one or more substantial industries ('leading sectors') with a high rate of growth to act as pace-makers. Criticism of Rostow has centred both on his general theory and his interpretation of the British experience. Thus it has been shown, for example, that the level of investment did not in fact reach 10 per cent of the national income until the 1840s, when there were heavy demands for railway building, by which time the Industrial Revolution was in an advanced stage. However, Rostow drew the attention of historians to new questions and showed how quantitative techniques might be used to find the answers. This statistical approach is exemplified by Phyllis Deane and W. A. Cole in their *British Economic Growth 1688-1959*, first published in 1962. Their method was to collect together every available statistic relating to economic development, particularly those of trade and population, which are available in great quantity, and to draw from them only those conclusions which the statistical facts permit. This approach is one which has many attractions although it has many dangers. The availability of the statistical evidence is a major problem. The first census was not taken until 1801; there are no official figures for coal output until 1854; no detailed agricultural statistics until 1866; nor adequate figures for unemployment before 1921. Even where figures are available doubt often exists as to their reliability, such doubt increasing as the period under investigation is pushed back. The statistical approach has another drawback in that it raises the temptation to push non-measurable factors into the background. If one accepts that the changes which occurred in the late eighteenth and early nineteenth centuries covered a large sweep of economic and social life, and are reflected as much as anything in a change of attitude, then the danger becomes acute. Similarly one might miss factors conducive to growth which are not open to statistical verification.

3 The debate on origins Present research on the origins and course of the Industrial Revolution still leaves certain issues in a state of controversy. The wrangle between those who favour an 'evolutionary' interpretation and those who prefer a 'revolutionary' one is perhaps of less importance, as the two schools of thought are seen to be not incompatible. The Industrial Revolution is now accepted as the culmination of centuries of economic growth, but there is still debate about the date at which the economy took the upswing. For a considerable time 1760 has been hallowed in the textbooks. Professor Ashton has pointed out that as the Carron ironworks lit its first furnace on 1 January of that year those who like to be really precise can date the Industrial Revolution in Scotland from then! In fact he sees the upswing occurring in the 1780s:

After 1782 almost every statistical series of production shows a sharp upward turn. More than half the growth in the shipments of coal and the mining of copper, more than three-quarters of the increase in broadcloths, four-fifths of that of printed cloth, and nine-tenths of the exports of cotton goods were concentrated in the last eighteen years of the century. (Ashton, 1959, page 125.)

Deane and Cole, on the other hand, push the turning point back to the 1740s. With claimants differing by as much as forty years, it has been observed that not only is the turning point difficult to locate, but also that its very existence must be doubted.

Controversy continues on issues raised by Rostow; whether for example, industrial growth proceeds by definable stages, and whether it proceeds from a broad base covering the whole economy or by way of leading sectors. The latter issue is clearly one which has to be faced by governments of developing countries today who wish to stimulate economic growth. Elements of both can be seen. Thus, changes in social attitudes and habits—the influence of Dissent, for example—affected the whole economy. On the other hand some industries, notably cotton, were quite definitely expanding at a faster rate than the economy as a whole and produced bottle-necks which demanded a solution.

The factors which led to the Industrial Revolution were diverse; yet although mono-causal explanations are less rigidly held, different historians still tend to stress the importance of particular issues. Ashton emphasises the importance of the rate of interest to capital formation, while Hobsbawm stresses the expansion of overseas trade. On the other hand David Landes has borrowed a metaphor from nuclear physics and has spoken of a 'critical mass', a piling up of various factors which triggered off a chain reaction. Before we see how far such a chain reaction might have proceeded by 1815 we must examine some of the factors involved.

4 Population   There is general agreement on the broad trends of Britain's population growth. The first (defective) census of 1801 showed numbers to be around 9 million for England and Wales, and 1½ million for Scotland. Gregory King's calculation of the population of England and Wales in 1688—accepted as a reasonable estimate—had shown 5½ million. Numbers had thus nearly doubled in little more than a century. The population of England and Wales had risen to 18 million by 1851; that of Scotland to 3 million—a twofold expansion in half a century. By 1901 the population of Great Britain had grown to 37 million (32½ million in England and Wales, and 4½ million in Scotland).

There is also a consensus of agreement on the trend in rates of growth. In England and Wales growth was negligible for the century prior to the 1740s. From 1741-81 numbers rose from 4 to 7 per cent per decade, while the rate from 1781 right through to 1911 remained at over 10 per cent per decade, the peak being between 1811 and 1821, when the decennial increase was 17 per cent. Great as this rate of increase was, it is not staggering by contemporary standards. In 1965 the population of Latin America, the fastest-growing continent, was increasing at not far short of double the rate of British growth in the last quarter of the eighteenth century.

Just as significant as the increase in total numbers is the difference in regional rates of growth, with counties such as Lancashire, the West Riding of Yorkshire, Warwickshire and Staffordshire growing appreciably, while the agricultural counties of the south remained stagnant. Between 1781 and 1801 the industrial and commercial counties grew by 31-34 per cent, as against 25-28 per cent in the previous thirty years, while in the agricultural counties the increase fell from 19-21 per cent in the period 1751-81 to only 10-12 per cent between 1781 and 1801.

Nor was this growth in the industrial regions to be explained entirely by migration. Natural increase appears to have been a major cause, with economic conditions favouring greater fertility in the north.

Certain questions are still a matter of debate. Thus, although population growth and economic development often go hand in hand, the exact nature of the link is complex and capable of different interpretations. That the two need not necessarily go together is apparent from Irish experience, while rapid population increase unaccompanied by industrialisation presents the contemporary world with one of its major problems. There is also disagreement over the causes of this increase in population. It is easy to see why this should be so for the issue is one which arises from the inadequacy of evidence. The significant changes occurred before the first census was taken, and we are thus forced to rely on estimates taken from parish registers of baptisms, marriages and burials, or other equally difficult sources.

The question is not only perplexing to historians; it was also a matter of controversy to contemporaries. Throughout the whole of the eighteenth century the accepted theory was that the population was decreasing, and various reasons were advanced why this should have been so. However, the quickening pace of economic activity in the last quarter of the century caused the opposite view to be put forward and led to a lively debate between 1770 and 1780. Arthur Young believed in the evidence which he perceived with his eyes rather than that obtained from figures:

View the navigation, the roads, the harbours, and all other public works. Take notice of the spirit with which manufactures are carried on . . . Move your eye on which side you will, you behold nothing but great riches and yet greater resources. . . . It is vain to talk of tables of birth and lists of houses and windows, as proofs of our loss of people: the flourishing state of our agriculture, our manufactures, and commerce, with our great wealth, prove the contrary. (Quoted in Mantoux, 1928, pages 344-5.)

After the optimism of Young a note of pessimism was sounded by Thomas Malthus, whose influential book *An Essay on the Principle of Population* was published in 1798. He agreed that the population was increasing; indeed, his fear was one of over-population, with the country doomed to pauperism. His theory of population was claimed to be of general application, and stated that population, increasing by geometric progression, always tends to outrun the means of subsistence, which progresses arithmetically. Although few of the facts upon which he built his theory were taken from Britain, the circumstances in which Malthus found himself must inevitably have helped to mould his ideas. The industrial towns were expanding and the class of factory workers was emerging. At the same time the country was going through a serious crisis, with a succession of bad harvests, accompanied by war at sea, pushing prices up to famine level in 1795-6. An increase in destitution occurred which is reflected in the growth of the poor rate, from £2 million in 1785 to £4 million in 1801. Malthus stressed the part played by a rising birth rate, but although his views were of great influence in the nineteenth century they are no longer held so dogmatically.

Only three factors can possibly affect the size of a country's population; the birth rate, the death rate, and migration. The latter can safely be ignored in this period for numbers were comparatively small; the net effect of migration into and out of the country is likely to have changed the quality of the population rather than its quantity. Thus the birth rate or the death rate must contain the answer—but they guard their secret well for they are almost inextricably linked. The most important factor is infant mortality; a child born one month and dead the next might figure in both the baptism and the burial figures. Infant mortality was high (and remained comparatively so until the twentieth century). Gibbon remarked that his father gave each of his sons the name of Edward so that the patronymic might have some chance of being perpetuated in the family. Yet a glance at tombstones reveals that if a child could survive the first few years of life he might expect to live as long as a person living today—especially if he lived in the country. A decline in the infant death rate would result in more children surviving to marriageable age, which might in turn raise the birth rate.

The controversy is of more than demographic interest however. Changes in the birth rate depend primarily on the proportion of women who marry and the age at which they marry. Both these variables are affected in the short run by economic changes; by changes in the structure of employment, for example, or by changes in wage rates. The increasing availability of employment opportunities for children might be another factor, but the essential point remains the same—the changes occur more commonly as the *consequence* of changes in the economy than as the *cause*. The same is not true of changes in the death rate. Part may be due to economic factors such as improvements in diet or environment, but there are powerful influences on the non-economic side. Of these, advances in medical knowledge and practice, and changes in the virulence and incidence of epidemic diseases are the most significant. It was particularly medical improvements—new techniques, more hospitals, and advances in medical education—which prompted G. T. Griffith to argue in 1926 that the increase in population was primarily the result of a reduction in the death rate. This view remained virtually unchallenged until the debate was reopened in the 1950s.

In 1953 Professor Habakkuk re-explored the possibility of a rising birth rate as the major factor, stressing once again the supposed stimuli in the form of rising incomes, opportunities for child labour, and a poor relief system incorporating a family allowance. The supporters of this view point to the breakdown of restraints on marriage. The practice of agricultural labourers 'living in' was in decline, while apprenticeship—which might lead to a postponement of marriage—was largely absent from the new trades. Griffith's hypothesis was subjected to a further onslaught in 1955 when the medical historians, McKeown and Brown, argued that the medical improvements of the eighteenth century were more apparent than real. Although there was a sevenfold increase in the number of hospitals in England between 1700 and 1800, the suggestion that this had an appreciable effect on the death rate seemed to them improbable. The importance of segregating infectious patients was not appreciated, and they noted that as late as 1854 persons infected with cholera were admitted to the general wards of St Bartholomew's Hospital. It was even possible that the hospitals did positive harm. A considerable number of lying-in hospitals were established in the last part of the eighteenth century, yet because of the vulnerability of new-born infants to infectious disease, mortality rates in hospital were actually greater than for home confinements. Surgery had an inappreciable effect on vital statistics until the advent of anaesthetics and antiseptics, while even in 1874 a surgeon could show that mortality following all forms of amputation was between 35 and 50 per cent. Vaccination against smallpox was not discovered by Jenner until 1789 and was not generally introduced until the beginning of the nineteenth century. Yet in spite of this swingeing indictment of medical improvements these writers still felt that the acceleration in the rate of population growth lay in a falling death rate. They observed that when, as in the eighteenth century, both rates are high it is very much easier to increase the population by reducing the death rate than by increasing the birth rate, while the reverse is true when the rates are low. Of all the possible causes of an increase in the birth rate the only one which they considered merited serious attention was a decrease in the age of marriage. However, for various reasons the effect on population growth was likely to be marginal. An increase in the birth rate would have been largely due to the addition of children to existing families rather than to a larger number of one-child families, and since infant mortality from infectious disease rose sharply with increasing family size any growth in the birth rate would have been largely offset by a higher level of post-natal mortality. They were thus forced to support a falling death rate, which they attributed to 'improvement in environment', higher standards of housing, clothing and diet.

There has been some reaction against McKeown and Brown's harsh dismissal of medical improvements. P. E. Razzell, for example, has claimed that inoculation against smallpox (a method introduced into the country in 1721, where the smallpox virus is injected into the patient, rather than the cowpox virus used by Jenner) could theoretically explain the whole of the increase in population.

Inevitably the debate hinges on the interpretation of statistical evidence. It should be remembered that before 1801 the only real source is the parish registers, which record not births and deaths but baptisms and burials. Some formula must therefore be adopted for converting the figures. There is also the possibility that the registers might be kept more or less effectively at different periods of time. Krause, for example, has claimed that clerical zeal in keeping registers waned between 1781 and 1820 when clergymen increasingly held more than one living. Non-residence was often a reason for not keeping the registers properly. Furthermore, there was not only a growth in the number of Dissenters, making the registers less representative, but there may also have been an increasing reluctance among Anglicans to pay church burial fees which could be three times as much as in non-Anglican graveyards.

The argument continues, but in all that has been said—be it concerning birth rate or death rate—the chronology of events is important, for only by establishing this can the relationship with economic growth be established. This relationship, often complicated, might take various forms, of which a major one is the impact on demand. Such a relationship is not direct, for the result of an increase in population might be a general decrease in the standard of living, depending on whether real income (the quantity of goods which the wage-packet will buy) is rising or falling. There is, however, little evidence that real income of any major groups fell for anything other than short periods in the eighteenth century, and for long periods demand was reinforced by rising real incomes. The improvements in agriculture which helped support the growing population greatly assisted this trend. When food cost less, more was left over in the family budget for spending on other things, and a common saying in Bradford in the nineteenth century was, 'When the poor live cheaply, they clothe well.'

The growing population was also accompanied by increasing urbanisation, and this encouraged social investment in such facilities as housing and transport. The Bridgewater Canal of 1759, for example, was built primarily to enable the Duke of Bridgewater to take advantage of a growing urban demand for coal. It is difficult to determine how far transport improvements were a direct *cause* of economic growth, for although the turn-piking of main roads was virtually complete by 1760, the canal mania of the 1790s was clearly a *response* to the expansion of industrial and agricultural needs. Nevertheless, transport improvements undoubtedly assisted in the problem of distribution and helped the industrialist to satisfy the increasingly concentrated demand.

5 The capital requirements of industry   One of the major changes brought about by the Industrial Revolution was the substitution of capital for labour as machinery took over many of the tasks previously undertaken by hand. Earlier methods of production required little in the way of capital equipment. Domestic industry is, by definition, carried on in the home, where little space is afforded for machinery, even if the worker could find the money to purchase it. Domestic industry must not be thought of as a 'prior stage' to the factory system—shipbuilding, for example, has never really been organised as a cottage industry—yet it remains true that an essential feature of the Industrial Revolution was the spread of factories requiring capital for their establishment far in excess of that which the individual worker or his family could afford.

It is important to distinguish between the forms which capital can take. The economist draws a distinction between what he calls 'fixed capital' and 'circulating capital'. Fixed capital consists of those items such as buildings and machinery which continue in production for a length of time, while circulating capital includes those items which are used up in a short period, such as stocks of raw materials, goods in the process of manufacture and unsold finished goods. These different capital requirements are met in different ways. Circulating capital may be supplied by short-term loans, for goods in the pipeline will eventually be sold, and the debts repaid. But the almost irredeemable nature of capital locked up in bricks and mortar, and machinery, means that fixed capital has to be supplied from a different source, and be met over a longer period of time. Britain was fortunate in that she underwent her Industrial Revolution at a time when fixed capital, which is usually more difficult to raise, represented only a small part of the total capital requirement. One example will perhaps illustrate this: Truman, Hanbury and Buxton's brewery in Spitalfields was, in 1760, one of the largest factory plants in the country; yet out of total assets of £130,000 the total value of the brewhouse, utensils, casks and leaseholds of public houses was only £30,000. Even in the later eighteenth century the proportion of fixed to circulating capital in the larger textile factories was only around 50 per cent. Admittedly the advances in technology tended to raise fixed costs. A steam engine, for example, was an expensive item, and Musson and Robinson have shown that the extra cost of £200-£300 which a Watt engine entailed persuaded many factory masters to invest in a cheaper if less efficient model.

Such is our experience of modern factories that it is easy to exaggerate the extent of capital required in the early stages of industrial growth. In 1792 a new 40-spindle jenny cost £6, although second-hand ones were frequently advertised at a lower price. When this is compared with the wages of hand spinners (2s to 3s a week) it is seen that a 40-spindle jenny cost something like two weeks' wages of the 40 women it replaced. The Walker brothers established an iron foundry near Sheffield in 1741 with very little capital, perhaps even as little as £10. Yet largely through the self-denial of the partners the concern was valued at £62,500 by 1754. And that was a large concern.

This does not mean that the raising of capital presented no problems, for if the scale of industry was small even at the height of the Industrial Revolution the factory master still had to face competing demands for finance. These came from investment in roads, inland navigation, enclosures and social requirements such as housing and 'improvements'. For example, investment in enclosing over three million acres between 1761 and 1801 may have been in the region of £7 million. The government was also competing for funds, and in the half century between the outbreak of the Seven Years War and the Peace of Amiens, government borrowing reduced the capital available for economic growth by about £10 million each year.

This being so, it is essential to examine the sources from which the capital needs of industry were met. The ploughing back of profits is one of the major sources from which modern industry obtains its capital, and that this was a major source during the Industrial Revolution cannot be denied. As Ashton has put it:

Whatever may be said against the early employers, the charge of self-indulgence can hardly be laid at their door. The records of firm after firm tell the same story as that of the Walkers: the proprietors agreed to pay themselves small salaries, restrict their family expenses, and put their profits to reserves. (Ashton, 1948, page 97.)

On the other hand Flinn has pointed out a difficulty which occurs here, for the key sectors of industrial expansion in the Industrial Revolution—engineering, canal-making, cotton manufacture, and iron-making by the new techniques of coke-smelting—were, because of their very newness, the ones which were least likely to have access to this source. Other possibilities must therefore be considered.

The profits from overseas trade are often quoted as a source of industrial capital, and it is true that quite definite links can often be traced. Abraham Darby's Coalbrookdale ironworks, for example, was financed by his Bristol merchant partners, and the New Lanark cotton mill derived from David Dale's accumulated profits as an importer of linen yarn. Yet there is no inherent reason why mercantile profits should flow into industry. In many cases they flowed into elegant but unproductive stately homes. However, in the late eighteenth century a shortage of suitable estates coming on to the market may have diverted a larger part of these funds into more productive uses.

On the other hand, there are many examples of landowners participating in industry, either passively or actively, so that it is clear that income from the rent of land played a significant part in financing the development of transport and industry; and rents tended to rise after enclosure. This participation is apparent in the case of canal-building; the Grand Junction Canal of 1793, for example, had its promotion led by the Marquis of Buckingham, the Earl of Clarendon, the Earl of Exeter and Earl Spencer.

The number of banks was expanding alongside industry, and their simultaneous evolution makes it impossible to distinguish cause from effect in the development of either. It is difficult to be exact on the number of country banks at any one time, for in the eighteenth and early nineteenth centuries they were less distinct from other enterprises than they are today. Drapers and mercers, hosiers and cloth merchants—all formed the ranks from which the bankers emerged. In Hertfordshire and Essex the maltster often turned to banking, 50 brewers becoming bankers. From not more than a dozen in 1750 the number of country banks rose to around 700 by 1815. The contribution which they made to the Industrial Revolution was to oil the wheels of business by facilitating payments and by making advances to businessmen. Such loans were usually short-term and helped to satisfy the need for circulating capital; as we have seen that this was the main capital requirement of industry the contribution was significant.

Long-term credit could remain a problem, and when the industrialist did not turn to the merchant or the landowner he often turned to his family or friends, any of whom might lend on a mortgage. Mathias has observed that where small capital sums were involved—as was most often the case—kinship contacts were usually the first to be exploited. 'Eighteenth-century business', he points out, 'flourished as a face-to-face society of friends, cousins and business associates.' He quotes the example of Mrs Thrale, who describes how her husband's brewery was able to survive the depression of 1772:

First we made free with our mother's money . . . about three thousand pounds 'twas all she had; and big as I was with child, I drove down to Brighton to beg of Mr Scrase . . . six thousand pounds more: dear Mr Scrase was an old gouty solicitor, friend and contemporary of my husband's father. Lady Thrale (Mrs Thrale's sister-in-law) lent us five thousand pounds more. (Quoted in Mathias, 1969, page 150.)

6 The progress of technology In 1814 Patrick Colquhoun expressed optimism about an increasing demand for British manufactures, which were 'now capable of being augmented almost to any extent, in consequence of the great improvements and incalculable mechanical powers of machinery'. Contemporaries could not fail to see the extent to which technical innovations were appearing. A writer of 1752 spoke of 'the infinite numbers daily inventing machines for shortening business', while Dr Johnson exclaimed, 'The age is running mad after innovation; all the business of the world is to be done in a new way.'

Some idea of the extent of innovation can be derived from the number of patents granted for new inventions. In the ten years 1771-80, the total number of patents granted was 297; in 1781-90 it rose to 512, and in 1791-1800 to 655. But although figures may indicate the quantity of inventions, their quality is of greater significance. Furthermore, an invention only comes to have practical effect when it is widely adopted. Indeed, the patent laws might impede development. While Watt made a tremendous contribution to the development of the steam engine, his opposition to high-pressure steam and the application of steam power to vehicles acted as a hindrance to profitable lines of advance. Steam power spread as fast as it did only because other manufacturers were prepared to pirate the Boulton and Watt engine, and because the older and more primitive Newcomen engines continued to be made. Musson and Robinson have shown that in Lancashire and Cornwall, the two counties which had made most use of steam before 1800, Boulton and Watt had, in fact, nothing like a monopoly. On the other hand Henry Cort's puddling and rolling process of 1784, which permitted the large-scale production of bar-iron with coal fuel, was adopted more rapidly than many successful eighteenth-century inventions because he was unable to protect his patent after 1789, when he was ruined by the bankruptcy and suicide of one of his main creditors.

It should not be thought that mechanical ingenuity and precision were new to the eighteenth century. An examination of time-pieces, scientific instruments or automata in the galleries of any major museum readily reveals this; while a close look at a windmill can still make us marvel at its ingenious (though largely wooden) mechanism. What was new was the introduction of machinery made of iron rather than the wood of the mills or the brass and precious metals of the instruments; and powered by forces greater than the spring or the human hand. The demands which were made on the engineer—itself a new profession—were great, and the marvel is that, by and large, the demands were speedily met. Engineers began to *think* precisely. In 1776 Watt could enthusiastically write, 'Mr Wilkinson has improved the art of boring cylinders so that I promise upon a 72-inch cylinder being not further from absolute truth than the thickness of a thin sixpence in the worst part.' Yet in 1805 Maudslay was using in his workshops a micrometer—nicknamed the 'Lord Chancellor' because any disputes over faulty workmanship were referred to it—capable of measuring to within 0.0001 of an inch.

It is apparent that technical advance during the Industrial Revolution proceeded on a wide front, while chronologically there are two important clusters. Kay's flying shuttle of 1733 marks off a period which had seen the development of coke-smelting in 1709 and the Newcomen engine in 1712. A greater concentration comes after 1764 and includes: Hargreave's Jenny (1764), Arkwright's water-frame (1769), Wilkinson's boring-mill (1775), Watt's improved steam engine (1776-81), Crompton's mule (1779), the improved seed-drill (1782), Meikle's threshing machine (1784), and Bramah's addition of the slide-rest to the lathe (1794).

Yet while a wide range of industries were affected by the new technology—and only some of the more important inventions have been listed—there were some (of which cotton and iron are the most important) which pushed ahead faster than others. There were certain non-technical reasons why there should have been a break-through in cotton. The supply of the raw material proved elastic in its response to increasing demand, and the fabric proved an attractive alternative to wool, being lighter, easier to wash, and potentially cheaper. Likewise the comparative insignificance of the industry at the beginning of the transformation worked in its favour, for there were few of the vested interests resisting change that there were in the woollen industry. But cotton also proved easier to mechanise for purely technical reasons, for wool is a more delicate fibre, while jute and flax are much stiffer. By 1812 the cotton industry had expanded so fast that it accounted for between 7 and 8 per cent of the national income and had outstripped wool in national importance. There were about 100,000 workers in cotton-spinning factories and probably another quarter of a million weavers and auxiliaries.

The relationship between technical developments in different industries, and the question why inventions occur when they do are complex issues. Sometimes inventions in one industry could be imitated in another. The use of rollers to produce bar-iron, for example, has an obvious similarity with their use in the spinning of cotton. More often an invention would break an equilibrium in a sequence of processes. The flying shuttle created such a demand for yarn that a tremendous incentive was given to the perfection of spinning machinery. Sometimes developments in more than one field were linked by mutual necessity. Darby's coke-smelting process required coal, yet coal production was hampered by the problem of pumping water from the mines. This was solved by the application of the Newcomen engine, which required large and intricate castings impossible to produce without the iron made by Darby's process. Darby in return required the Newcomen engine to obtain the greater blast which he needed.

Many attempts have been made to produce a theory of invention explaining why they appear when they do, but none has been generally accepted. Yet we need to know the answer before we can tell if economic growth is due to technical innovation (as was once assumed) or whether it is the response to prior economic expansion. It is clear that technical advance is not *simply* a response to economic pressure. In the case of iron smelting, for example, Flinn has observed that 'the whole cycle from the first awareness of the cost advantage of coal in the late sixteenth century to the final general adoption of coke smelting in the third quarter of the eighteenth century occupied nearly two hundred years'. Nor does the idea that technical advance is merely a response to demands show why weaving was pushed forward by the flying shuttle when the great pressures were on the spinning process, the hand-loom weaver requiring the services of a number of spinners.

Yet if the timing of inventions is difficult to explain, the results for industry are clear; the replacement of scarce by less scarce resources. In coal mining the high labour cost of loaders, putters, winders and waggoners was reduced by the simple expedient of laying rails. Often it was natural resources which needed to be economised. Ashton has pointed out the dependence of the eighteenth-century economy on water; improvements in the water-wheel and the use of steam engines to throw back the water resulted in spectacular economies. In other cases the effect was to liberate capital. 'When iron', says Ashton, 'took the place of copper and brass in engine parts, of stone or brick in bridges, and of timber for the beams and pillars in factories, there was a considerable capital saving.'

7 Business enterprise As technical innovations have no practical effect until they are adopted, a person of equal importance with the inventor is the entrepreneur—the man who is willing to undertake the risks inherent in production and to organise the productive process. While comparatively few inventors were also entrepreneurs there are important similarities between the two types. Both are individualists and are interested in novelty and innovation; both display an appreciation of future possibilities; and both possess more than average energy.

The importance of examining the entrepreneur in the Industrial Revolution is all the greater because, except in the field of transport (which required abnormally large amounts of capital) the eighteenth century saw no new developments in business organisation. The creation of joint-stock companies had been severely restricted by the Bubble Act of 1720, so that until well into the nineteenth century the one-man business or the small partnership was typical of British industry. The individual entrepreneurs therefore played an enormous part in industrial expansion and have rightly earned the description given to them by Mathias—'the shock troops of economic change'.

The problems of organisation which the factory masters faced were great and many were of a new sort. The factories often grew up on isolated sites, wedded to water power or cheap coal. The new technology required a large labour force which often had to be housed by the industrialist, who also had to provide shops and other services. When, as sometimes happened, employment opportunities in the factories existed mainly for women and children, alternative employment had to be found for the men. Nor was the payment of wages as simple as it is today, for the Mint failed to keep the provinces supplied with a sufficient quantity of small change. Thus the evils of payment in kind (truck) and the 'tommy shop' run by the factory were partly the result of the tremendous problems which the entrepreneur faced.

It is difficult to generalise about the origins of the entrepreneurs, and Ashton has indicated the wide field from which they came. Some, like the Duke of Bridgewater and Earl Gower, who created new transport systems, were aristocrats. Edmund Cartwright forsook the pulpit for the power loom and the cotton mill. John Roebuck gave up medicine for the ironworks; Richard Arkwright started off as a barber; Peter Stubs, an important file manufacturer, had been an innkeeper. Even the schoolmaster made good, Samuel Walker becoming a leading figure in the north of England iron industry. Entrepreneurs were sometimes joined by the bonds of marriage, with ironmasters marrying the daughters of ironmasters and potters marrying the daughters of potters. 'Hence arose dynasties (such as those of the Darbys and the Wedgwoods)', wrote Ashton, 'as powerful in industry as royal houses in international politics.'

Diverse as their origins may have been, one thing is immediately striking—the large number of Dissenters who became captains of industry. So apparent is this that some have seen in Dissent a contributory factor to the Industrial Revolution itself. It is difficult to be precise; but Flinn quotes figures which show that out of a fairly random sample of the principal entrepreneurs and inventors of the Industrial Revolution, 49 per cent were Nonconformists.

The relationship between Dissent and enterprise may have taken a number of forms. It has been held that the religious teaching of Protestant nonconformity is conducive to business, while the individualism of Protestantism has been contrasted with the authoritarianism of the Catholic Church. Others have seen the connection mainly in the social position in which Dissenters found themselves in eighteenth-century and much of nineteenth-century Britain. Nonconformists who were strict to their faith were excluded from civil and military office, and could not go to Oxford or Cambridge. This blocked certain careers to them but left the way open in business and industry. Denied entry to the English (but not the Scottish) universities, the Nonconformists established their own academies, which provided the best commercial and scientific education available in England at the time. The curriculum was broad, and many of the greatest industrialists such as Roebuck, Wilkinson and Boulton received their education there. The recent work of psychologists has taken some of these suggestions a step further by postulating that the withdrawal of status respect which was the experience of Dissenters gave rise to psychological needs which motivated individuals to achieve success, while parents might inculcate these drives through their pattern of child-rearing. Such theories are of great interest but are difficult to validate; at present the historian must be satisfied with other demonstrable evidence.

8 The role of the government   In comparison with countries such as France, Germany and Sweden, British industry in the eighteenth century was relatively free from government interference. Even so there were many apparent restrictions. The Statute of Artificers of 1563, which was still in force, laid down elaborate provisions concerning the training of skilled labour, labour mobility and the regulation of wages, while the Law of Settlement placed further obstacles in the way of labour migration. The Bubble Act of 1720 put severe limitations on the creation of joint-stock companies, and the Usury Laws set a limit of 5 per cent on the rate which could be charged for loans. The export of a number of goods was prohibited, while duties were imposed on the importation of a great many more.

Much importance has therefore been attached to the publication in 1776—the year in which Watt's improved steam engine made its appearance—of Adam Smith's *Wealth of Nations*. Smith advocated *laissez-faire*: the belief that the government should stand aside so that the wealth of the nation might be maximised through the collective efforts of individuals pursuing their own best interests. Yet apart from the rationalisation of import duties in the 1780s, and some modifications to the Navigation System and colonial regulations consequent on the loss of the American colonies, there was no serious abandonment of the so-called 'mercantilist' policies until the second decade of the nineteenth century, and even then the change came about gradually. Chronology alone, therefore, would indicate that the adoption of *laissez-faire* could have had little influence on the origins of the Industrial Revolution.

In reality, however, the regulations which remained in force throughout the eighteenth century were more apparent than real. The Statute of Artificers was a dead letter, while recent research has shown that the hindrance to migration imposed by the Law of Settlement was minimal. The ban on joint-stock enterprises presented little hardship on account of the low requirements of fixed capital which were typical of industrial undertakings, while turnpike trusts and canal or tramway companies could obtain the powers they needed by Act of Parliament. There were various ways of getting round the Usury Laws, and it was not difficult to evade restrictions on overseas trade. The smuggler, indeed, was a highly respected member of the community, while one manufacturer after another cheerfully admitted to being a law-breaker when the laws regarding Yorkshire woollens were under review before a Select Committee in 1821.

While no changes in government policy can be discerned which might have acted as a direct stimulus to growth, to the extent that existing regulations were not, or could not be enforced, a congenial environment for growth was provided.

9 The impact of war The long-term effect of war on the economy is a matter over which historians argue. The beneficial effects are clear. War was a great consumer of iron, and Henry Cort, who revolutionised its manufacture, was a Navy agent in the 1760s, anxious to improve the quality of the product 'in connection with the supply of iron to the navy'. A number of ironworks depended on government contracts for cannon; the Carron Works developed the famous carronade, used against the American rebels, while Wilkinson's boring-machine—which proved so essential to the manufacture of steam-engine cylinders —was initially designed for the boring of cannon. The output of pig-iron increased spectacularly during the French Wars; in 1788 the estimated production was 68,000 tons; eight years later it was 125,000 tons; and by 1802 the figure had risen to 170,000 tons.

The Navy stimulated technical developments in a number of other fields. There was a great demand for ships' pulley-blocks. Maudslay, who had begun his career in the Woolwich Arsenal, built 44 machines to the design of Sir Marc Isambard Brunel which were set running at Portsmouth in 1809. A fully mechanised production line was introduced which turned elm logs into pulley-blocks and enabled ten men to produce 160,000 blocks a year. Previously 110 men were employed at a cost to the Admiralty three times as great.

The number of beasts coming to Smithfield increased in war-time because of naval purchasing there, and the earliest English cannery, established at Bermondsey, supplied preserved meats and soups to the Navy during the War of 1812. Certain branches of the textile industry, such as those providing canvas, cheap shirt-cloth and woollens, benefited from government contracts; such contracts in general had to be filled on time, and it was worth a businessman's while to introduce innovations if they would help him meet an order.

The effect of the wars of the eighteenth century on the export trade varied, but after 1793 the French Wars probably did more good than harm. Exports to Europe grew faster than those to other markets, while Britain's command of the high seas enabled her to deny markets to French and French-occupied competitors. Exports between 1793 and 1815 expanded at 3·8 per cent per annum, faster than that before or subsequently. On the other hand, the losses which war entailed, while less obvious, may have been equally or more substantial. War brought distortion to trade and a dislocation of peace-time economic activities. The construction of houses, workshops, canals and highways declined; the national debt increased and represented investment which was largely unproductive, as the greater part met current expenditure, much of it overseas. It is impossible to balance all the gains against the losses, and one must agree with Ashton that 'the case for war as a stimulus to economic expansion is, to say the least, unproven'.

10 The need to keep a balanced view Great changes had undeniably occurred by 1815. The population had soared and towns had grown apace. Yet although industry had undergone a great expansion, a greater change was yet to come. The Industrial Revolution was by no means complete; in some industries it had hardly even begun. The typical Englishman was still a countryman (and was to remain so until mid-century), and agriculture remained the greatest source of wealth. In 1812 the proportion of the national income derived from agriculture was 27 per cent while cotton contributed around 6 per cent—and cotton had shown the greatest advance in the industrial sector. In 1815 the export of cotton textiles made up 40 per cent of the value of British domestic exports. There had been a great advance in the use of steam power; yet as late as 1839, while there were 3051 steam engines in the textile factories of the United Kingdom, there were still 2230 waterwheels. The really massive growth of steam power did not occur until later in the century. All the engines built by Boulton and Watt up to 1800 totalled only 7500 h.p. Total steam power was 500,000 h.p. in 1850, rising to 9,650,000 h.p. in 1907. The early engines were also small; even in the 1820s a 60 h.p. mill engine was considered large, while by the early twentieth century steam engines of 3000-4000 h.p. were to be found in the big cotton mills.

It was easier to travel around the country. The canal mania of the 1790s had been the climax in canal building, while the peak in the passage of turnpike Acts occurred between 1791 and 1810. Although the great days of Telford and Macadam had only just begun, 20,000 miles of road out of a total of 120,000 miles had been turnpiked by 1815. Mail coaches ran with a clockwork precision which reflected a new sense of time throughout the community; a strict discipline and regular hours were necessary features of the factory system.

The strains on the economy and society which the beginnings of industrialisation imposed inevitably caused stress, and an industrial structure based essentially on one sector of the textile industry could be neither stable nor secure. Growth pains were evident, of which the most obvious symptom was what Hobsbawm has described as 'the high wind of social discontent' which blew across Britain in waves between the last years of the French Wars and the middle 1840s.

Chapter II

Signs of Strain

1 Industrial Revolution: first or final stage? After two centuries of industrial development, it is clear to us that the period to which we refer as the Industrial Revolution was the initial stage of industrial capitalism. But to contemporaries, lacking our hindsight, it was just as easy to see these changes as the *final* stage. Such a suggestion may seem absurd to us, for they obviously were not. But Dr Hobsbawm says:

This is to underestimate the instability and tension of this initial phase—particularly of the three decades after Waterloo—and the malaise of both the economy and those who thought seriously about its prospects. Early industrial Britain passed through a crisis which reached its stage of greatest acuteness in the 1830s and early 1840s. That it was not in any sense a 'final' crisis, but merely one of growth, should not lead us to underestimate its seriousness, as economic (but not social) historians have persistently inclined to do. (Hobsbawm, 1969, pages 72-3.)

There were obvious signs of strain in the system: Luddism between 1811 and 1818, the East Anglian riots of 1816, the March of the Blanketeers in 1817, Peterloo in 1819, the Swing Riots of 1830 and the Rebecca Riots in 1838-9. 'At no other period in modern British history', writes Hobsbawm, 'have the common people been so persistently, profoundly, and desperately dissatisfied.' Widespread trade union activity, Radical journalism, the factory reform movement, and the variety of movements which made up Chartism all reflect the stress.

Capitalism was not seen as the only possible economic structure, and many alternative systems, based on ideas of co-operation and community, were put forward—some being more utopian than others. The way in which the ideas of Robert Owen caught the popular imagination reveals the discontent which the existing order provoked. E. P. Thompson writes:

> It was not Owen who was 'mad', but, from the standpoint of the toilers, a social system in which steam and new machinery evidently displaced and degraded labourers, and in which the markets could be 'glutted' while the unshod weaver sat in his loom and the shoemaker sat in his workshop with no coat to his back. (E. P. Thompson, 1963, page 804.)

If only the worker could find the capital required to set up business, he could organise production in a more equitable fashion, with the simple needs of all being met, and labour receiving its due reward. Hence the great interest in co-operation as a means of acquiring capital to establish socialist communities. There were two strong incentives: the despair born of poverty, and the belief that capitalism (a mere infant) would speedily show its inherent sickliness and pass away. But Professor Pollard has shown that co-operation falls into two phases, the second marked by the coming together of the Rochdale Pioneers in 1844. Their innovation was the payment of dividends—an abandonment of the idea that trading surpluses should be used to raise the capital required to opt out of capitalism and to establish instead the co-operative community of friends. The new phase assumed that capitalism was a healthier child than had been anticipated. Co-operation now became one of the many aspects of Victorian 'self-help', a lever by which the worker could raise himself up *within* the system.

It is not strange that this change should have come about when it did, for by the late 1840s the worst was over, and the fruits of industrialisation fell in greater abundance to the workers, whose standard of living clearly began to rise. By 1851 Britain was sufficiently confident in its progress to invite all the world to celebrate, at the Great Exhibition, human ingenuity, industry and enterprise.

In the previous chapter it was stressed that the extent of economic change by 1815 should not be exaggerated. A similar warning needs to be repeated, for there is a temptation to see the strains imposed by the early industrial economy, and the discontent which followed, too much in terms of the factory system. Luddism was the work of skilled men in small workshops, and outworkers were as prominent in radical agitation as the factory hands. Within the labour movement it was the artisans who tended to take the lead, and even where the unrest was rural it was often this class which exerted the leadership. Conditions in many of the factories were terrible, but so were conditions in domestic industry and in agriculture. Farmers as well as factory owners had their problems, and it is to them that we must first turn.

2 Agriculture in the early nineteenth century

Industrialisation requires increasing numbers of workers who do not grow their own food; while one of the factors in the complicated process of economic growth is a rising population. This being so, the importance of agriculture cannot be over-stressed. While it is difficult to point to ways in which agriculture was a direct stimulus to the Industrial Revolution, it remains true that such a dramatic change could not have occurred without the firm foundation of an efficient agriculture and an expanded production of food.

So strong were the debts which the Industrial Revolution owed to agriculture that it seems curious that the debts which agriculture owed to the Industrial Revolution should, before the middle of the century, have been so small. With the exception of the threshing machine, very little machinery was used in farming before the 1840s. It was not until 1841 that a portable steam engine intended for agriculture was exhibited (at the 'Royal' show in Liverpool) and although it was estimated in the year of the Great Exhibition that there were eight thousand portable steam engines in use, most were used for driving threshing machines or barn machinery (for grinding, chaff-cutting, or preparing animal feed). Small farms and small fields remained an obstacle to the general introduction of steam cultivation. Similarly, there was as yet little application of chemistry or biology to farming. Only in its use of the new means of transport did farming make much use of the industrial innovations.

It was in other ways that agriculture achieved its great increase in production. The best traditional methods were applied more widely. Even the breeding methods of Bakewell, and the crop-rotations of Townshend (which were popularised at the end of the eighteenth century) had been practised, here and there, much earlier. More important still was the bringing into cultivation of new land which had existed either as waste or rough pasture.

Much of the land reclaimed for agriculture was taken over during the French Wars. The Board of Agriculture claimed in 1795 that 8 million acres were still waste land. In 1815, most of the wastes and moorland which remained were uncultivable. E. L. Jones has observed:

The edge of cultivation was pushed beyond even the obliterating limits of the Second World War's reclamation campaign, so that abandoned Napoleonic ploughing rig survives far up on the chalk downs and Dartmoor and out on the New Forest heaths. (E. L. Jones, 1968, page 10.)

A large part of the increase in cultivable land was associated with enclosure, which rose to one of its peaks during the wars; for whereas over 1000 Acts for Parliamentary enclosure were passed between 1760 and 1800, a further 800 were passed between 1800 and 1815. Landlords and farmers enjoyed prosperous conditions, benefiting from a scarcity of foodstuffs, and profits and rents rose. There was a sharp upswing in prices, most marked in the case of wheat (which is generally subject to the greatest fluctuations). In the early 1790s the price hovered around 48-50s per quarter. It shot to over 90s in 1795 and with intermittent falls rose to 126s 6d in 1812. In only six of the 23 years between 1793 and 1815 did the average price fall below 65s, and in only ten years did it fall below 75s. A similar story is true of barley and oats, while meat prices also rose.

It is tempting to attribute these price rises to the wars. But wars can prove troublesome to the theorist, for they often obscure other factors which may be more relevant. Napoleon must take some of the credit for the great rise in agricultural prices, but the heavens must also take theirs. The upswing of 1795 (the year of Speenhamland) resulted from one of the three worst seasons of the eighteenth century, which, combined with the unusual cold of the following summer, produced a harvest between a fifth and a quarter less than normal. The whole period from 1795 to 1800 was remarkable for poor seasons, and although the first few years of the new century saw improved weather conditions there was a disastrous run of five bad seasons between 1808 and 1812. The summers of 1808 and 1809 were wet, and serious outbreaks of sheep rot added to the devastation of spoilt harvests. That there should have been few good seasons was one thing; that the bad ones should have been blocked together in long runs was quite another. The absence of reserve supplies of grain, and the reduction of flocks and herds, sent prices up to famine level. The inflationary consequences of the war merely exacerbated the situation. Ironically, the French harvest of 1809 was a bumper one, and faced with a glut of corn and discontented farmers, Napoleon allowed large quantities of French corn to be exported to England, thus helping to relieve the effects of a very critical food situation. Throughout the war period imports rose, although the price of imported grain was raised considerably by the high transport costs together with insurance and other charges. The chance run of wet seasons hid the fact that the potential supply of grain was greatly over-expanded by the vastly increased acreage under production. The bumper harvest of 1813 revealed the problems which the war-time expansion was bound to produce, for with an inelastic demand for bread there was a catastrophic fall in prices. With only brief reversals wheat prices continued to tumble until 1835.

Corn laws had existed for centuries, with the aim of stabilising home prices, and were calculated to foster imports when home prices were high and encourage exports when they were low. Not until the end of the war years did protection become a live issue, for it was only then that the prospect of peace presented the threat of imports from the Continent. It was now argued that although continental farmers could produce their wheat at 40s a quarter, English farmers could not show a profit at less than 80s—a famine price in pre-war days. Farmers insisted on regarding the abnormal war years as the norm, and pre-war days seemed too remote to contemplate. The life style of many of them had changed, and Cobbett was but one of those who mocked the fancy ways of the farmers and their families. Broader arguments for protection were, of course, brought forward, and it was pointed out that large capital sums had been expended on enlarged and improved production. Malthus, one of the more disinterested advocates of protection, argued that it was necessary in order to keep farming profitable; a vital matter for the country as a whole since agriculture contributed rather more than a third of the national income, and gave employment to roughly the same proportion of the employed population, whose purchasing power was essential for the maintenance of domestic demand. That a great many farmers engaged in livestock production (to whom corn is an *input* and not an output) had an interest in low corn prices was generally overlooked.

The voice of the agricultural interest as a whole was nevertheless loud, and the Corn Law of 1815, which allowed imported wheat to be sold only when the home price reached 80s a quarter, and barley and oats when they respectively reached 40s and 27s, marked a new phase in protection for the farmer. It does not follow that prices would have been any lower had the laws not been passed, for that would be to suppose that foreign corn could have been imported at a lower price than that at which the home producers could supply it. But this was not to be possible until new sources of supply became available in the middle of the century. Indeed, it could be claimed that the Corn Laws were repealed just at the time when they might have begun to produce a material effect on prices. Until then foreign producers were hardly in a position to undercut the home suppliers, for climatic conditions tended to produce similar harvests amongst our traditional suppliers on the Continent, and the cost of freight and allied charges had to be added to the price of their corn.

The post-war talk of 'agricultural depression' was largely due to the habit of drawing comparisons with the abnormal war years, for an examination of the prices which farmers actually received shows that as a rule, wheat prices were consistently higher than those which had prevailed before the wars, while meat prices also settled down to an average above the pre-war level. Lord

Ernle wrote: 'Between 1813 and the accession of Queen Victoria falls one of the blackest periods of English farming. . . . Farms were thrown up; notices to quit poured in; numbers of tenants absconded. Large tracts of land were untenanted and often uncultivated.' This, however, is a generalisation made from evidence taken from the worst-hit districts in the worst spells of depression. The reader of the Board of Agriculture's report of 1816 and the Parliamentary Commissions of 1821, 1833, and 1836 needs to interpret his evidence with care. It is a fundamental law of human nature that the man with a grievance is a noisier animal than the one who is contented. The loudest representations to all these enquiries were made by large arable farmers and landowners of southern and eastern England, anxious to secure relief from rates and taxes (which tended not to fall in line with grain prices), and to increase their protection against imported cereals. The depression, which was intermittent (becoming severe and widespread only in the two brief periods of 1821-5 and 1833-6), mainly affected arable farmers. The more contented livestock producers made much less fuss.

Much of English farming was mixed, and while there were many pasture farmers with little or no arable land, there were few arable farmers who did not keep some sheep or cattle. This was assured by the miscellaneous demand of the large towns for food, as well as the enduring defects of the transport system, which, before the railway boom, made it impossible to transport perishable commodities over very long distances. Many parts of East Anglia and the Home Counties were therefore concerned with fattening livestock driven up from the more specialised rearing counties.

Ernle argued that 'prosperity no longer stimulated progress' after the Napoleonic Wars. Yet he failed to notice that progress can be stimulated by adversity. Chambers and Mingay note:

It is not often appreciated how much agricultural development stemmed from the stimulus of low prices, bad seasons and the threat of bankruptcy. . . . The difference between improvements in periods of low prices and those in periods of prosperity was really one of emphasis. Both low and high prices resulted in a search for greater efficiency; but in the first the emphasis was on greater economy through reduction of costs; in the second it was more concerned with expansion of the cultivated acreage and higher output.

When it was appreciated that at the post-war levels only efficient farming could be made to pay, there was renewed interest in techniques and improvements and a willingness to invest in them. (Chambers and Mingay, 1966, pages 130-1.)

That agricultural labourers were in a distressed state cannot, however, be questioned, and their plight is considered later in the chapter. The extent to which the supply of labour for both agriculture and industry was affected by enclosure has been much debated, and we cannot leave a consideration of agriculture without a brief examination of this question and the related one of enclosure and the small landowner.

The era of Parliamentary enclosure, from about 1760 to 1830, has received great attention. Primarily interest has centred in the relationship between enclosure, improvements in farming methods, and industrial growth. Great significance was also attached to enclosure by Marx, who regarded it as a key factor in the robbery of communal lands by the landlords in order to create large capitalist farms and, by throwing large numbers off the land, to set free a proletarian labour force for manufacturing industry. By 1887 only about 12 per cent of the occupiers of agricultural land were the owners of it, and the concern which this supposed loss of a peasantry aroused led, in the years preceding the First World War, to a number of major studies of eighteenth- and early nineteenth-century enclosure by such historians as Hasbach, Gonner, Ernle, and the Hammonds, of which the last's *The Village Labourer*, published in 1912, is the best known. The work is a classic and deserves to be read as such, although it is now seen to be very biased and is superseded by modern research. The Hammonds could hardly have painted a blacker picture of enclosure, which they saw as an evil force—a gigantic swindle by which wealthy owners rode rough-shod over the rights of small men. Typical of their strong views is the following:

The enclosures created a new organisation of classes. The peasant with rights and a status, with a share in the fortunes and government of his village, standing in rags, but standing on his feet, makes way for the labourer with no corporate rights to defend, no corporate power to invoke, no property to cherish, no ambition to pursue, bent beneath the fear of his masters, and the weight of a future without hope. (J. L. and Barbara Hammond, 1948 edn., page 101.)

In subsequent years traditional views on enclosure have been modified on many points, through the work of a number of historians including W. E. Tate, J. D. Chambers and G. E. Mingay. It is now felt that the effects of enclosure have often been over-stated. Recent research has tended to diminish the effect which it had on agricultural practice, there being much evidence that it had little or no impact on the character of farming, which rarely changes in any sudden or dramatic manner. G. E. Mingay writes:

Full-scale enclosure, when it came, often represented the final rather than the first stage in the process of reorganisation, and its effects on farming methods and on the village community were not always very great. Frequently, parliamentary enclosure was the logical conclusion of the piecemeal creation of separate closes from the waste and the gradual modification of the common fields that had been going on for a century or more. . . . The farming itself was not always much affected: the general effect was to extend or intensify the local specialisation that was determined by natural factors; many farmers had already a large proportion of enclosed land and had already adopted leys, legumes and roots, and in arable areas the nature of the soil did not always allow the farmers to depart from the ancient two crops and a fallow. (G. E. Mingay, 1960, pages 10-19, by permission of Macmillan, London and Basingstoke.)

Again, enclosure is now regarded neither as the creator of a rootless labour force which was driven into the factories, nor as the destroyer of the small farmers. As early as 1912, E. C. K. Gonner was impressed by the complexity of the task of enclosure and the fairness with which the commissioners carried it out. This view has since won general acceptance, and J. D. Chambers and G. E. Mingay write that 'parliamentary enclosure represented a major advance in the recognition of the rights of the small man'.

Undoubtedly the cottagers and the squatters lost their access to the common land and the waste, which may have provided the keep for a cow or some pigs or geese, as well as a supply of fuel. Yet although this was a factor in the impoverishment of the rural labourer, it is easy to exaggerate its importance. To some extent compensation may have been afforded by the increase in both the volume and regularity of employment which followed enclosure, for new demands for labour were created by the extension of the cultivated area, as well as work on the erection and maintenance of fences and hedges, the laying down of new roads, and the construction of new farm buildings. Nor did labour-saving machinery, with the possible exception of the threshing machine, do much to diminish this demand. Wheat was still dibbled in Norfolk as late as 1831, and for even longer the scythe and the sickle reaped the harvest.

Arthur Redford, in a study of labour migration in England, demonstrated that far from there being a movement of rural depopulation in the early nineteenth century, the population of the countryside actually increased. He noted that, 'During Cobbett's life-time no single county . . . reported a decreased population at *any* of the successive census returns. Cobbett countered this argument by flatly refusing to believe the census returns.' How then does one account for the permanent and crippling surplus of labour which was a sad feature of the countryside throughout the first half of the century? The answer is not hard to find—the natural increase in population created a labour supply which agriculture, although its demand was expanding, could not absorb. Population pressure rather than enclosure was the major cause of the distress which followed.

Similarly, the major cause of the decline in the number of small landowners lay elsewhere. The trend developed over a much longer period than that covered by Parliamentary enclosure, and Mingay argues that many of the causes of decline date back to the seventeenth and eighteenth centuries. The Hammonds had supposed that the small farmers were forced out through the burden of enclosure expenses, yet they produced no evidence (beyond mentioning some enclosures where the cost was unusually high) to prove that the burden was crushing. One of the major aims of enclosure was to raise land values, and the small owner benefited from this, so that for an expenditure of between £50 and £100 he might increase the value of his land from £450 to £900. The alternatives open to the small owner were therefore varied. He might, with little difficulty, raise a mortgage to meet his enclosure expenses, he might sell off a few acres to meet his costs, or he might sell all his land at its improved value and use the proceeds to set himself up as a really substantial tenant farmer. What was more important than enclosure to the small farmer was the level of prices. There was a long-term trend towards larger farms, which enjoyed economies of scale and in most cases were more efficient and flexible. The lower prices which prevailed after the Napoleonic Wars are thought to have subjected the small owners to greater pressure than enclosure. The small tenant farmers were also in a weaker position than their more substantial brethren for, being easier to replace, they were less likely to be granted those abatements of rent which were fairly common in the case of larger tenants.

However depressed English agriculture may have appeared after the Napoleonic Wars it managed (with little help from imports), through an increased yield per acre, to feed a population which rose from just over 11 million in 1815 to nearly 15 million twenty years later. This ability of English farmers to supply the needs of the expanding population is one of the factors which bears upon the standard of living controversy.

3 The economic and social costs of industrialisation

Between 1801 and 1851 the national income per head at constant prices almost doubled. This might suggest, at first glance, that there was a substantial rise in the standard of living, yet in reality it merely indicates that such a rise is a feasible hypothesis. Whether or not it represented improved living standards would depend on the proportion of the national income diverted from consumption to investment, and it was shown in Chapter I that this rose from below 5 per cent in the 1750s to nearly 10 per cent by the 1840s. Similarly, whether the majority of the population benefited depends upon the way in which the proportion of the national income devoted to consumption was distributed between the rents and profits going to the property owners, and the wages and salaries going to the workers.

Like many problems of historical interpretation, the question of whether industrialisation brought with it a higher standard of living was a matter of controversy even to contemporaries. The factory system was hotly debated—so that some, like Dr Ure, could liken factory children to 'lively elves' at play, while others, like Cobbett, could hardly refrain from 'cursing a system that produces such slavery and such cruelty'. Economists assumed that the life of the labouring masses would be miserable, and much of their theory was aimed to show why this was inevitable. In a situation where it was clearly and visibly untrue, it would have been impossible for Malthus to argue that population must grow faster than the means of subsistence, so that the poor remain on the verge of famine.

On the whole, the weight of literary evidence, whether in the Parliamentary reports or in other contemporary sources, suggests that there was a widespread feeling that conditions both in agriculture and industry were deteriorating. Some care needs to be taken, however, in interpreting this material. It may be argued that the Parliamentary Papers deliberately present a black picture, having been drawn up by men whose great concern was to see conditions improved, and who needed to shake those in power from their apathy. Nor does the great feeling of discontent (although it is difficult to explain away) necessarily imply that conditions were getting worse. It has been argued:

The idea of progress is largely psychological and certainly relative; people are apt to measure their progress not from a forgotten position in the past, but towards an ideal, which, like an horizon, continually recedes. The present generation is not interested in the earlier needs and successes of its progenitors, but in its own distresses and frustration considered in the light of the presumed possibility of universal comfort and of riches. (A. L. Bowley, quoted in R. M. Hartwell, 1960, page 415.)

Yet not all historians are ready to accept that a 'revolution of rising expectations' is as familiar in reality as it is in books. The debate has witnessed a predominantly 'pessimist' period, followed by an 'optimist' period, which in turn has been succeeded by a new confrontation of the two schools of thought. The pessimistic view has a heredity stretching back to contemporary observers, and it was given a great boost by the social investigations of Booth and Rowntree at the very end of the nineteenth century. Despite half a century of undisputed progress, they demonstrated that nearly a third of the population of London and of York existed in poverty. It was in this atmosphere that the Webbs and the Hammonds wrote, and it is from their writings that much of the support derives for the view that conditions were deteriorating in the early stages of industrialisation. Their views were expressed with deep passion:

The bleak and sombre landscape that gives its sad tone to the life and art of the Brontës seems to speak of the destinies of that world of combers and croppers and spinners and weavers on whom the Industrial Revolution fell like a war or a plague. For all these classes of workers it is true that they were more their own masters, that they had a higher range of initiative, that their homes and their children were happier in 1760 than they were in 1830. Surely never since the days when populations were sold into slavery did a fate more sweeping overtake a people than the fate that covered the hills and valleys of Lancashire and the West Riding with the factory towns that were to introduce a new social type for the world to follow. (J. L. and Barbara Hammond, 1920, page 4.)

E. P. Thompson has shown that much of the 'optimist' revision has taken the course of a running critique of the Hammonds, who, he concedes, were 'too willing to moralise history'.

It was not surprising that the response to the moral indignation of the pessimists should have taken the form of a number of empirical studies, firmly based (so their authors believed) on fact. Representative of such writers are Sir John Clapham and T. S. Ashton, who argued that while economic change left some workers displaced and distressed, the majority benefited from falling prices, more regular employment, and a wider range of employment opportunities.

From the 1950s the debate has reopened, and has consisted very largely of a confrontation between the 'pessimist', Dr Hobsbawm, and the 'optimist', Dr Hartwell, with contributions from many others. At times the controversy has degenerated to one of apologetics rather than history, for it is easy to see the question in terms of an attack on or a defence of capitalism. The argument has been fierce—indeed, it has been suggested that so far the controversy has generated heat rather than light.

More light and less heat might result from a clearer agreement on the criteria involved. What exact period is under examination, whose standard of living are we talking about, and what do we include in the term? Ashton began by considering the period 1790-1830. Hobsbawm extended it to 1850, but later concentrated on the period from the early 1790s to the early 1840s. A. J. Taylor took the period 1780-1850, while Hartwell has taken 1800-1850. These differences are more than trivial, for they may affect the answers which are produced, 1780-1830 favouring the pessimists, and 1800-1850 favouring the optimists. However, with concessions made by both sides, the area of greatest disagreement can be narrowed down to the period from the 1820s to the early 1840s. As to those whose standard of living is under discussion, Clapham referred to 'every class of urban or industrial labour about which information is available'. Ashton, Taylor and Hartwell refer to the 'workers' or the 'working class', while Hobsbawm prefers sometimes 'the labouring poor' and at others 'the British labouring population'. All such definitions present the difficulty of the 'average worker', who is an elusive creature. It is too easy to see 'labour' as more homogeneous than in reality it was. This is true of both agriculture and industry. In farming, the 'yearly men' with responsible positions fared much better than the day-labourers. Likewise there was a great range of skills in industry, each rewarded differently. The difficulty of talking about the 'average worker' is apparent when it is observed that in the 1841 census 1225 sub-divisions of heads of employment were enumerated for cotton manufacture *alone*. There is also the hasty assumption, indicated above, of assuming that the typical worker of the period was a factory hand, whereas the census figures reveal the continued dominance of the artisan. It therefore pays to take care when attempting generalisation, just as it pays to ascertain whether statements about standards of living include the Irish or not. 'The argument for declining living standards', writes A. J. Taylor, 'is patently strongest when the experience of Ireland is added to that of Great Britain, and correspondingly weakest when attention is confined to England and, more specifically, to its new industrial North and Midlands.' The point was not lost on contemporaries. The Select Committee on Emigration declared in 1827:

It is vain to hope for any permanent and extensive advantage from any system of emigration which does not primarily apply to *Ireland*; whose population, unless some other outlet be opened to them, must shortly fill up every vacuum created in England or in Scotland, and reduce the labouring classes to a uniform state of degradation and misery.

One last cautionary point needs to be made, for it underlies much of the current debate. That is to distinguish between the *standard of living* which, representing material well-being, is an economic phenomenon, and *way of life*, which is basically a social matter. The Industrial Revolution was not a mere economic expansion; it marks one of the most profound social changes in the history of Britain, and imposed strains which we are only now coming to appreciate as we see emergent nations struggling to overcome them. Contemporaries were not concerned only with wages or the cost of living. Instead they were concerned about the breakdown of traditional values, by loss of status and security, and by all those issues which affected the *quality* of men's lives. The point is simply put by E. P. Thompson:

From food we are led to homes, from homes to health, from health to family life, and thence to leisure, work-discipline, education and play, intensity of labour, and so on. From standard-of-life we pass to way-of-life. . . . The first is a measurement of quantities: the second a description (and sometimes an evaluation) of qualities. Where statistical evidence is appropriate to the first, we must rely largely upon 'literary evidence' as to the second. A major source of confusion arises from the drawing of conclusions to one from evidence appropriate only to the other. It is at times as if statisticians have been arguing: 'the indices reveal an increased per capita consumption of tea, sugar, meat and soap, therefore the working class was happier', while social historians have replied: 'the literary sources show that people were unhappy, therefore the standard of living must have deteriorated.' (E. P. Thompson, 1963, page 211.)

There are three lines of approach which may be taken in order to attempt an evaluation of changes in the standard of living. The statistical ideal would be an authentic money wage index and an authentic price index. The latter divided by the former would give us *real wages*—an indication of what money will buy. Secondly, it is possible to take the physical quantities of certain commodities consumed and express these per head of population. To these results can be added the estimates and views of contemporaries, which are illuminating, if somewhat subjective.

Finally, economic theory can be invoked to demonstrate which estimates are mutually consistent and which are not, and sometimes to fill in, provisionally, some of the gaps in the data.

Sir John Clapham's optimistic assessment was based on Silberling's cost-of-living index, which has since been subjected to heavy criticism. However attractive this quantitative approach may appear, it is now generally felt that the difficulties involved are too great, and that it must be abandoned. The problems relate mainly to the available data. Most price indices are based on the wholesale prices paid by institutions such as Eton College or Chelsea Hospital, usually in the south of England, and it is possible that they bear little relationship to weekly retail prices paid in the industrial districts. There are also problems in drawing up the 'basket of goods' (a list of representative goods purchased by the consumer) used in a cost-of-living index to represent the pattern of spending. As these patterns change, so the basket of goods becomes less and less representative as an index of prices, for new commodities appear while others decline in importance. One can change the 'weighting' of the items—but then comparability is lost. Peter Mathias has indicated the inadequacies of the most famous cost-of-living index, that of Professor Silberling:

The 'basket of goods' upon which [it] is based suggests that the 'Silberling man' did not live in a house (at least he paid no rent); he did not drink, he did not gamble and he did not smoke. He was scarcely representative, therefore, of the English working man. (Mathias, 1969, p. 217.)

Similar problems arise when one attempts to measure changes in money wages. In the first place the available indices may not be representative of workers as a whole. Secondly, money wages give no real indication of the amount of money which the worker actually has to spend at any particular time, for they take no account of unemployment or supplementary earnings. Likewise, we know too little of the actual earnings of workers employed on piece-rates, for their wages depended on the amount of work available, as well as on their own inclinations and aptitudes.

It is startling how little we know about unemployment. Yet, speaking of the first half of the nineteenth century, Pollard and Crossley estimate that 10 per cent of the population was permanently pauperised, while every major crisis rendered perhaps a third of the working classes unemployed and entirely dependent on charity and the poor laws. Hobsbawm gives figures for Leeds in 1838 which show the degree to which weekly wages must be corrected to take account of unemployment. He lists trades working twelve months, eleven months, ten months, and only nine months. Thus, for example, a tailor earning 16s a week, but working only eleven months, has a corrected wage of 14s 8d. Two months' unemployment brings the 13s a week wage of a weaver down to an average of 10s 10d, while a dyer, employed for only nine months, received an average weekly wage of only 16s 6d, as compared with a nominal wage of 22s. Supplementary earnings might increase the family income. Their amount depended on individual family circumstances, but, generally speaking, in the textile industries the earnings of a wife, a son and a daughter might double the husband's wage.

Emphasis amongst historians concerned with the standard of living debate has turned increasingly towards changing patterns of consumption. That this should be so is partly due to the technical difficulties involved in establishing cost of living indices, and partly to an awareness that consumption is likely to come under pressure during the process of industrialisation. Resources have to be diverted to investment, and the greater the proportion allocated in this way, the smaller the part left to satisfy the consumer. The example of Soviet Russia, where living standards were held static while the foundations of heavy industry were laid, is a dramatic example of the sacrifice of present comfort to future wealth and prosperity. However, Japanese industrial expansion after the First World War showed the possibility of reconciling industrial growth with improved living standards, so that it is dangerous to press the argument too far. Hartwell has supported his optimistic case with the point that the cost of investment was low during the British Industrial Revolution, while Hobsbawm has argued that as the investment mechanism was inefficient, with a large proportion of accumulated savings not directly invested in industry at all, a greater burden was thrown upon the rest of the community.

One might suppose that the growth of industry would provide a greater quantity and variety of goods for the masses, yet it remains difficult to make firm statements. As the textile factories were able to produce more cheaply than the former hand methods of spinning and weaving (while raw material costs also fell) there must have been a fall in the cost of clothing. But as fashions and materials changed, and as few people bought new clothes anyway, it is difficult to be certain how great an advantage this proved to be for the workers. Likewise, there was an increase in the supply of soap and candles, and a variety of household goods; but while some of these improvements must have percolated down to the mass of the population, a disproportionate amount was no doubt taken by the middle and upper classes.

Fuel was increasing in availability and falling in price, as improvements in transport assisted in the exploitation of inland coalfields. In 1815 the price of best coal in Newcastle and Sunderland was 13s a ton, while it cost 39s a ton in London; by 1845 the price had fallen to 8s a ton and 17s 3d a ton respectively.

We know less than we would like to about house rents, although, in relation to the labourer's wages, rents probably rose rather than declined between 1800 and 1850. Conditions in the towns were appalling, yet the jerry-built houses were often better than the rural slums from which many of the workers had come. The overcrowded conditions of the industrial towns revealed that supply failed to keep up with demand. Private builders tried to fill the gap, but many who wanted houses could not afford to buy them. Compared with the quick profits which might be made in trade or industry, house-building was not particularly attractive as an investment. A back-to-back cottage built in mid-century might cost £150-£200, and was expected to repay its capital cost after about 20 years at a rent of 4s a week. The weakness of much of the model housing movement, which stressed the need for economic rents, was that it failed to appreciate how little the majority of workers could afford. Yet even if he could afford better housing, it was difficult for the worker to improve his lot, as was revealed in Chadwick's Report on the Sanitary Condition of the Labouring Population, of 1842:

The workman's 'location' as it is termed, is generally governed by his work, near which he must reside. . . . The individual labourer has little or no power over the internal structure and economy of the dwelling which has fallen to his lot. If the water be not laid on in the other houses in the street, or if it be unprovided with proper receptacles for refuse, it is not in the power of an individual workman who may perceive the advantages of such accommodations to procure them. (Quoted in *English Historical Documents*, Vol. XII(I) Eyre & Spotiswood 1966 page 784.)

More attention has been focused on changes in the consumption patterns of food. Much of the argument hinges on the interpretation of the statistical sources, while there is disagreement as to the actual significance of the changes which can be demonstrated. It has been argued, for example, that foodstuffs differ not only in their nutritional value but also in the status which they hold in the eye of the consumer. Hobsbawm puts the point clearly:

A new food can be regarded as evidence of a rising standard of living only if it is adopted because believed to be superior (nutritionally or socially) to the old, and if bought without sacrificing what people believe to be necessities. Thus the mere fact that a new diet is nutritionally inferior to the old one is irrelevant, except to the nutritionist. If white bread is adopted because it is *believed* to be a sign of a higher standard, then its adoption must be regarded as a sign of improvement. Conversely, if—as was widely held in the early nineteenth century—labourers take to tea in order to make an increasingly grim diet tolerable, an increase in tea-drinking cannot prove a rising standard of living. (Hobsbawm, 1968, page 94.)

Meat is one item where a decline in per capita consumption might be taken as a *prima facie* case for a deterioration of living standards. A major source of information consists of the Returns of the Collector of Beasts Tolls at Smithfield Market. From these Dr Hobsbawm has argued that consumption declined after 1800. Yet the figures are difficult to use, for they indicate the number of beasts rather than their weight, and while G. E. Fussell has disproved that the weight of animals at market more than doubled during the course of the eighteenth century, as was formerly alleged, it would be dangerous, without an equally close examination, to assume that this conclusion could be carried over into the nineteenth century. Nor do the figures include all classes of meat—the most serious omission being the pig, which provided the major form of meat for the working class. Again, the figures apply only to London, whose economic progress did not run in the same way as that of the industrial north or the agricultural south. Furthermore, Hartwell has argued that the Smithfield Returns do not even represent an accurate estimate of meat consumption in the capital, in that there were other important markets such as Newgate and Leadenhall. John Burnett argues that there appears to be no evidence of a general rise in consumption trends over the period 1815-50. The trend in sugar and beer was downwards until 1845, tea remained stationary throughout the period, while bread consumption rose only after 1847. He suggests that sugar and beer are better indicators of working-class standards than tea (which was regarded as a near-necessity, and in consequence had an inelastic consumption) and that the evidence therefore points to a fall rather than a rise. After 1845, however, there is evidence of a sharp upswing in most food trends. As W. H. Chaloner has pointed out, the 1840s (in spite of popular belief) were no hungrier than preceding decades had been.

One cannot turn from an examination of diet without considering food adulteration, for while it clearly existed before the nineteenth century, there is much evidence that it increased during this period. It is, as Burnett has pointed out, very much a phenomenon of urban society, and exists where the producer and consumer are widely separated. A *Lancet* enquiry of the 1850s revealed the appalling extent to which adulteration had taken a grip on the food market. All bread tested in two separate samples was adulterated; over half the oatmeal was adulterated; all but the best quality tea was invariably adulterated, while a little over half the milk and all the butter was watered. Over half the jam and preserves included deleterious matter, and while 90 per cent of the sugar appeared to be straight, it was often filthy.

In some cases the adulteration represented merely a fraud on the pocket (although it grew in response to a demand for cheapness). In other cases the ingredients used to adulterate food were positively harmful to health, and made a direct contribution to the degradation of the workers. The response of some of them was co-operative shopkeeping, which, as Checkland has observed, 'was, in part, an attempt to avoid toxic Prussian blue in tea, plaster of Paris in bread, red lead in pepper and mahogany sawdust in coffee'.

Compared with the progress in working-class standards of living after 1850, the conclusion to which one is drawn is that there was comparatively little change during the first half of the century. Whether living standards actually declined, or whether there was a marginal increase, is debatable; all that one can say is that the record is unremarkable. As E. P. Thompson puts it:

In fifty years of the Industrial Revolution the working-class share of the national product had almost certainly fallen relative to the share of the property-owning and professional classes. . . . In psychological terms, this felt very much like a decline in standards. His own share in the 'benefits of economic progress' consisted of more potatoes, a few articles of cotton clothing for his family, soap and candles, some tea and sugar, and a great many articles in the Economic History Review. (E. P. Thompson, 1963, page 318.)

We need not consider at such length those changes which affected the way of life of the workers, for they are sociological rather than economic. Yet the two are so closely linked that the one cannot stand without the other. Only by considering both aspects of the condition of the people can one fill in the background to Luddism, the agrarian revolts, and the development of workers' organisations.

The task of adjusting to urban life faced many workers with a challenge which they were rarely able to meet. Traditional patterns of spending and saving were quite inappropriate for the demands of the factory towns. The traditional pattern had been that a man had a right to earn a living, and if unable to do so, a right to be kept alive by his community. Cash was of less importance, for he had access to other means of subsistence. Now only the wage packet stood between him and distress, and few had either the skill or the discipline to discount present benefits for the sake of the future. Yet the very irregularity of earnings made it difficult to take a long-term view of the future. In consequence, the worker often adjusted his expenditure to his lowest rather than his average earnings, and squandered any surplus which might accrue. Drink no doubt made the poor even poorer, yet it is difficult to condemn the worker for seeking some consolation, while the public house was often a warmer and more comfortable place than home.

The middle classes frequently made suggestions as to how the masses might budget more effectively, yet often with a total lack of understanding of the difficulties which they faced. Esther Copley's *Cottage Comforts* and *Cottage Cookery* circulated widely in the 1820s and 1830s, condemning the beer-house and the tea kettle, and suggesting that the labourer should drink infusions of rue or strawberry. *Cottage Cookery* was a collection of economical recipes for such delicacies as stewed ox-cheek and scrap pie. The recipe for mutton chitterlings suggested that they should be obtained immediately after the animal had been killed, scoured many times in salt and water, and put to soak, the water being frequently changed for twenty-four hours; this would make them quite white and free from smell. Such advice completely neglected the fact that the wives of many men were also at work in the factory and had neither the time nor the inclination to cope with food which required extensive preparation. The difficulties facing factory wives were brought out in evidence before the Factories Commission in 1833:

Brought up in the factory until they are married, and sometimes working there long after that event has taken place, even when they become mothers they are almost entirely ignorant of household duties, and are incapable of laying out the money their husbands have earned to the best advantage. They are equally incapable of preparing his victuals, in an economical and comfortable manner. . . . Every apology, however, may be offered for some of these unfortunate creatures for they have never had the opportunity of learning better. (Quoted in E. Royston Pike, 1966, page 233.)

Dicticians might concern themselves with propagating the nutritional value of particular foods, but the kind of food which commended itself to the workers was that which needed least preparation, was tasty, and if possible, hot. Anyone who experienced the depression of the 1930s knows the truth of this. George Orwell described the attitude in *The Road to Wigan Pier*:

When you are underfed, harassed, bored, and miserable, you don't *want* to eat dull wholesome food. You want something a little bit 'tasty'. There is always some cheaply pleasant thing to tempt you. Let's have three pennorth of chips! Run out and buy us a twopenny ice-cream!

Put the kettle on and we'll all have a nice cup of tea! . . . White bread-and-marge and sugared tea don't nourish you to any extent, but they are *nicer* (at least most people think so) than brown bread-and-dripping and cold water.

Just as the worker had to learn the new skills of the urban consumer, so he had to adapt himself to the burdens of factory discipline. He was not the only learner in this situation, for perhaps the major problem of the new industrial entrepreneurs was that of labour management. The employer quite often fell into the habit of regarding his capital equipment as his major concern, and thinking of the worker as expendable. Many of the excesses of the factory system were the result.

Machinery required a new regularity from workpeople, and the practice of celebrating 'Saint Monday' by starting work on Tuesday was the despair of the masters. Absenteeism was rife. As late as the 1840s it was estimated in South Wales that the workers lost one week in five, while in the fortnight after the monthly pay-day only two-thirds of the time was worked. With a tradition of working for subsistence, the worker now had to be made obedient to the cash stimulus. Regularity was frequently enforced by fines, which were meant to hurt. Fines of 6d to 2s were typical for ordinary offences, and were equivalent to between two hours' and a day's wages. No assessment of the worker's wage is complete which ignores this.

Of all the evils of the factory system, that which we find most appalling is the employment of children, the greatest problems being produced in the textile mills. Silk mills were dependent almost exclusively on child labour, with two-thirds to three-quarters of the hands often under eighteen. In flax and the woollen and worsted industries the proportion was around 50 per cent, while in cotton it was around 40-45 per cent. There is some evidence that the introduction of child labour was a concession to the earlier family-based economy, mill owners striking up bargains with heads of families for the labour of the whole unit. Family discipline was imposed on the children, and it may be noted that Peel's Factory Act of 1802 applied only to pauper apprentices who were outside the kinship system. Technological advance eventually broke up these kinship links. The automatic mules of Richard Roberts, introduced into the mills after 1824, meant that an adult spinner needed as many as nine young assistants in place of the one or two required before. On the other side of the industry, power-loom weaving similarly broke the tradition of family employment. Attitudes swung radically when foremen and managers came to impose discipline, instead of the father as before. The kinship system was broken to pieces by the 1833 Factory Act, which limited the hours of work of children, and snapped the link between the children's shifts and those of the adults. The reactions of the workers were initially to demand either the bringing down of adult working hours to those of the adolescents (12 hours per day with no night work) or a 12-hour day for the children. The movement then swung behind the demand for a ten-hour day, which was gained in 1847. However, down to 1853 the Factory Acts were confined to textile mills, and although in practice the Ten Hours Act meant that men had to stop work with the women and the children, no limitations were imposed on the adult male workers. Gradually the evidence of the blue books broke through public apathy, and although Lord Londonderry, a leading owner of collieries in County Durham, regarded them as 'extravagant . . . disgusting, and in some cases of a scandalous and obscene character', the pictures which accompanied the report to Parliament on the employment of women and children in mines aroused great indignation. Here there could be no mere amelioration, and the Mines Act of 1842 prohibited entirely the employment underground of women and boys under ten.

4 The hand-loom weavers But what if the worker should resist the changes in his way of life implied by the factory system, and cling to the old traditional ways? The result could be nothing short of disaster, as the plight of the hand-loom weavers was to prove. They represent a group to whom new economic incentives proved weaker than the old bonds of independence and family unity.

The cotton hand-loom weavers are an interesting group in that they are sometimes represented as though they were domestic workers, lingering on from an older economic system, and finally destroyed by the factory system. Yet in reality they were both created and destroyed by the Industrial Revolution, the traditional time limits of which coincide almost exactly with their rise and decline. 'In three generations', writes Duncan Bythell, 'the process of economic change had first created and then destroyed a new type of labour.' Once the new cotton fabric could be made, its cheapness and variety immediately commended itself to home and foreign markets, and to meet the ever-growing demand, a labour force of cotton hand-loom weavers had to be called into being, for whereas spinning was early mechanised, the power-loom, though invented in the 1780s, was not, for various technical and economic reasons, quickly introduced. In the early nineteenth century there were serious attempts to improve the *hand-loom*, and not until the 1820s was it generally felt that the power-loom had come to stay and would eventually triumph in the industry. Even as late as 1830 it was estimated that there were in England and Scotland not more than 60,000 power-looms, while there were 240,000 hand-looms.

Contrary to popular belief, hand-loom weaving was not a skilled trade. Three weeks was reckoned sufficient time to learn plain weaving, while of muslin weaving a manufacturer claimed that 'a lad of fourteen may acquire a sufficient knowledge of it in six weeks'. Many weavers from the older fustian trade entered cotton weaving, as did many domestic spinners displaced by the new machinery. Irishmen also entered the trade, although their importance has recently been questioned by Duncan Bythell. At first the high wages proved attractive, but the ease of entry led to distress, as hand-loom weaving came to be seen as a last refuge. As more and more entered the trade, so piece rates fell. From a peak of 23s per week in 1805, wage rates dropped to 6s by 1831. It was this demoralising competition amongst themselves, rather than competition with the power loom, which led to their distress, for it can be shown that their misery was great even before the power-loom came to be more widely adopted in the 1820s. It is to the period immediately after the Napoleonic Wars that the bitter indignation of the anonymous weaver-poet relates:

> Aw'm a poor cotton wayver as many a one knows.
> Aw've nowt t'eat in the house, an aw've wore out me clo'es.
> Me clogs are both brokken an' stockins aw've none.
> Yo'd hardly gie tuppence for all aw've got on. . . .

As piece rates fell, so the weavers produced more, merely adding to their own degradation. It is a plausible estimate that in the 1820s output per weaver increased by about 25 or 30 per cent. The manufacturer was happy to employ both power-looms and hand-looms, for he could base his steady trade on the former, and give out more work for the latter when trade was brisk. In this way he kept his own costs down (for the weaver provided his own loom and paid his own rent) and in times of slackness he could reverse the process, dispensing with the services of the hand-loom weaver first.

Why then did not more weavers leave the trade instead of hanging on—especially after the writing was on the wall in the 1820s? There were many reasons why the hand-loom weaver might have difficulty in finding alternative employment in the factories, even if he could overcome his deep antipathy towards them. In the first place there were geographical difficulties, as the earliest power-looms were located outside the old weaving districts; for whereas the latter tended to be in the rural areas, the new weaving mills tended to grow alongside the sources of power, and in many cases side-by-side with the spinning mills. Secondly, the demand in the mills was mainly for the labour of women and children, and adult males might experience difficulty in getting work. John Fielden, one of the best-disposed of masters, recalled of 1835:

I was applied to weekly by scores of hand-loom weavers, who were so pressed down in their conditions as to be obliged to seek such work, and it gave me and my partners no small pain to . . . be compelled to refuse work to men who applied for it. (Quoted in E. P. Thompson, 1963, page 309.)

In addition, the attitude of trade unions in other sections of industry, if not downright hostile, was at best unhelpful, and there was a natural fear that employers would use hand-loom weavers as blacklegs. There was nothing idyllic about the life of the hand-loom weaver in his cottage, and even his independence was more illusory than real; yet, however poor, he felt that he had a certain status which no factory 'hand' ever had, for he could regard himself as the real *maker* of cloth. Where social losses compete against economic gains, it is never inevitable that the latter will win.

5 Workers' movements in the first half of the nineteenth century The remainder of this chapter is concerned with some of the ways in which workers in the first half of the nineteenth century combined to maintain or improve their position. Such organisation might, in the main, take four forms. In the first place, the period reveals the first effective attempts to form trade unions to take collective action, by negotiation or strike, in disputes with employers. On the other hand, when this proved impracticable or ineffective, workers might proceed to what Dr Hobsbawm has called 'collective bargaining by riot'—putting pressure on employers by damaging property, and in particular by breaking machinery. Thirdly, action might be taken to better conditions through some form of 'self-help'—friendly societies might be formed to provide some means of social insurance against sickness and death, and co-operative societies which might offer better trading facilities, as well as promise benefits of a higher order. Finally, the workers might resort to political action, which might itself take a number of forms. In addition to demanding a say in the government of the country the workers pressed Parliament both to pass new laws, and to enforce existing laws, for their protection. These varied approaches to the common problem predominated in different places and at different times. London workers concentrated on political reform, while trade union activity was strong in the north. On the other hand, the greatest outbreak of machine-breaking was concentrated in the agricultural counties of the south. Broad trends are also discernible chronologically. Activity of all kinds was widespread in the troubled years after the Napoleonic Wars, while the 1820s and early 1830s saw a great growth in trade union activity. The poor law question came to a head just as the great trade union agitation of 1830-4 was dying down, and this turned attention back to politics in general, and Chartism in particular. While these divisions, both chronological and categorical, are useful, they should not of course be regarded as mutually exclusive, for there were many shared characteristics. To take a notable example, friendly societies and trade unions were often difficult to differentiate, while many ostensibly political movements pursued economic ends.

6 Ned Lud and Captain Swing The Luddites have received a poor press. In the popular mind, Luddism lingers on, as E. P. Thompson has put it, 'as an uncouth, spontaneous affair of illiterate handworkers, blindly resisting machinery'. There is the view noted by Hobsbawm, 'that the early labour movement did not know what it was doing, but merely reacted, blindly and gropingly, to the pressures of misery, as animals in the laboratory react to electric currents'. Classical middle-class economists assumed that the workers must be taught not to pit themselves against economic inevitability. Even the Hammonds and the Webbs, pioneer students of the movement, found difficulty in sympathising, for their Fabian persuasion made them view the labour movement in terms of a progression towards the T.U.C. and the Labour Party, and it was difficult to fit the Luddites into this framework. The work of Dr Hobsbawm, and more recently of E. P. Thompson, has done something towards redressing the balance.

Luddism proper was confined almost entirely to three areas and to three occupations, and was an active force for only a limited period. The areas chiefly affected were the West Riding, where the croppers of the woollen trade rose in revolt; South Lancashire, where the cotton weavers were active; and Nottinghamshire, Leicestershire and Derbyshire, where the movement sprang up among the framework knitters. The unrest began in 1811, and continued intermittently down to about 1818, although in 1826 there were serious outbreaks of loom-breaking in Lancashire. It is important to distinguish between the movements in the three areas, for the characteristics of these groups of workers varied, and for only one of them did machine-breaking represent direct antipathy to the introduction of machinery.

The croppers or shearmen of Yorkshire were skilled and privileged workers, who were amongst the aristocracy of the woollen industry. Their task was concerned with the vital finishing processes of cleaning, tentering (or stretching), pressing, and the key process by which the nap of the cloth was raised, and then cropped or sheared. The nap was raised by teazles, and the shearing was done by heavy hand shears which might weigh 40 lbs and be four feet in length. So skilled was their craft, and so important the processes, that it was claimed that their work could make a difference of 20 per cent, for good or ill, in the value of cloth. The croppers' skill was directly threatened by two machines—the gig-mill and the shearing-frame. The gig-mill was a device whereby the nap was raised by cylinders set with teazles, instead of by hand. It was not a new invention; in fact it had been banned by a statute of Edward VI. Indeed, much of the conflict leading up to Luddism hinged on the failure of the authorities to enforce this law. The shearing-frame was simply a device which, by mounting two or more shears in a frame, dispensed with the need for skilled craftsmen. Petitions to Parliament in 1802-3, and again in 1806, failed to secure an enforcement of the protective legislation. The threat imposed by machinery now appeared greater: 'Now gigs and shearing frames are like to become general', complained the croppers, 'if they are allowed to go on many hundreds of us will be out of bread.' Not only did Parliament allow the trend to continue; in 1809 all the protective legislation in the woollen industry—covering apprenticeship, gig-mills, and the number of looms—was repealed. Here was an example of *laissez-faire* proving a burden rather than a benefit to the workers.

The condition of the cotton weavers and the frameworkknitters was somewhat different. They were outworkers, experiencing a devastating loss of status, to whom machine-breaking represented little more than a method (and an effective one at that) of putting pressure on their employers. The conditions of the cotton weavers have already been described, but something needs to be said of the framework knitters. The hosiery trade was highly localised. Nearly 90 per cent of all the frames in the United Kingdom in 1812 (and over 60 per cent of the estimated number of frames in the world) were situated in the Midlands. There was a certain amount of specialisation between counties, Leicestershire's trade being mainly in wool, while the cotton trade was concentrated in Nottinghamshire, with silk divided between that county and Derbyshire. The industry was preponderantly rural, more than 82 per cent of the frames being scattered amongst 253 manufacturing villages. The isolation of the frames did much to make the work of the machine-breakers easier.

The grievances of the framework-knitters were complex. Few owned their own looms or frames, the majority renting them either from a hosier or from an independent speculator. This gave the hosier two methods of cutting wages, for he could either lower the piece rate or raise the frame rent. The framework-knitters claimed that they were defrauded in a variety of ways; piece rates depended on the quality of the articles produced, which the hosier could determine arbitrarily, numerous deductions from earnings were made, and in some villages payment in wages had been almost entirely displaced by 'truck'. More serious than any of these complaints were those against 'cut-ups' and 'colting'. Cut-up stockings and other articles were but one of a number of means whereby hosiers attempted, by shoddy methods, to meet the demands of a boom market. Cut-up stockings were manufactured from large pieces of knitted material which were then cut out and sewn to the shape of the leg. Although at first they might be difficult to distinguish from the genuine article, they soon lost shape and had a tendency to split. The worker, with his craftsman's pride in his trade, resented these shoddy goods, which he felt destroyed the confidence of the consumer. Moreover, the cheap new techniques of production encouraged an influx of cheap, unskilled labour. The displacement of skilled men by employing unskilled labour or too many apprentices ('colting') pushed the craftsman further down the pathway of decline.

Abuses within the trade, rather than the introduction of machinery, therefore underlay this branch of Luddism.

The restriction of foreign markets by Napoleon's Continental System, and the closure of the American market in 1811, caused a collapse of demand, and as stocks piled up in warehouses, distress became very real. This was the spark which led to the outbreak of machine-breaking in Nottinghamshire which spread throughout the Midlands and into other areas. Ned Lud's right hand man was 'Enoch', the giant sledge hammer used to smash doors and machinery. Many of the frames (as well, ironically, as the hammers) were made by Enoch Taylor, of Marsden. 'Enoch made them', cried the Luddites, 'Enoch shall break them.'

> Great Enoch still shall lead the van
> Stop him who dare! stop him who can!
> Press forward every gallant man
> With hatchet, pike, and gun . . .

In the first phase of Nottinghamshire Luddism, between March 1811 and February 1812, perhaps 1000 frames were destroyed, at a value of between £6000 and £10,000. The Luddites showed remarkable organisation and great discrimination in what they destroyed, frames not used for cut-ups or colting being usually spared. Geography gave to Luddism different characteristics in Lancashire and Yorkshire, where the machines were chiefly to be found in mills, which were easier to defend, and made the masters less easy to intimidate. It was in these areas that the legendary pitched battles were fought.

It is not easy to judge how effective Luddism was as a workers' movement, although Hobsbawm argues that it was at least as effective as other means of bringing pressure might have been, since men with little scarcity value could gain nothing from strike action, and were forced to adopt violent defensive tactics. Luddism proved an effective method of enforcing group-solidarity (as anyone who has experienced the behaviour of gangs will know) while the destruction of property—or the constant threat of destruction—might prove an effective means of intimidating smaller employers. At least a temporary redress of grievances was granted everywhere except in Lancashire and Cheshire. Yorkshire woollen masters withdrew their shearing-frames, and in the Midlands negotiations between the men and their employers quickly followed.

The country cousin of Ned Lud was Captain Swing; he was equally desperate and in some ways more effective, Indeed, the 'Swing' rising of the agricultural labourers in 1830 has been described as the greatest machine-breaking episode in English history. As with the earlier Luddites, the revolt represented more than *just* antipathy to labour-saving machinery. It was an explosion for which the combustible material had been piled up for several decades, and as with the Luddites, the causes were both social and economic.

During the Napoleonic Wars farmers and labourers drifted apart, the one class enjoying high profits and learning to acquire the trappings of the gentry, the other gradually sinking into depths of misery. It was the widening social gap, as much as anything, which accounted for the decline of living-in, one of the traditional means of supporting the labourer:

> At the kitchen table formerly, the farmer he would sit,
> And carve for all his servants, both pudding and fine meat,
> But now all in the dining-room so closely they're boxed in,
> If a servant only was to peep, it would be thought a sin.

The demobilisation of 400,000 servicemen at the end of the war added to the rural surplus of labour, and the riots in East Anglia in 1816 showed the explosiveness of the situation.

It is often alleged that the impoverishment of the farm labourers was largely the result of the poor law—in particular, the Speenhamland system of allowances, and to a lesser extent the settlement system. It is claimed that the latter prevented the labourer from travelling in search of work by confining him to the parish in which he was legally 'settled', but it has been shown that the laws were never applied as severely as they might have been, while inertia was a greater bar to the mobility of the worker. Likewise, most recent opinion plays down the supposed effect of the Speenhamland system, heavy poor law expenditure now being seen as the consequence of low wages and unemployment rather than the cause.

It was in 1795 that the Berkshire Justices of the Peace, meeting at Speenhamland, near Newbury, made an honest attempt to deal humanely with the rising tide of pauperism and the threat of famine. Rejecting the expedient of a minimum wage, they decided to subsidise low wages out of the poor rates in cases where the labourer's income fell below subsistence level, either because the number of his children was too large or the price of bread too high. Although never given the basis of law, the sliding-scale system of allowances was soon widely adopted except in the extreme north and west. The outcome had not been anticipated; farmers found that by paying low wages, even where able (if only temporarily) to pay more, they could throw some of the burden on to the parish. Likewise, the labourer had little incentive to exert himself, for his income was pinned to a subsistence level. Traditionally the argument has tended to stop here, but attention is now focused more on the large stagnant pool of surplus labour and the high structural and seasonal unemployment. The importance of the existence of alternative forms of employment in determining agricultural wages is borne out by the differential between the wages of farm labourers working in the north, where industry offered alternative employment, and the south, where the local economy was almost entirely dependent on agriculture. There, under-employment was constant, except perhaps at the height of the harvest. Possibly a quarter of the entire annual labour requirement of a farm was taken up with threshing, which went on throughout November, December and January, if not longer. These winter months coincided with the time of greatest burden to the men, when their need for fuel, food and clothing was greatest. The introduction of threshing machines—slowly at first because human labour with the flail was so cheap—enabled farmers to stand off more men at the time of their greatest need. It is not difficult to see why the machines should have been so hated by the labourers.

The opportunities for self-defence or protest open to the labourer were few. The very surplus of labour made mere protests against wage cuts, or demands for higher wages, unlikely to succeed unless they were accompanied by a mass movement. He could fall back on the poor law, until what had started as a temporary expedient sank into such chaos that something had to be done. More positively, he could turn to crime, either as a means of social protest, or in order to eke out his budget. Poaching possessed both of these qualities. Cobbett once asked a young Surrey labourer how he managed to live on the half-crown dole he got from the parish for breaking stones. 'I poach', was the reply, 'it is better to be hanged than starved to death.' Country people could see no sin in poaching, and in some years nearly two-thirds or more of all convictions were under the Game Laws. Poaching represented a blow to the farmer and the squire. If such blows failed to achieve much, outright terror might achieve more; hence the labourer was led to arson and the destruction of buildings and machines.

There were thus many reasons why the labourers should have rebelled. That they did so in 1830 may have been due to the worsening economic conditions of the previous two years, and may have owed something to the revolution in France and the political tension at home. At all events, the revolt began in Kent in the summer of that year, and exploded throughout the southern and eastern counties in the following months. The exact pattern varied from district to district. In some places the stress was on wages and allowances; in others men resorted to the flaming torch and the crashing hammer. Between August 1830 and September 1832, a total of 387 threshing machines and 26 other agricultural machines were destroyed in 22 counties. It is difficult to assess the total damage, but a figure of £100,000 has been suggested for damage caused by incendiary fires, while it has been estimated that over £20,000 of agricultural and industrial machinery was destroyed by the farm labourers.

The rising did achieve something. Wages were temporarily raised in the southern counties, although the state of the labour market made a permanent improvement impossible. Similarly, the spread of threshing machines was held up. As late as 1843 it was claimed that in many agricultural districts of the south the threshing machine could not be used 'owing to the destructive vengeance with which the labourers resisted its introduction'.

There were other effects upon the labourers themselves. Nineteen swung from the gallows, while nearly five hundred were torn from their families and shipped 12,000 miles away with virtually no hope of ever returning. In subsequent years others were to follow them abroad, the more desperate as transportees, the more enterprising as emigrants. For those who remained there was continued bitterness and hatred, reflected in sporadic rick-burning and machine-breaking; but not until the rise of Joseph Arch's union in the 1870s was there an effective movement of the farm workers. Instead the more active drifted to the towns.

7 The organised worker   Friendly societies, co-operatives and trade unions were three organisations whereby those without political power sought to protect themselves in an increasingly industrialised society. The movements are not always easy to separate, for, in their initial stages at least, they grew in that atmosphere of secrecy fostered not only by the hostile attitudes of those in power, but the colour which secret rites could bring into otherwise drab lives. At times the confusion between the different movements was deliberately exploited by the workers, as when the illegal trade unions used the organisation of a friendly society as a mask for their activities. When Francis Place joined a Breeches Makers Benefit Society in the 1790s, he found that it was in fact 'intended for the purpose of supporting the members in a strike for wages'.

The facility with which English working men formed societies in the early nineteenth century was formidable, and E. P. Thompson has described them as the most 'clubbable' working class in Europe. 'It seems at times', he says, 'that half a dozen working men could scarcely sit in a room together without appointing a Chairman, raising a point-of-order, or moving the Previous Question.'

8 Friendly societies and co-operative societies   The democratic organisation of the trade unions was probably derived from the friendly societies, which, in terms of both time and numbers, represented the pioneers amongst the three groups. Some measure of the importance of friendly societies is given by the estimate in the early 1870s that there were some 4 million members of friendly societies as against no more than 1 million trade unionists.

The friendly societies differed greatly, both in organisation and strength. On the one hand there were small village clubs, each with its own emblem and customs; while on the other, there were the massive affiliated orders, like the Manchester Unity of Oddfellows, whose appeal was to better-paid workers. There were the highly centralised societies, like the Hearts of Oak and the Royal Standard, devoid of the 'friendly' spirit and operating simple insurance business; and there were societies associated with particular trades whose interests went beyond social benefits into the realm of industrial relations.

By and large, the societies served the two distinct purposes of social solidarity and social welfare. It was difficult for middle-class critics to appreciate the former—that to many of their members they were *friendly* societies, real societies of friends. Thus the convivial 'box nights', when the funds were counted, were frowned on, as was the practice of holding meetings in public houses. In contrast, the social welfare activities were greatly encouraged (so long as they were adequately supervised) for if the workers made their own provisions against ill-health and unemployment, the burden was removed from the community at large. Indeed, the Registrar of Friendly Societies came to be described as 'minister of self-help to the whole of the industrious classes', for his administrative functions eventually came to cover not only friendly societies, but also trade unions, savings banks, building societies and co-operative stores. He was, it was claimed, 'the embodiment of the goodwill and protection of the state'.

Co-operative shopkeeping (as was suggested at the beginning of this chapter) began as a means to an end; the raising of capital to establish productive co-operative communities. Yet, as Professor Pollard has put it:

It is one of the strengths of the co-operative idea that its appeal to human beings, then as now, is at many different levels. At the lowest, it offers immediate advantages in employment, saving and pure goods for sale, without any special demands on the members; next, it offers the social and educational values of co-operating with others on a local basis; further, it was expected to put all the paupers to useful work, and increase national output; at a higher level still, it proposed to offer the attractions of communal, harmonious relationships in life and work; it offered justice in the distribution of wealth; it promised a rational, happy, and more social commonwealth; and at its highest, it presented a new religion which could combine the aspirations of the soul with a rational explanation of society, and promised to lift the life of man on to a higher plane of existence. (Pollard, 1967, page 89 by permission of Macmillan, London and Basingstoke.)

So long as capitalism was regarded as ephemeral, the vision of co-operative communities remained feasible, but as capitalism gained strength—and was seen to offer hope of progress to the workers—the vision became more and more utopian. In the co-operative movement, the watershed was marked by the decision of the Rochdale Pioneers to pay dividends on purchases, instead of saving profits to establish communities. Revolutionary aims were abandoned, but the movement continued to develop both as a field for working-class investment, and as an expression of the Victorian ideal of self-help.

9 The development of trade unions The growth of trade unions is often seen as a response to the Industrial Revolution and, of course, in many ways it was. Yet it was a response not merely to the factory system, but to the fundamental changes in society and the economy which the Industrial Revolution entailed. The pioneers were not factory workers, and the first unions were almost all of skilled artisans anxious to maintain their status and their standard of living rather than of labourers. There were obvious reasons why this should have been so. Such men possessed a scarcity value which enabled them to put pressure upon their employers; their earnings more frequently allowed something to spare for union subscriptions, and they possessed in their ranks a greater proportion of literate persons able to fulfil the administrative requirements of an organised body of men. It was inevitable, therefore, that regional differences should appear in trade union organisation. It was in the south that craft unionism found much of its strength, while the general union better suited the demands of the factory workers of the north. Even there, the more skilled workers took the lead: the mule spinners in the cotton mills, for example, and the skilled miners in the collieries.

The early unions were weak, yet their weakness sprang from economic conditions rather than the opposition of the law. Continuity of combinations was weakened by the rapidly expanding labour force and rapidly changing industrial location. As industries grew apace an enemy appeared in the small, newly-established master, who often undercut in price, overworked his employees, and broke apprenticeship agreements. Fluctuations in the economy revealed the weaknesses of the unions, and wage levels were never so high as to allow the accumulation of large funds to sustain a long strike action. Funds were soon exhausted, and even a minor strike could ruin a union for years.

There are other reasons why the effects of the Combination Laws should not be over-stressed, for there was a substantial body of common law, as well as over forty statutes, which prevented men from combining at the end of the eighteenth century. The number of statutes is indicative of two things; that there had been a widespread existence of unions over a number of years, and that Parliament was ready and willing to support the labour policy of the employers. It was the introduction in 1799 of a Bill similar to the many which had already been enacted which led to the passage of the Combination Act of 1799 (modified in 1800); although the legislation of those years was more a response to the critical political situation.

The Combination Acts did not make illegal what had been legal before. Instead, they represent an administrative reform, designed to check a growing and illegal practice. In contrast to the seven years' transportation to which members of unlawful combinations could be sentenced under existing legislation, the three months' imprisonment or two months' hard labour provided by the new Acts was mild. Few prosecutions took place under the Acts, although the process of summary conviction which they contained could prove successful in the hands of determined employers. In 1801, for example, some of the workers of Messrs. Bulmer's ship-yard at South Shields sent their employer, in the course of a strike, an anonymous letter:

You Bulmer, if you do not give the carpenters a *guinea* a week as sure as Hell is hot O before winter is done you must be shot O . . .

Bulmer had little difficulty in speedily identifying some of the striking workmen, who, when threatened with prosecution under the new Acts, publicly apologised, thanked him for his leniency, and promised good behaviour for the future. For more serious offences, it seems, the Common Law continued to be applied.

In theory the Acts of 1799 and 1800 also forbade combinations amongst the masters, but this section remained a dead letter. In 1811, in one of the few recorded actions against masters under the Acts, evidence was produced before the magistrates that some of the Nottinghamshire hosiers had combined to reduce wages, but the authorities refused to take action.

By this time it was becoming increasingly clear that the law was failing to put down combinations of workers, and in the post-war years the illegal trade unions began openly to display their strength. In Manchester, during the great strike of 1818, the spinners 'marched By piccadilly on Tuesday and was 23½ minets in going Bye', while in the following year the miners at Dewsbury proceeded through the town with bands playing and banners flying.

The repeal of the Combination Laws owed much to the exertions of Francis Place, although he was not alone in advocating reform. It was not that Place was a supporter of trade unions; on the contrary, he felt that wages tended to find their own level according to the laws of supply and demand, and that combinations existed because of the law of the land, rather than in spite of it. He wrote:

Repeal every troublesome and vexatious enactment, and enact very little in their place. Leave workmen and their employers as much as possible at liberty to make their own bargains in their own way. This is the way to prevent disputes.

Place was a great wire-puller, and with the support of Joseph Hume, M.P., a Select Committee was set up in 1824 to consider repeal. The committee was packed with supporters, and with great patience Place rehearsed the workmen who appeared as witnesses. In its report the committee endorsed the view that the Combination Laws 'had a tendency to produce mutual irritation and distrust', and recommended not only their repeal, but an amendment of the common law to allow peaceful combination. As a result, legislation was passed in the same year, sweeping aside all statutes concerning combinations from the reign of Edward I onwards. 'Combinations will soon cease to exist', wrote Place:

Men have been kept together for long periods only by the oppression of the laws; these being repealed, combinations will lose the matter which cements them into masses, and they will fall to pieces. All will be as orderly as even a Quaker could desire. (Quoted in E. P. Thompson, 1963, page 519.)

But he was soon proved wrong. The Act came into force just at the beginning of a period of good trade and rising prices, with the result that there was a great crop of strikes, some of them violent. The government quickly counter-attacked, and a new Select Committee was established in 1825. This committee heard rather more evidence than its predecessor, and it required great effort on the part of Place and Hume to prevent the laws being re-enacted. In the event, a compromise was reached, for while repeal was upheld, the provisions against violence and intimidation were made much more stringent. 'Molesting' or 'obstructing' persons at work was forbidden, and the legal purposes of combinations were narrowly defined. However, trade unions and strikes were no longer illegal as such. The existence of unions was still precarious: they could be sued for breach of contract or action in restraint of trade, and if union funds were stolen (as they quite frequently were) no action could be taken in the courts unless the subterfuge of registering as a friendly society had been adopted.

In spite of their precarious position, trade unions developed in the later 1820s in a remarkably ambitious way, with attention focused not only on national unions of particular trades but also on national general unions of all trades. After a cotton spinners' and weavers' strike in 1818 a general union called the Philanthropic Society was established in Lancashire, while in the following year a similar society known as the Philanthropic Hercules was set up in London. Neither possessed anything like herculean strength, and they were both short-lived. It was ten years before there was another serious attempt to form a general union, but again the initiative came from the Lancashire textile industry.

After a disastrous strike in 1829, delegates from the spinning trade met in the Isle of Man, under the leadership of John Doherty, and established the Grand General Union of All Operative Spinners in the United Kingdom, which has been described as the first really national trade union of the modern type. In Doherty's mind the Spinners' Union was only part of a more ambitious plan, and, in the following year, he established in Manchester a general union of all trades which went by the name of the National Association of United Trades for the Protection of Labour. Twenty trades were represented at the inaugural meeting, and soon the number of affiliated societies rose to 150. Its strength lay mainly in the Lancashire textile towns, although its net was soon spread as far as Huddersfield, Birmingham, and Newtown in Montgomeryshire. By 1831 the N.A.P.L. claimed a membership of 100,000. The name, however, suggests the inherent weakness of the union, for it was concerned with 'protection' rather than 'advancement'. The rules stated:

That the funds of this Society shall be applied only to prevent reductions of wages, but in no case to procure an advance. Any trade considering their wages too low may exert themselves to obtain such advance, as they may think necessary and can obtain it by their own exertions. (Quoted in Cole & Filson, 1965, page 253.)

It was difficult to get one trade to support another, and even different sections of the same trade proved unwilling to offer mutual assistance. Thus when, engaged in a strike to prevent a reduction of wages, the Lancashire spinners called on their fellow-workers for support, not only did the Scottish and Irish spinners fail to comply, but even the other English workers made only a partial response. By March 1831 the strike had failed, breaking up the Spinners' Union and weakening in consequence the N.A.P.L., which was further damaged when its secretary ran off with the bulk of the remaining funds. By 1832 the N.A.P.L. had ceased to exist as a truly national and general union, and had broken up into a number of separate sections, most of which soon merged themselves into the Grand National Consolidated Trades Union.

The years 1829-34 saw a great ferment amongst working class movements, and although activity took a variety of forms, it is possible to see behind them the common influence of Owenism. Robert Owen (1771-1858) is one of the most fascinating characters of the nineteenth century. He grew up with the new industrial age, and was one of the first to see its evils. 'All the world is queer save thee and me', he is reputed to have said to a business partner, 'and even thou art a little queer.' Phrenologists agreed that Owen's 'bump of benevolence' was unusually large, and it was his practical benevolence and philanthropy which made his New Lanark mills the destination of thousands of admiring visitors. The solution of two problems facing him as an employer underlay his ideas; the creation of an efficient labour force in his factories, and the curse of unemployment and pauperism.

The labour force of New Lanark fluctuated around 1400-1500, and in terms of numbers employed it was the largest cotton mill in Britain. Wages were low in comparison with other mills; but were counterbalanced by superior social welfare benefits. Housing was provided at a moderate rent, a contributory sickness and superannuation fund was maintained, free medical services were available, and there existed a remarkable school for the children. In addition, a large store and a savings bank existed for the benefit of the workers, whose social and recreational needs were also met. All of these facilities arose from Owen's overriding belief in the importance of environment on character-formation; yet idealist though he was, New Lanark was held up not only as a fine example of enlightened philanthropy but also of enlightened management. The measures were in no sense 'charity', and there could be no mistaking that New Lanark was, first and foremost, a profit-making cotton-mill.

There was also much middle-class interest in Owen's solution to the problem of poverty. He felt that with the industrial advance of Britain, poverty was not only wicked, but unnecessary—for already every man could produce more than enough to keep himself and his family in comfort. This could be proved by setting all paupers to work on sufficient land and capital, living in communities and trading their products with each other, and the surplus with the outside world. This had an immediate appeal to many of the governing powers, for not only would the poor rates be reduced, but the wealth of the country would be increased. Gradually, however, the subversive character of Owen's plan for 'Villages of Co-operation' became clearer, and it was seen that it struck at the very root of the profit system. Likewise, it came to be appreciated that Owen meant them not as a mere measure of relief for the unemployed, but as the basis of a whole new social and economic order. Very quickly Owen's rich friends began to desert him, with the result that his appeal to the working class increased. Owenism, says J. F. C. Harrison, 'provided a kind of reservoir from which different groups and individuals drew ideas and inspiration which they then applied as they chose'. The workers dipped increasingly into that reservoir in the early 1830s.

At the heart of Owen's ideas lay the *labour theory of value*, an idea supported by the economists Adam Smith and Ricardo. The theory postulated that the measure of the value of commodities was the quantity of labour incorporated in their production. But, whereas the 'orthodox' theory gave the capitalist a share in the product of labour, in the 1820s it was used by the enemies of the existing system as a weapon against capitalism. Interpreted by them, the labour which was the source of all value was the productive labour of the worker alone. Capitalists were regarded as parasites whose role could be eliminated by co-operative production.

From this idea arose the Labour Exchanges, of which the chief example was Owen's National Equitable Labour Exchange, which opened its doors in 1832, and was followed by others in Birmingham, Liverpool, Glasgow and elsewhere. In such labour exchanges the workmen or producers' co-operative societies could directly exchange their products in such a way as to dispense altogether with the capitalist employer or capitalist merchant. An entrance fee was charged on joining the exchange, and a small commission on each article deposited. The system worked in this way:

A tailor will bring—say, a waistcoat, or topcoat, say it cost four shillings for the cloth, etc. and six hours' labour; we give him a note to this amount; he turns round and sees a pair of shoes; they cost four shillings and six hours' labour; he gives his labour note the same as we give a shilling over the counter; the shoes are taken away, and the note destroyed, because it ceases to represent real wealth. (Quoted in J. F. C. Harrison, 1969, page 202.)

Labour notes were also used to give change. However laudable its aims, the system was hampered by certain weaknesses. It was impossible for Labour values and ordinary commercial values to exist side by side, for goods which the exchange sold for less than the private tradesman were quickly disposed of, while those for which it asked more remained on the shelves. Unlike the ordinary shops, the exchanges could not control their stocks to fit the demand. They had to take what was brought to them, and the movement was limited to handicraftsmen who were able to produce their goods in small workshops without the need of large amount of capital or equipment. It was thus natural that the movement flourished most in places like London and Birmingham where tradesmen predominated. It was the independence which Owenism offered which constituted its appeal for the artisan.

However, similar ideas influenced workers in the building trades, where in the early 1830s the growing practice of 'general contracting' threatened the independence of the various building craftsmen. Local trade clubs had long existed amongst these crafts which had, by this time, begun to unite into national organisations. In 1827, for example, the General Union of Carpenters and Joiners was formed. In 1831 or 1832 the various crafts drew together into a federal body, the Operative Builders' Union, which, with a membership at its peak of over 40,000, leapt to the forefront of the trade union movement. At the Builders' 'Parliament' in 1833 Owen put forward a plan of action on a most ambitious scale. The Builders' Union was not merely to commence co-operative building in competition with the master builders; it was to *take over* the entire industry and re-organise it as a Grand National Guild under the direct control of the union. Master builders would be allowed to join the Guild as its servants. Those who refused to join would be frozen out, for no one would work for them. Plans were laid to launch the guild, and at Birmingham designs were drawn up by Joseph Hansom (of cab fame) for a Guildhall. The master builders did not sit back waiting to be swallowed up, however, and speedily retaliated with lock-outs and the 'document', a written promise which workers were forced to sign, renouncing member-ship of the union. Such tactics proved stronger than the grandiose schemes of the union, and by the middle of 1834 the Operative Builders' Union had fallen apart into its constituent elements. In spite of this, it left a legacy to the Grand National Consolidated Trades Union, which took both its federal constitution and its grandiose aims.

At a London conference of trade union delegates in February 1834, the G.N.C.T.U. was formally established. Before the year had passed it had faded away. Yet at the peak of its strength half a million members had been enrolled, including even women and farm labourers. The G.N.C.T.U. nevertheless remained heavily biased towards the London trades, the great majority of unions affiliated being of more or less skilled crafts-men, and its connections with the previous general unions of the Midlands and North being few. Time was not on the side of the G.N.C.T.U., for the Derby 'Turn-out' proved a drain on the funds, while within little more than a week of the union being founded, the government aimed a crushing blow at the whole labour movement with the arrest of six Dorchester labourers who, after their trial and sentence in March, became the 'Tol-puddle Martyrs'. The G.N.C.T.U. had come into existence largely because of the Derby 'Turn-out', which had followed a strike by a smallish number of silk workers in November, 1833. Locked out by their employers, the unionists determined to do without them by commencing co-operative production. The help of other unions was called for, and it was largely in order to continue support that the G.N.C.T.U. was formed in the following February. After four months' struggle, the Union could no longer finance the strike, and the workers were compelled to go back to work on their employers' terms.

The trial of the Tolpuddle Martyrs for administering illegal oaths, and their sentence to seven years' transportation, have long held a place in the folklore of the labour movement. The events made it quite apparent that despite the fact that trade unions had been legalised in 1824-5, their position was more than precarious. Before their trial, Owen had not officially been a member of the G.N.C.T.U., but he joined soon afterwards, and, at the end of April, riding on horseback at the head of a throng, he led a procession to the Copenhagen Fields in London as a protest. Nothing was achieved by this, the strains within the union and the dissension amongst the leaders increased, and soon the union was in ruins. But it was not the end of Owen:

Owen possessed an unconquerable optimism, even in the hour of utter defeat. In fact, he never knew that he had been defeated. He simply collected a fresh audience, and went on saying the same thing. His connection with the great Trades Union uprising of these years had been, in a sense, an accident. He was by nature neither a Trade Union organiser nor a revolutionary leader, but a prophet. (G. D. H. Cole, 1953, page 151).

The aims of the G.N.C.T.U., which included the use of the general strike (or 'Grand National Holiday') to overthrow the whole social and economic order, were far in excess of its organisation. It is not surprising, therefore, that the development of unionism in the following years was more cautious and less spectacular. The idea of a general union was pushed to the background for a while, and, instead, unionism developed either amongst those workers little affected by the industrial changes, or amongst those who, like the engineers, actually benefited. The mass of the workers were disillusioned both by the failure of the trade union movement in 1834, and the passage of the new Poor Law in the same year, and directed their attention back to politics. Chartism became the new means to the same end.

Chapter III

Mid-Victorian Prosperity

1 The Great Exhibition of 1851   In its issue of 3 May 1851, the *Illustrated London News* carried a report of the opening of the Great Exhibition in Hyde Park, and at the same time indulged in historical reflection and speculation on the future. If any space of one hundred (or even two hundred) years in the history of Britain, or any other nation, were taken, it would not be found, claimed the paper, that progress in all the 'arts which elevate and adorn humanity' could compare with that in the twenty years since 1830:

The ball of improvement has rolled with accelerated velocity, increasing its impetus as it went; and we may reasonably anticipate, if no war arise in our time to destroy the auspicious work that has been begun, that the next twenty years will afford us triumphs still more substantial and more brilliant than those which we already enjoy.

The paper precisely captured the feeling of progress that was in the air, and a belief in the dawning of a new age of international peace and prosperity—the same feeling as was expressed in a song by Dr Charles Mackay and Henry Russell (the Lennon and McCartney of the Victorian Age):

Gather, ye Nations, gather!
From forge, and mine, and mill!
Come, Science and Invention;
Come, Industry and Skill!
Come with your woven wonders,
The blossoms of the loom,
That rival Nature's fairest flowers
In all but their perfume;

Come with your brass and iron,
Your silver and your gold,
And arts that change the face
of earth,
Unknown to men of old.
Gather, ye Nations gather!
From ev'ry clime and soil,
The new Confederation,
The Jubilee of toil.

Yet if the Great Exhibition was intended to be international, it was also designed as a display of Britain's national wealth and prosperity. 'We strive not for dominion', ran the second verse of the song:

> Whoe'er the worthiest be,
> Shall bear the palm and garland,
> And crown of victory.

There could be no question as to who would receive the palm and garland—if there had been the least doubt that Britain would excel, the Exhibition would not have been held. The prevailing attitude was one of supreme self-confidence and complacency. A trial of some of the agricultural machinery to be displayed was held even before the Crystal Palace opened, and allowed the *Illustrated London News* to boast how satisfactory it was to know that 'in the first step of the industrial contest, British pre-eminence stands undisputed in a branch of industry of such immense importance'. The same smugness was displayed with our industrial machinery and hardware.

The French section in the Crystal Palace was enormous and impressive, but excited admiration through the display of craftsmanship rather than industrial strength. Most of the exhibits of the German *Zollverein* were described as 'not above mediocrity', while the *Economist* held that 'in machinery—except perhaps field-pieces . . . the Germans appear very deficient'. More space was given over in the press to contemptuous descriptions of the American contribution. The most obvious target for the jibe of the wits was the failure of the United States to fill the space allotted to it. *Punch* suggested that the Americans should utilise the empty space by letting it as lodgings:

By packing up the American articles a little closer, by displaying Colt's revolvers over the soap, and piling up the Cincinnati pickles on the top of the Virginian honey, we shall concentrate all the treasures of American art and manufacture into a very few square feet, and beds may be made up to accommodate several hundreds in the space claimed for, but not one quarter filled by, the products of United States industry.

But if the American exhibits lacked quantity, the United States nevertheless succeeded in displaying several of the most significant exhibits of all, including the Colt revolver (a mass-produced precision article with fully interchangeable parts), the McCormick Reaper, and a sewing-machine of 'astonishing velocity'. In addition, the Goodyear Company presented an impressive array of articles made in rubber, a material of the future, while the exhibits also included a new refrigeration process. Not all were blind to the American potential. In March, the *Economist* observed that 'the superiority of the United States to England is ultimately as certain as the next eclipse', although, as Clapham has pointed out, no indication was given as to the estimated time the ultimatum had to run.

For a while Britain was able to enjoy the confidence of being the world's leader in industry and trade. Her exports multiplied by leaps and bounds; valued at £53 million in 1848 (only £1 million or so more than in 1815), the declared value of exports reached £122 million in 1857, and after a brief interruption in the depression of 1858, reached £136 million in 1860. The pace still did not slacken, and in the next twelve years the value doubled again. By then, however, complacency was out of place, for at the Paris International Exhibition of 1867 the British cut a poor figure, and were given what Professor Armytage has described as 'convulsive therapy'.

As a display of national supremacy, therefore, the Great Exhibition was a success, if only a temporary one. As herald of the dawn of an era of international peace it was less successful. Few paused to observe that while the thousands were flocking to Hyde Park, Britain was at war with the Kaffirs. Colonial Wars were far away, and were being made less troublesome by the very technology which the Great Exhibition was celebrating; the triumph of such destructive progress was seen at the battle of Omdurman in 1898, where, with 20 Maxim machine-guns, 44 field-pieces, and a flotilla of gunboats firing a new high explosive (lyddite), Kitchener was able to dispose of 11,000 Dervishes in $4\frac{1}{2}$ hours, at a cost of 48 of his own men. Within three years of the Great Exhibition, and two months before the Crystal Palace was reopened at Sydenham, Britain was plunged into the Crimean War, and the assumption that progress could only come through peace was soon proved wrong as the demands of war came to be felt. From 1854 to 1856 the Navy added some 284 steam vessels to the fleet, as against 26 from 1850 to 1853, steamships being able to make the run from Portsmouth to Constantinople in 12-15 days, as against the 40-50 days taken by sailing vessels. The Army was supplied with the newly developed Minié rifle (which gave the Thin Red Line its withering fire-power), and when the Royal Small Arms Factory at Enfield was re-equipped with American machinery, it quickly revealed the advantages of the production line. Technological spin-off was further illustrated in the need to produce giant iron sheets to provide armour for the floating batteries, and later used in the construction of steamships; even the supply of canned food for the troops provided a stimulus to the expanding tin-plate industry.

However, in 1851 there was much to justify both confidence and excitement, and the Crystal Palace, in which the Exhibition was housed, was itself a symbol of the triumph of industry and technology. Two hundred and forty-five plans were submitted for the temporary exhibition building, but none satisfied the organisers, who produced a monstrous plan of their own. It was only at the eleventh hour that Joseph Paxton sent in his design for a building which was to be constructed almost entirely of iron and glass (a material which had only been released from a crippling excise duty in 1845). Paxton's ideas were breathtaking, both in their scale and in the techniques he proposed to adopt. The estimate of the contractors included 900,000 square feet of glass, in larger panes than had ever been made before; 3300 iron columns; 2224 girders; and 205 miles of sash-bars. The length of the building was the same as the year—1851 feet (nearly twice the length of the liner *Queen Mary*). Perhaps more mar-vellous even than the scale was the speed with which the building was constructed. The contractors had a mere twenty-two weeks to enclose a space of twenty-three acres, and their ability to do so was a triumph of mass-production and prefabrication. Pick-ford's vans plied between Euston Station and Hyde Park, delivering fifty girders and tons of columns a day. It took only four minutes to test each cast-iron girder for size and strength as it arrived on the site, and Paxton once witnessed the erection of three columns and two girders in only sixteen minutes. Each day the glaziers put up as much iron and glass as went into a good-sized railway station, the workers (who numbered about 2000) being aided by a battery of machines, including a morticing-machine which could cut seven or eight mortices in the time that one could be cut by hand.

The building was supremely functional, which is more than can be said of many of the exhibits which it contained. Ranging from the sublime to the ridiculous, they demonstrated the best in Victorian inventiveness and the worst in Victorian taste. Yet of all the sections, Machinery was the most popular. This need not surprise us, for the mid-Victorians regarded engineers as their folk-heroes. Samuel Smiles' *Lives of the Engineers*, which sang their praises, was a best-seller; and Gladstone agreed with Smiles that 'the character of our engineers is a most signal and marked expression of British character'. He even found time to read the book 'in little fragments at midnight hours each night, as a composing draught'.

Also in 1851 was held the fifth decennial census, significant in many ways, not least in that it showed for the first time more people living in towns than in the country. It is at first surprising that occupations not particularly characteristic of a machine age should come so high in the list. Just over 20 her cent of the occupied population was employed in agriculture, and 13·3 per cent in domestic service. It is of course true that machinery freed people to work in such occupations, just as it is true that the abundance of domestic help enabled engineers and businessmen to devote so much energy to their work. George Hudson, the 'Railway King', replied promptly to the hundred or so letters he received each day, while Paxton succeeded in developing his idea for the Crystal Palace in only seven days from blotting paper doodle to detailed drawings. Without their maids and their men-servants, such tasks would have been nigh impossible.

Carlyle had spoken of the 'Age of Machinery' in 1829, while Disraeli coined the phrase 'Workshop of the World' nine years later. These descriptions remained valid for the mid-Victorian period, although others came to be applied—'Railway Age', 'Coal Age', 'Iron Age', or 'Steam Age'. All such titles illustrate factors in that prosperity which became increasingly apparent from the 1850s, and it is to them that we must now turn.

2 **Railway development** That arch-enemy of the Crystal Palace, Colonel Charles de Laet Waldo Sibthorp, M.P. for Lincoln, did not think highly of railways. Indeed, he exclaimed that 'next to civil war, railways are the greatest curse to the country'. However, by the 1840s his was a lone voice crying in the wilderness, for railways touched the popular imagination, and 'railway' became a synonym for ultra-modernity as 'electric' became at the end of the century, and 'atomic' was to be after the Second World War. Sibthorp might invoke the devil when he spoke of railways, but the popular view was inclined the other way. 'Nothing', said a director of the Great North of England Railway, *'next to religion* is of so much importance as a ready communication'—and it was 'ready communication' that the railways, above all, gave.

There had been a steady improvement in communications before the railway arrived on the scene, although roads and canals still remained deficient. By 1838, out of nearly 105,000 miles of public road only 22,000 miles had been turnpiked, and the quality of many of these roads left much to be desired. Even as late as 1856 the Metropolitan Commission, a model authority managing all the chief Middlesex roads out of London, had not half its mileage macadamised with broken granite, though it had been served by three generations of Macadams. Even so, the United Kingdom led other European countries, having at the end of the 1860s rather more than five miles of metalled road per thousand of population, as compared with less than three in France and only two and one-third in Prussia.

With the notable exception of the Manchester Ship Canal, there was little expansion of canals after 1850, but at their greatest extent (in 1858) the inland waterways had a length of about 4250 miles, as compared with 1000 miles, consisting of river improvements only, just over a century before. Coastal shipping was also important, especially for bulk cargoes such as coal, and thousands of ships of all sizes and descriptions still plied up and down the coasts. Even as late as 1872 it was reckoned that goods charges from three-fifths of the railway stations in the country were affected by the competition of transport by sea.

The broad outline of railway history is well known. In the eighteenth century there was considerable development of the use of railways in collieries while, ironically, their use was further spread by the canals themselves—either as feeders or as temporary links, such as that used for the Grand Junction Canal during the construction of a tunnel from Stoke Bruerne to Blisworth. By 1811 it was claimed that South Wales had nearly 150 miles of railway 'connected with canals, collieries, iron and copper works', while Tyneside was said to have had 225 miles before the Stockton and Darlington Railway was projected.

All these railways (none of which used mechanical power) were run in conjunction with other undertakings, so that the credit for the first public railway in its own right goes to the Surrey Iron Railway, running from Croydon to the Thames at Wandsworth, which obtained its Act in 1801, and was opened in 1803. Like its predecessors, its sole concern was with the carriage of goods, and it was not until the Swansea and Oystermouth Railway was opened in 1807 that a passenger service began to operate. The Stockton and Darlington Railway, opened in 1825, drew together several of the earlier strands of development. Locomotives were employed from the start, although horses continued to be used for some of the work, and while the company provided wagons for the carriage of goods, all the passenger traffic was carried by a contractor using horsed coaches. Outside its own locality the railway at first aroused little interest, and even in the next county, the *Yorkshire Gazette* devoted only eight lines to the opening. Nevertheless, 25 railways were authorised between 1826 and 1830, when the Liverpool and Manchester Railway was opened. This can justifiably claim to be the first modern railway, in the fullest sense of the word. A triumph of civil engineering, the railway linked two of the most important towns in the country, with a combined population of 350,000. It was the first to convey both passengers and goods solely by mechanical traction, the traffic being handled entirely by the company itself; and it was the first to be built in direct competition with a canal.

That there was not an immediate multiplication of railways was due partly to a cautious wait to see if the Liverpool and Manchester would fulfil its early promise, but probably more to the discouragement of enterprise by the political disturbance of the country at the time. Only ten new lines were sanctioned by Parliament in 1831 and 1832, and their significance was small. In the following years, however, four major lines were projected. The London & Birmingham and the Grand Junction (from Birmingham to Warrington, where it would link with the Liverpool and Manchester) were successful when they re-submitted their Bills in 1833, while in 1834 the London & Southampton was authorised, to be followed by the Great Western in 1835. These formed the first trunk lines out of London, and whereas the Liverpool and Manchester was only 30 miles long, these four together totalled 380 miles.

The launching of these trunk lines was followed by the first railway 'mania' of 1836-7, when 1500 miles of new railway were authorised and the outlines of a railway network ('system' would be too strong a word) began to appear. By the end of 1843 there were more than 2000 miles of railway in operation throughout the country. Then, in 1845-7, the country was gripped by a second speculative mania. Interest was whipped up by the press—the number of railway journals alone increased from three to twenty—and the newspapers were swollen with advertisements. In the one week ending 18 October 1845, *The Times*, which in its editorials warned its readers against the mania, received £6687 in advertising revenue, while on 15 December, the *Gazette* put out 583 pages. The extent of the frenzy can perhaps be judged by the wild scenes on 30 November 1845, fixed by the Board of Trade as the last date by which plans must be submitted if Bills were to go through during that session. As more than 800 groups made a last-minute rush, the roads to

London were blocked with coaches, and the trunk lines with express trains—one of which actually steamed 118 miles in an hour and a half. Established companies naturally tried to refuse facilities to the promoters of competing lines, to get round which the agents of one projected railway procured a hearse with all the paraphernalia of mourning, placed plans and clerks inside, and sped to London by special train. In the three Parliamentary sessions of 1845-8, some 650 railway Acts were passed, authorising the construction of nearly 9000 miles of line; but not all were built, and in 1850 it was found necessary to pass an Act by which projected railways could be abandoned and companies dissolved. Over 3500 miles were given up, yet although the mania was undoubtedly wasteful, given the legislative machinery of the time it is a wonder that so much was achieved without complete breakdown. By 1850 there were some 6000 miles of railway open for public traffic in Great Britain, and by 1852, when nearly all the chief main lines of the country had been completed or authorised, the most important English towns not yet served were Hereford, Yeovil and Weymouth. The construction of the 1850s was mainly of feeder or connecting lines, and by 1870, when 13,500 miles were open, the network had been largely completed.

Compared with those built elsewhere, the British railways were expensive to construct, costing on average £40,000 a mile, which was something like three to four times the cost of building the American and Continental railways. The cost of land was high, although the oft-quoted instance where the Eastern Counties line paid Lord Petre of Ingatestone Hall, Essex £120,000 for land worth at most £5,000, is probably exceptional. However, the London & Birmingham paid out £750,000 to landowners as the easiest way to soften potential opposition. Pollins has shown that 27 principal railway companies spent some £7 million on land between 1825 and 1850, out of a total of £50 million spent on construction—about 13·9 per cent (although J. R. Kellett holds that the figure was more likely 16·5 per cent). While this is a large proportion, it is by no means excessive, and helps to keep in perspective the enormous sums which are sometimes given as examples. Heavy legal and Parliamentary costs must also share the blame, although again, Pollins has shown that in nearly all cases they were less than 5 per cent of the whole. Parliamentary costs are alleged to have cost the Great Northern £432,600 'before a spade was put to the ground'; and where there was opposition from rival companies, the total sums involved were indeed huge—over £500,000 was spent as a result of the un-availing opposition which Hudson led against the London & York, for example. More important, perhaps, was the bidding up of the price of materials and labour as a result of the rush to construct. One of the staff of Thomas Brassey, the leading con-tractor, illustrated the effect of the mania on wages; a mason who in 1843 earned 21s a week was earning 33s a week in 1846; carpenters were earning respectively 21s and 30s; while the navvies who did the spadework found their wages increased from 15s to 22s 6d. The impact of these increases is appreciated when it is recalled that in 1847, at the height of the mania, 300,000 men were at work constructing the railways. Nor were these the only men whose services were bid for. There was a shortage of surveyors and engineers, such that at one time Robert Stephenson was employed by 34 lines. As the leaders of the field, Britain also had to bear the cost of experiment, and for this reason the civil engineering costs of most of the early railways were un-usually high. George Stephenson once remarked that engine and road were like man and wife, the two went hand in hand; thus, until engines became powerful, gradients had to remain slight. Experiments in 1833 showed that if a locomotive could draw 67 tons on the level, it could draw only 15 tons on an in-cline of 1 in 100, and could not move at all at 1 in 12. Thus, in the early days (and most of the major lines were built then) a railway had to be built level, which involved expensive earthworks. The Great Western Railway, for example, was a mammoth piece of engineering, and with a mean gradient of only 1 in 1380, became known as Brunel's Billiard Table. As more powerful engines came to be developed, engineers found that they could cut costs by permitting steeper gradients, but by then much of the network was completed. Sometimes the opposition of landowners involved costly earthworks, as when they prevented the London & Birmingham from passing through Northampton. The digging of a tunnel at Kilsby Hill became necessary, for which an estimate of £90,000 was accepted. But when an unsuspected patch of quicksand was encountered, the contractor threw up his contract, took to his bed, and died. Stephenson took over, and with 1250 men, 200 horses and 13 steam engines, completed the work—at a cost of £300,000.

It was inevitable that the railways would have a profound effect on the economic life of the country. The older forms of transport were among the first to feel the effect. The canals could not hope to compete unless they improved their service. They were slow (canal boats could rarely travel at more than 2½ miles an hour) while the frequency of locks further slowed progress; locking up the two miles to Devizes on the Kennet & Avon Canal could take half a day, for example. Most tunnels had to be 'legged' by the boatman, lying on his back in the darkness and kicking against the roof, a practice which continued in the three-mile-long Standedge tunnel until 1928. Long-distance traffic was hampered by the lack of standardisation in width, depth, and length of lock. The Leeds & Liverpool could lock a boat of 76 feet from Liverpool to Wigan; from Wigan to Leeds only a 66 foot boat could travel; while at Leeds the canal met the Aire & Calder Navigation, whose locks would only take a 53 foot boat. As late as the 1880s whichever of the three canal routes between London and Liverpool was taken entailed tolls to nine separate undertakings. All this involved transhipment of cargoes far more frequently than on the railways (even with different guages), raising costs and increasing the already high risk of pilferage. On top of all these drawbacks, the canals suffered from the natural hazards of flood, drought, and frost. Bad management is the most serious charge that can be brought against the canals. Their first serious competitor, the Liverpool and Manchester Railway, was projected largely in order to break the canal monopoly which held merchants and manufacturers to ransom, and resulted in cotton taking longer to reach the mills from Liverpool than it had taken on the voyage from New Orleans. Yet, faced with fresh competition, the canals put more resources into opposing the railways than into improving their own services. Price cuts were forced upon them, but they lost the initiative, and in the three years 1845-7 over 900 miles of canal, one-fifth of Britain's navigable waterways came under railway control.

Whereas the canals had been most important for the carriage of goods, the roads had been predominant in passenger traffic. By the 1830s, when it was estimated that there were 3000 coaches on the road, it was claimed that a person had 1500 opportunities of leaving London daily. Forty coaches a day went to Birmingham, 54 to Manchester. Although usually promoted to facilitate the distribution of goods, the early railways immediately revealed the enormous potential of passenger traffic. Half a million people travelled on the London & Birmingham in its first year, increasing to one million by 1845. This had an immediate impact on the roads, and inevitably resulted in the coach proprietors cutting their fares, although this could provide only a temporary respite. Some put up a good fight; in the Spring of 1838 the *Wonder*, a Shrewsbury coach, left Euston just as the Birmingham train departed, and waited 20 minutes for it at the other end. But such efforts could not be kept up for long. The mail coaches of the Bath Road ceased running when the Great Western Railway was opened from Paddington to Bristol in June 1841; and the last of the old London mail coaches (from Norwich and Newmarket) pulled in on 6 January 1848. By then most of the coach operators had gone bankrupt, or had converted their businesses into feeders for the railway. Some of the major concerns had gone completely over to the enemy camp. Chaplin & Horne, amongst the biggest coach proprietors, took a goods agency with the London & Birmingham Railway (Chaplin eventually became chairman of the London & Southampton) while Pickford opened the first railway goods station in London, for the same company. Firms such as these had a wealth of practical experience of great value to the new undertakings, and they provided many of the early railway staff.

The decline of long-distance road traffic had an immediate effect on the revenue of the turnpike trusts. On the London and

Birmingham road, eight trusts took a total of £28,500 in 1836; the revenue in 1839, after the railway had opened, was £15,800. By 1854, the net reduction in annual toll receipts for the country as a whole was £470,041 as compared with 1837. But if long-distance traffic declined with the advent of the railway, local traffic increased, both feeding the stations with passengers, and delivering the increased volume of goods which the railways transported. Far more people in 1851 were dependent on the horse of flesh and blood than upon his iron brother; and if the census could enumerate 34,306 railway labourers and 14,559 railway officers, clerks and station-masters, it could also list 56,981 carmen, carriers and draymen, 29,408 horse-keepers, non-domestic grooms and jockeys, and 16,836 non-domestic coachmen, guards and postboys—not to mention thousands of blacksmiths, wheelwrights and saddlers.

The impact of the railways on industry was diffuse. The construction and operation of railways exerted a demand for the products of other industries, such as iron and coal, while the completed railways affected the location of industry and permitted an easier distribution of raw materials and completed goods. A growing quantity of goods was carried, but it was not until 1852 that the revenue from freight charges exceeded that from passenger fares, while the reduction in carrying costs was achieved partly by forcing canals to bring their charges down.

The variety of goods carried by the railways was vividly illustrated by the *Railway News* in 1864, in a description of the morning routine at Camden Goods Station:

In the grey mists of the morning, in the atmosphere of a hundred conflicting smells, and by the light of faintly burning gas, we see a large portion of the supply of the great London markets rapidly disgorged by these night trains: fish, flesh and food, Aylesbury butter and dairy-fed pork, apples, cabbages and cucumbers, alarming supplies of cats' meat, cart loads of water cresses, and we know not what else, for the daily consumption of the metropolis. No sooner do these disappear than at ten minutes' interval arrive other trains with Manchester packs and bales, Liverpool cotton, American provisions, Worcester gloves, Kidderminster carpets, Birmingham and Staffordshire hardware, crates of pottery from North Staffordshire, and cloth from Huddersfield, Leeds, Bradford, and other Yorkshire towns, which have to be delivered in the City before the hour for the general commencement of business. At a later hour of the morning these are followed by other trains with the heaviest class of traffic: stones, bricks, iron girders, iron pipes, ale (which comes in great quantities, especially from Allsopps', and the world-famous Burton breweries), coal, hay, straw, grain, flour, and salt . . . (Quoted in G. R. Hawke, *Railways and Economic Growth in England and Wales, 1840-1970* O.U.P. 1970, page 59.)

Coal used by railways for steam raising was less than 2 per cent of the national production, but higher demands were made indirectly through the use of coal to produce metal and bricks intended for railway contracts. The Victorians delighted in useless statistics, and, like them, we may marvel that the number of bricks used in the Kilsby tunnel alone was 36 million, 'sufficient to make a good footpath from London to Aberdeen (missing the Forth) a yard broad!' At the height of their construction in the 1840s railways may have been consuming one-third of the total output of bricks. Railway demand dominated both the home and export markets for iron, and whereas the improved fuel economy of new locomotives kept the demand for coal in check, the steadily increasing weight of iron in rails and chairs multiplied the demand for iron. By 1841 the weight of iron in rails and chairs for a mile of single track was 156 tons as against $53\frac{1}{2}$ tons in the early days. Making allowance for double track and sidings, each route mile of line must have required 300 or more tons of iron. Thus, in the five years from 1846-50, when 4000 miles of line were opened in the British Isles and about 2500 locomotives (weighing some 25 tons each) were running, allowing for the iron required for rolling-stock, bridges, buildings, and maintenance, one cannot suppose that less than a million and a half tons was consumed. This was more than the total British output in 1844. B. R. Mitchell has estimated that 18 per cent of the U.K. output of iron went on permanent way between 1844 and 1851; a more than proportionate part of this demand was diverted to South Wales.

As railways set new technical (and management) problems, new solutions had to be discovered. Sometimes the solutions were novel, if unlikely to lead to further progress, as when parrots were used on the Edinburgh and Glasgow railway to call out the name of the station as trains arrived; (as a means of communication, the telegraph was perhaps more efficient—of the seventeen

London offices of the Electric Telegraph Company in 1854, eight were at railway termini). On the other hand, solutions to railway problems often had applications elsewhere. One may take the example of the huge arched roofs of the termini, made necessary by the need to move crowds of people and innumerable packages in a confined space while locomotives waited with steam up. The iron and glass roof of St Pancras station, opened in 1868, was of 240 ft. span, and was then the widest in the world.

Agriculture as well as industry felt the impact of the railway. The farmer's transport costs for his feed, fertilisers, seed and implements were greatly reduced, while he was able to market his produce more easily, and could take advantage of the growing urban demand for perishable foodstuffs. Livestock farmers were particularly affected, for the railway facilitated the transport of cattle to market, as well as dairy produce. At the Falkirk 'tryst', or wholesale cattle market, in 1849, it was considered a novel feature that the London & North Western Railway had a marquee in which orders could be taken for shipping stock to all parts of England. In the following decades the railways eliminated the old droving trade which had resulted in such a loss of weight, bullocks driven by road from Norfolk to Smithfield, for example, losing four stone. Railway charges were admittedly higher than the old droving charges, but it was estimated in 1856 that the Norfolk farmer now gained 20s a head on every bullock sent to town, while he was enabled to take advantage of a dear market. There was also a great increase in milk shipments, especially after the cattle plague of 1866, which decimated the insanitary town dairies of London. It is estimated that in the course of that year 7 million gallons of milk were brought by rail to London from 220 country stations, while by 1880, 20 million gallons were said to arrive in the capital each year.

The attitude of the state to the railways down to at least 1844 was to hold a watching brief. The only experience which the government had was of canals, and although there was little evidence in the 1830s that the railways were abusing their position, it was expected that as the canals had done so, railways would also—so long as they were not adequately controlled. The spectre of monopoly power haunted Parliament for the remainder of the century, although little effective was done to lay the ghost. As early as 1839, a Committee of the House of Commons examined the railways, as a result of a petition from traders complaining of the alleged monopolistic policies of the London & Birmingham Railway. By that time competition from the roads was almost dead, while competition from canals was effective only at times. Yet the committee was aware that different methods would be required to check the railways from those used on the canals. Until 1845 canal companies were not allowed to carry goods on their own waterways, but had to rely instead on tolls from independent carriers, whose rivalry, it was supposed, would exercise some competitive control. Such a system could not work on the railways, and the Select Committee held that, for the safety of the public, railways must control their own lines 'although they should thereby acquire an entire monopoly'. In view of this, they concluded that some supervising authority would be necessary, the need for which was a central feature of successive reports right down to 1872.

Two Acts did follow the report of the Select Committee. In 1840 the Railway Regulation Act was passed, by which the Board of Trade was to be notified of the opening of all lines, which were to be inspected by its officers. In addition, toll, rate, and accident figures had to be submitted, together with by-laws. Concern for the safety of passengers was well-founded. Accidents involving injury and loss of life were so frequent that *Punch* suggested a new invention to be called 'the Railway Pocket Companion, containing a small bottle of water, a tumbler, a complete set of surgical instruments, a packet of lint, and directions for making a will'. Many accidents were avoidable and were the result of careless operating or, more serious, of attempts at economising by cutting safety measures to a minimum. The second Act (passed in 1842) entitled the Board of Trade to postpone the opening of a passenger railway until satisfied as to its construction. No power was given to issue regulations, but from 1858 onwards 'Requirements' were issued, outlining the basis upon which the Department intended to use its discretionary powers of postponement. Although they had a very dubious basis in law, the Requirements gradually extended the control of the Government, and they represent an interesting example of quasi-legislation, usually thought of as a twentieth-century development.

While these two Acts did much for the safety of the railways, in the opinion of the Select Committee of 1872 they 'contained nothing which had any effect in checking or regulating monopoly'. A further Regulation of Railways Act was passed in 1844, and is better known as the Cheap Trains Act from the sections which required new lines to provide at least one train a day in each direction, stopping at all stations, and conveying third-class passengers in coaches protected from the weather, for not more than one penny per mile. The Bill was emasculated in Parliament, and the major provisions, which included nationalisation, never came into effect. As finally passed, the Act provided for state purchase of all lines sanctioned after the Act, after the lapse of twenty-one years from the respective authorising Acts. The limiting clause excluded 2300 miles already sanctioned, and as these included most of the main trunk lines, the acquisition of the rest became impracticable.

The lack of effective Parliamentary control was largely due to the speed at which railways developed, and to the strength of the 'railway interest'. By 1847, 178 M.P.s were directors of railway companies, while there were 172 in both Houses in 1872. Parliament was wedded to the Private Bill procedure, whereby each projected line was treated on its merits, and while this system undoubtedly spread the railways more rapidly than would otherwise have been the case, the result of virtually unrestricted private initiative was the absence of a nationally planned network.

3 Shipping The development of British shipping is hardly less interesting nor less important than that of railways. Not only was shipbuilding a major industry in its own right, but the revenue from shipping was one of the most important 'invisible' earnings which helped to convert a deficit in the balance of trade into a surplus in the balance of payments. For example, in 1851-5, while the average annual excess of imports over exports was around £33 million, net shipping revenue of about £19 million did much to redress the balance. Net shipping earnings grew steadily from the 1830s, making their major contribution to the national income in the decade from 1875, although the set-back in the late 1880s represented only a small fall in absolute values, which was made up in subsequent decades.

Crucial to this development was the winning of trade, especially in the Atlantic, from the United States. The challenge of the Americans was serious, for they put to good use their abundant raw materials, and produced softwood ships which were not only cheap, but extremely well built. In fifty years the Americans contributed as much to the sailing ship as the whole world had contributed in three hundred. While the average British ship engaged in the Atlantic trade was about 250 tons (not much larger than a modern lightship), in the twenty-five years from the end of the Napoleonic Wars to 1840 the Americans built a fleet of packet ships of size steadily increasing from 500 to 1200 tons. The design of the ships was revolutionised by increasing the ratio of the length to the beam, thus giving better lines, permitting a greater spread of sail, and increasing speed. The ships were not only better built, but better handled; American master mariners were generally better educated than their British counterparts, and while seamen enjoyed better conditions and higher pay, fewer were required to man each ship. To the shame of British shipbuilders, even Lloyds offered American ships a lower insurance rating.

A frontal attack on this entrenched position would have been impossible; instead, the front was turned with the aid of the newly-developed steam engine. However, although most of the major technical problems of steamships were solved in the thirty years 1808-38, the transition from sail to steam was not rapid; and it was not until the 1870s that new steamship tonnage began to exceed new sailing-ship tonnage. The opening of the Suez Canal in 1869 was one of the decisive factors, for its success-ful navigation required a controlled power which the sailing-ship could not command.

The only sustained effort to develop the ocean-going steamship was made in Britain. A stimulus was provided by the interest of coastal shippers and companies plying on short sea routes; in 1826, for example, the recently-formed General Steam Navigation Company put steamers into the London-Portugal service. More important still was the stimulus to development given by the British government through its award of postal contracts. The significance of this is seen in the reconquest of the Atlantic trade, in which two men were prominent—Isambard Kingdom Brunel and Samuel Cunard.

Brunel must surely rank as one of the most fascinating men of the nineteenth century, many of his ideas being so far in advance of their time that they had to be re-invented years after his death. His interest in the Atlantic crossing arose from his connection with the Great Western Railway, for, having built a railway from London to Bristol, it seemed logical to him not to stop there but to push on to America. In 1835 a company was formed at Bristol to back him, while at the same time a rival company was formed in London. Competition was further encouraged in 1837 when the government granted a mail contract for the Peninsular run, and an Atlantic contract was in the offing. Excitement mounted when, as Brunel's *Great Western* was nearing completion, the engine-makers for the rival London company went bankrupt. Determined to be first, the London company chartered the *Sirius*, a small Irish Channel steamer. She sailed on 4 August 1838 (three days before the *Great Western*) and made the crossing in 18 days 10 hours, being the first vessel to cross the Atlantic under continuous steam power. At New York 'she met a firm welcome— she ran aground', but was floated off without damage. Despite her earlier start, she beat the *Great Western* by only about four hours.

Following these successful voyages, the British government, in October 1838, invited tenders for the Atlantic mail contract. The Great Western Steamship Company, with sound finance and a good ship giving a regular service of 15 days out, 13 days home, was firmly convinced that it would win the contract. But the government and the company failed to agree on terms, and it went instead to a new company floated by Samuel Cunard, a prominent shipowner of Nova Scotia. Beginning with four 1000-ton wooden steamers, the first of which was launched in 1840, the company began to build up its fleet. The need for government subsidy was amply revealed by the fact that the *Britannia*, the first of the Cunard steamers, needed to allocate 640 out of its capacity of 865 tons to carrying its own fuel.

The repeal, in 1849, of the Navigation Acts, which had confined certain areas of trade to British ships, acted as a further stimulus to the industry. The legislation had been no mere dead letter, for Britain still faced serious competition from the Americans, and her superiority in iron steamships was at that time by no means assured. In 1851 only 185,000 tons of steam tonnage existed in Britain, and most of that was in wooden ships in the coastal and short sea trade. By comparison, she possessed 3,600,000 tons of wooden ships under sail.

The repeal of the Navigation Acts was closely followed by the discovery of gold in Australia, and a consequent growth of trade with that continent. To meet this trade, the merchants of Liverpool acted promptly by ordering fast American sailing vessels. The Australian run was particularly suited to the sailing ship for two reasons: there was an absence of suitable coaling stations (the haul from the Cape to Melbourne was double the distance of the Atlantic crossing) while sailing vessels benefited from the prevailing westerly winds of the southern hemisphere. Not until the end of the century was sail ousted from this trade.

The search for greater efficiency in the use of fuel remained a major problem in the development of the steamship. Auxiliary steamers (which carried sail as well as steam-engines) were built as a compromise, but were never fully successful. As an alternative to the 'pure' steamer they were not fast enough, while the economy of days (or even weeks) as compared with sail was not of great significance before the development of the international telegraph—if you did not know when a ship had left port, you were less concerned about when it would arrive. An alternative solution was that of Brunel, the brilliant theoretician. He followed up the *Great Western* with the *Great Britain*. This ship, the hulk of which was towed back to Britain from the Falkland Islands in 1970, chalked up a notable list of 'firsts'. It was the first ocean-going ship driven by screw propulsion; the first with the remote-indicating electric log; the first capable of lowering all masts in a head wind; first with a double bottom; and first with watertight bulkheads. As technological spin-off, the first shipyard intended to work iron had to be constructed, while Nasmyth invented the steam-hammer to cope with the materials. In the words of Dr Ewan Corlett, the naval architect largely responsible for the ship's salvage, the *Great Britain* 'could be likened in technological advance to the supersonic Concordes of today'. But Brunel did not stop there, and in 1851 conceived his idea for a 'Crystal Palace of the Sea'. In his mind the solution to the problem of steamship operation was a simple one, for a few calculations convinced him that, in theory, if you build a ship large enough, the uneconomic features of the steam engine in relation to cargo capacity disappear altogether. He therefore planned to build a ship six times the size of any contemporary vessel. His *Great Eastern*, as the ship was to be called, was to have paddle-wheels, screws, and six masts capable of carrying 6500 square yards of canvas. Her passenger capacity was to be just double that of the *Queen Mary* of 1936, and she was to have cargo space for 6000 tons. When the ship was built, only one problem remained—getting it into the water, for it was far too long to be launched stern first into the Thames. The crowds therefore gathered on 3 November 1857 to see the *Great Eastern* launched sideways. Things immediately began to go wrong, and the ship did not finally float until the last day of January 1858. For Brunel, 'it was a simple, if stern, conflict between a Victorian father and the recalcitrance of a monstrous child. He won.' But the company lost, for by the time the *Great Eastern* was launched it had gone bankrupt, while the builder, John Scott Russell, lost his yard. After four publicity voyages across the Atlantic, the *Great Eastern* became a cable ship, and ended as a showboat on the Mersey.

The great defect lay in the under-estimation (to the extent of 75 per cent) of the coal required to fuel her 6600 h.p. engines.

The victory of steam over sail depended on improvements in marine engines. Developments in steel-making after 1856 enabled steel boilers to be made capable of pressures three times as great as those common in the early 1850s, but the decisive break-through was the triple-expansion engine, first employed in the *Aberdeen* of 1881. Compound engines, using a high- and a low-pressure cylinder, had been in use from the 1860s, and had led to a saving of nearly 60 per cent in coal consumption; the use of three cylinders, successively driven by steam at decreasing pressures, resulted in fuel economies which could at last drive the sailing ship from the seas. In 1887 the scientist and politician Lyon Playfair wrote:

Not long since a steamer of 3000 tons going on a long voyage might require 2200 tons of coal, and carry only a limited cargo of 800 tons. Now, a modern steamer will take the same voyage with 800 tons of coal, and carry a freight of 2200 tons. While coal has thus been economised, human labour has been lessened. In 1870 it required 47 hands on board our steamships for every 1000 tons capacity. Now only 28 are necessary. (Court *British Economic History, 1870-1914* C.U.P. 1965, page 165.)

At the same time there was a growth in the construction of specialised ships. The first oil tanker (to carry 5000 tons of oil) was launched in 1886, and by 1912 Lloyds' Register listed 300 such ships. Refrigerated ships for the frozen meat trade also increased, and of these there were some 200 in 1914. From the early 1900s oil began to replace coal for steam raising—the Navy did not start until 1903—but progress was not at first fast, and by 1914 only 2·6 per cent of British tonnage was oil-fired.

By 1890 Britain had more registered tonnage than the rest of the world put together, and even in 1910 over 40 per cent of tonnage entered and cleared in world trade was British. The record was impressive, and shipping represented one of the only sectors of the economy where Britain kept the world dominance after 1870 that she had enjoyed over a wide field in 1850.

4 Coal Writing in the 1860s, the economist Stanley Jevons criticised those who spoke of the period in which they lived as the 'Iron Age' or the 'Steam Age'. 'Coal alone', he said, 'can command in sufficient abundance either the iron or the steam, and coal, therefore, commands this age.' It was its strategic position as a basis for successful industrialisation which gave coal its importance. As an employer of labour it ranked only eighth in the 1851 census (immediately after milliners and dressmakers), rising to sixth in 1871 (again following the same trades). As an export, it represented less than 5 per cent of the total value right down to the 1870s and rose to 10 per cent only at the beginning of the twentieth century.

Nevertheless, a steadily increasing demand pushed up coal production from an estimated 16 million tons in 1816 to 65 million tons in 1856, 117 million tons in 1871, and 185 million tons in 1891. Domestic demand probably grew faster than the fast-growing population, as more and more people were brought within range of fuel at possible prices. As industry became more dependent on steam power a great demand for coal arose for steam raising. It was this demand in the 1840s for a steam coal to burn fiercely with a clean ash which partly accounts for the revival of the industry on the north bank of the Tyne, where the coal was particularly suited to this demand. By the middle of the century probably about one-third of all coal raised was used in iron works and for refining metals. However, while smelting demand was one of the most important, it was prevented from growing as fast as the output of pig-iron by the development of fuel-economising techniques. The hot blast, discovered by James Neilson in 1828, made it possible by 1833 to make a ton of iron with only one-third the amount of coal previously required. Scottish ironmasters were quick to take advantage of the invention, which gave them an immediate cost advantage. Further fuel economies were obtained from mid-century when the French practice of using the waste gases of combustion was employed, not for lighting up the countryside (as in Loutherbourg's dramatic painting of Coalbrookdale), but in order to raise steam to heat the blast.

The changing distribution of coal production is illustrated by the table on p. 102. (Errors introduced by 'rounding off' prevent the second column from adding up to exactly 100 per cent.)

**Estimated distribution of coal
in the United Kingdom**
(as percentages of U.K. tonnage raised)

	1840 %	1869 %	1887 %
Iron industry	25	30	16.5
Mines	3	6.5	6.5
Steam navigation	1.5	5	12.5
Gas and electricity	1.5	6	6
General Manufacturing	32.5	26	26
Domestic	31.5	17	17.5
Exports	5	9	15

Figures taken from Deane & Cole, page 219.

As the depth of working increased, so too did the technical problems of mining. The problems of lighting and drainage had been tackled earlier in the century, and had been largely overcome by the use of the safety-lamp and the steam pump. The major problems which remained concerned winding, haulage and ventilation. Down to 1840 winding engines were small, and in Scotland some pits did without machinery altogether, women carrying the coal on their backs up ladders of incredible length. In the deep pits of Lancashire and the North, engines of 100-175 h.p. were coming into use by the 1840s, and by the 1880s 1500 h.p. was sometimes required. A satisfactory method of coal-raising in cages rather than wicker corves was not worked out until the middle 1830s, and even then it remained far from perfect; at about the same time, wire rope was developed, and by the 1840s this was being fitted to the more powerful winding engines in the more progressive collieries. Ventilation was a problem of supreme importance, both to circulate fresh air to the miners and to minimise the risk of explosion. By the 1840s the use of furnaces at the bottom of the upcast shaft was universal in the deeper pits of the northern field, and as with other improvements, the experiments were made in Northumberland and Durham. In other districts little attention was paid to ventilation before 1845, because the pits either were not 'fiery' or were shallow. Furnace ventilation was both crude and risky. The upcast shaft was not always a mere chimney, for it might carry traffic, in which case the temperature could not be allowed to rise above 80-90°F. If the furnace got too much air it might set light to the adjacent coal-face, and if it got too little it might cause an explosion. The slightest upset to the planned balance of the pit's circulatory system could cause the out-going current, gas-laden after its long journey through the workings, to be thrown directly on to the flames. After 1840 considerable experiment was made with alternative methods— including the use of high-pressure steam, air-pumps and fans, much of the inspiration coming from Belgium.

By the 1880s most of the coal was raised from pits completely mechanised for winding, ventilation, and (at least on the main 'roads') underground haulage. Mechanical coal-cutting was slow to develop, however. The difficulties were first to find a steel for the pick which would not wear out after a few hours' work, and second to develop a safe and efficient form of power. The steam engine was of little use underground, as there were formidable transmission problems, apart from questions of safety. The first practical coal-cutter of 1863 used compressed air, but this was only a partial solution, for again there were tremendous power losses in transmission. These were not the only obstacles, however, for the size of the business unit hindered change. While the average size was increasing, and the major collieries were on a mammoth scale (Lord Londonderry and the Earl of Durham, for example, each had more than £500,000 invested in pits) there remained a vast number of small undertakings. While there was an abundance of skilled miners—and the British were regarded as the best in the world—and while there was little effective competition from abroad, colliery owners were reluctant to invest in the capital equipment which mechanical coal-cutting required.

5 Iron, steel and engineering Total iron production for Great Britain rose from a little over 100,000 tons per annum in 1802 to over 2 million tons by 1850. By then Scotland was producing over 25 per cent of the whole, whereas it had produced under 5 per cent in the 1820s. Traditional markets expanded—the catalogue of the Great Exhibition shows how much the Victorians managed to fabricate out of iron—while new markets developed in all kinds of constructional uses, in engineering and in railways, both at home and abroad.

Steel is an alloy of iron and carbon; it is harder and stronger than wrought iron, which contains no carbon, but much less brittle than cast iron, which has a higher carbon content. In spite of the fact that for nearly all purposes steel has been proved superior to iron, its production did not expand greatly until the second half of the nineteenth century. Its manufacture remained a small-scale and laborious process, in which no notable improvement had been made since the Huntsman crucible process of the mid-eighteenth century. In 1850 the entire British output of steel was only about 60,000 tons; and the material, which was not entirely faultless, was expensive. Whereas at that time pig-iron cost around £3-£4 a ton, the price of steel was around £50 a ton. In consequence, the demand for a malleable iron, later to be satisfied by cheap steel, was met by wrought or 'puddled' iron. The process of puddling was developed by Henry Cort in 1784, and consisted of raking and stirring a mass of molten pig-iron with a long iron rod poked through a hole in the side of the furnace. As the air was given full and rapid access to the molten metal, the carbon was burned out until a lump of malleable iron was left. The puddler became one of the key industrial workers of the next hundred years, and it has been held that the weight of metal and the temperature involved made this the heaviest regular task ever accepted by man. The arduousness of the work is illustrated by the life-span of 31 years which was all that puddlers in Sheffield could expect in the late 1860s. Yet puddling was difficult to mechanise, for while machines could be made to stir the bath of molten metal, only the human eye and touch could separate out the solidifying decarburized metal. Iron-making, like cooking, says David Landes, requires 'a feel for the ingredients, an acute sense of proportion, an "instinct" about the time the pot should be left on the stove'. Even as late as 1886, a Royal Commission was told that fully half the iron and steel required in a malleable form continued to be made in the puddling furnace.

The problem of manufacturing cheap steel was investigated by a professional inventor, Henry Bessemer, who published the results of his experiments in a paper delivered to the British Association in 1856, entitled 'The Manufacture of Malleable Iron and Steel without Fuel'. The fuel to which Bessemer referred was that used in puddling, and other processes by which small quantities of steel could be made. His original plan was to run molten iron straight from the blast furnace into a 'converter', to burn away all the chemical impurities (mainly carbon and silicon) if he wanted malleable iron, and to burn out all but an appropriate proportion of carbon if he wanted steel. The novelty of his process was the forcing of air from below, in great quantity and at great speed, into the iron while molten. In the existing methods of refining for steel, as in puddling, the iron was almost viscous. In Bessemer's process the rapid combustion of the silicon and carbon raised the temperature to such a degree that the mass of iron was kept perfectly fluid.

Difficulties arose, however, which Bessemer (an engineer rather than a metallurgist) had not foreseen. By chance, his experiments had been made with an iron ore remarkably free from phosphorus. When repeated with phosphoric iron his process failed to remove this impurity, more than a very small proportion of which makes the steel non-malleable. Bessemer began to look for a suitable non-phosphoric ore, and found what he wanted in the Cumberland haematite, while it could also be imported from Spain and Sweden. A second difficulty was that Bessemer found no effective way of ascertaining the exact moment of the 'blow' at which the metal had just enough carbon in it to be steel. Furthermore, the first Bessemer steel was brittle, and contained many air-holes. A remedy was found by R. F. Mushet, who realised that the addition of spiegel (an alloy of manganese and iron) which had a de-gasifying effect, would remove the excess oxygen introduced into the metal, while as it was a 're-carburizer', it could also be used to adjust the carbon content. Even so, Mushet's discovery was only a partial answer to Bessemer's difficulties, since the use of spiegel was limited to the making of steel with a relatively high carbon content. A third difficulty was mechanical, and was solved by Bessemer himself. The first converters had been fixed, but to secure exact results, Bessemer had to be able to stop or re-start the full blast at will, and during the stoppage the air-pipes under a fixed converter might get clogged. The converter was therefore swung on its axis, so that it could be tilted until the pipes led in above the surface of the molten metal.

When the engineer Rennie had first seen Bessemer's process—before it was made public—he assured him that the ironmasters could be relied on to solve all the difficulties that remained. In fact, they lacked the initiative, and as no Sheffield man would adopt his methods, Bessemer decided to force the trade to take it up by underselling. He started with a partner in 1858; and undersell he did. His quotation for high-class tool steel was £42 a ton, as against £50-£60 asked by other makers. However, the things which were made most successfully were those that had hitherto been made, not of tool-steel, and not at Sheffield, but of the finest Yorkshire or Black Country wrought-iron—such as locomotive cranks and axles, railway tyres and ships' propeller shafts. For these, pure Swedish iron, and later 'Bessemer iron' were employed, but as neither of these was smelted at Sheffield, pig-iron had to be melted, so that the plan of running molten iron from blast furnace direct to converter had to be dropped.

There was no mushroom growth in the production and use of steel. Comparative cost remained an important factor. Bessemer charged a high price for patentee's licences, which settle down at £1 a ton on steel rails, and £2 a ton on steel for other purposes. The licence fee, together with the greater expense of the raw material, made steel rails and plates much dearer than their iron competitors. The steel/iron rail price ratio was 2·65 to 1 in 1867, but fell to 1·50 to 1 in 1871, and 1·16 to 1 by 1875. Yet, long endurance tests were required to prove that the dearer material was in fact more economical, and attitudes remained conservative. The War Office and the Admiralty were slow to accept steel, while its use in bridge-building was not authorised by the Board of Trade until 1877. Finally, there was an enormous amount of capital and human skill locked up in puddling, in which Britain had undisputed dominance. It was not until this semi-monopolistic position was lost by foreign competition in the 1870s that the ultimate transition was made.

It was in that decade that the rapid strides in the use of steel were made. In 1872, for example, the North Eastern Railway used steel rails only at points and crossings, but by 1877 it had ceased to order iron rails at all. The Great Western used steel rails on four-fifths of its main line by 1878. Shipbuilding witnessed the same changes. As iron had only come to be generally adopted in the 1850s and 1860s, the reluctance to experiment with another new material is easily understood. The launching of two steel despatch vessels for the Navy in 1876 marked the moment of rapid change. In September 1875 there had been no steel ships under construction; in 1880 Lloyds' surveyors inspected a steel tonnage of 35,000; and in 1885 a steel tonnage of 166,000 (but also 934,000 tons of iron shipping).

The growing use of steel owed much to technical developments made after Bessemer, of which Sir William Siemens' regenerative gas furnace and open-hearth process were of major significance. In the regenerative gas furnace (which could be used for any purpose) a current of burning gas heats the firebrick labyrinth of the regenerative chambers. Through them go the next incoming currents of gas and air, sucking in heat, and burning at a far higher temperature than the first current, and so on. Currents and temperature can be exactly controlled, and as much heat can be generated as the fabric of the furnace will stand. Such a furnace was introduced at Ormesby, near Middlesbrough, in 1860, with the result that temperatures were raised to 256°C—never before achieved—and the output of pig-iron was increased by 20 per cent. From the first, Siemens had suggested that his furnace might be used for steel-making, but the early experiments of licencees were failures. However, in 1865 the Martins of Sireuil, in France, successfully made cast steel by melting scrap steel in a bath of molten pig-iron on a Siemens open hearth. In the same year Siemens started his Sample Steel

Works in Birmingham to make his process known, and with a group of associates he founded the Siemens Steel Company at Landore, Swansea, in 1869. Here, Siemens' own method of steel-making (more fundamental than the Martins') was applied. Into the molten pig, at full heat, was fed a pure ore in relatively small quantities. The perfect control of the gaseous fuel and hence of the temperature in the open-hearth furnace enabled the steel-maker to work very exactly. Ore was fed in to keep the 'boiling' constant, the contents of the furnace were sampled at intervals, and at the right moment the molten mass was 'physicked' with manganese. By 1873, when the Landore works owned its own blast furnaces and collieries, 1000 tons of steel were being made each week. Siemens' process had many advantages over that of Bessemer, which was gradually overtaken. By 1900 the for mer was more widely used, while the last two Bessemer converters in Britain are scheduled to go out of production in 1972-3.

The open-hearth process still left unsolved the problem of phosphoric ores, which was finally solved by a police-court clerk and his cousin between 1875-8. Sidney Gilchrist Thomas (described by Landes as 'the last and perhaps the most important of the line of tinkerers that had made the Industrial Revolution') was an amateur scientist, whose experiments led him to discover that in the existing processes the phosphorus in phosphoric ores formed a phosphoric *acid*, which would not combine with the acid (silica) lining of the converters. The solution was therefore simple, namely to fit a *basic* lining, in the form of limestone, to the converter. Not only would the phosphorus separate out, leaving a pure steel; the resulting basic slag would form a most valuable fertiliser. This production of a valuable by-product makes it all the more surprising that Thomas's invention was not an immediate commercial success in this country. Again, conservatism played its part, while the industry was also less dependent on phosphoric ores. However, the process was eagerly taken up in Belgium, France, Germany and the United States, where there was abundant phosphoric ore, with the consequence that the British industry, for the first time, became seriously threatened by foreign competition.

Alongside developments in iron and steel, and the expansion of steam power, went the growth of the engineering industry. In both civil and mechanical engineering Britain often gave the lead, although in the latter part of the century many technical advances were made abroad, especially in the United States. Joseph Whitworth, one of the leading British mechanical engineers, was able to point to one of the root causes of the advance of American technology when he reported that 'the labouring classes (there) are comparatively few in number, but this is counterbalanced by, and may indeed be regarded as one of the chief causes of, the eagerness with which they call in the aid of machinery. . . . Wherever it can be introduced, it is universally and willingly resorted to.' It was little wonder that the process of mass-production of products with fully interchangeable parts became known in this country as 'the American System.'

One of the intriguing elements in the development of the British engineering industry is the way in which skills and ideals were passed down from one leader to another. Joseph Bramah (whose foolproof lock was first picked at the Great Exhibition, sixty seven years after it was patented) employed Henry Maudslay in his workshops. In his turn Maudslay employed Joseph Clement, Richard Roberts, Joseph Whitworth, and James Nasmyth. Maudslay impressed upon his pupils the need for simplicity as well as what he called 'get-at-ability'—the need to be able to get at any part of a machine which might need repair, without having to dismantle the whole. Whitworth's great contribution was in his crusade for standardisation. He collected sample screws from as many British workshops as possible, and, by taking the average of their measurements, put forward his proposals for screws of a standard angle of $55°$ between the sides of the thread, and a specified number of threads to the inch for different diameters. His recommendations became standard British practice in the 1860s. Beyond such basic requirements as this, however, standardisation came much more slowly. Even apart from the battle of the gauges, the railways, for example, showed a remarkable lack of standardisation. As late as 1917 an official enquiry showed that British railways had over 40 different types of handbrake in use on their wagons and no fewer than 200 types of axle box. Inconvenient as this lack of standardisation was, in some respects it was all to the good, in that the precipitate adoption of one standard type could well have stifled further technical progress. This was one of the reasons why the Board of Trade was reluctant to lay down requirements for specific types of brake or signalling equipment for the railways.

As machines advanced, a greater quantity of goods could be produced at a lower cost. By 1875, for example, two girls with two machines could turn out 240,000 screws a day, as compared with 20,000 a day by twenty men and boys in 1840. Yet if machines replaced some skilled labour with less skilled labour, engineering itself saw the rise of a body of highly skilled craftsmen, and it is not surprising that it was from this sector of industry that important new developments in trade unionism came.

6 The organisation of industry and banking   It is not to be thought that the great increase in output was entirely due to technical advances, for it was just as important that the organisation of industry and the financial system should develop.

In Chapter I it was seen that in the early stages of Britain's industrial growth there was little need for joint-stock organisation. Not until at least mid-century did the scale of manufacturing industry increase to such a point that it came to be seen as a growing necessity. The Bubble Act had been repealed as a result of pressure during the boom of 1824-5, and in 1837 the Letters Patent Act was passed. This gave the President of the Board of Trade, as representative of the Crown, the discretionary power to grant certain privileges by Letters Patent which could previously be obtained only from Parliament; but the attitude remained that incorporation should be a privilege rather than a right. Most of the applications came from public utilities rather than manufacturing industry, and many serious industrialists still considered joint-stock companies to denote irresponsible management, defective finance, or even fraud.

A Select Committee investigated the law relating to joint-stock companies in 1844, and concluded that as the development of this form of organisation was inevitable, Parliament should seek to control it. As a result, the Joint Stock Companies Act was passed in the same year, by which any association of 24 or more members could register as a company, with power to sue and be sued. Registration was in two parts; a company first gained provisional registration, and might then be fully registered if the Registrar of Companies was satisfied as to its structure and genuineness. Limited liability—whereby the liability of each shareholder is restricted to the amount of his investment—was not provided for, although some companies sought to provide it by various legal devices. The passage of this Act was followed immediately by the railway mania, which did much to change attitudes to joint-stock companies, for although there were many instances of loss, on the whole investments were secure. Many provincial stock exchanges were opened during the years of the railway mania, including those at Glasgow and Edinburgh in 1844, and at Leeds, Bristol, Birmingham and Leicester in 1845, as well as several others.

As the prosperity of the country increased, there came to be a mass of savings seeking profitable investment, but unlimited liability remained a deterrent. As the question was more and more discussed, there was increasing criticism of the discretionary power of granting limited liability which had been given to the Board of Trade by the Act of 1837. Either the principle was a good one, in which case it should be available to all, or it was a bad one, in which case, as Robert Lowe put it, he would 'as soon think of allowing the Secretary of the Treasury to grant dispensations for smuggling or the Attorney-General licenses to commit murder'.

In 1851 a Select Committee on the Law of Partnership made a recommendation for limited liability, citing the advantages that would be obtained from companies promoted for social welfare purposes, such as housing. At last, an Act of 1856 (following a clumsily worded Act of the previous year) enabled any seven men to start a joint-stock company with limited liability—although banks were excluded until 1858, and insurance companies and discount houses until 1862. There was no immediate rush to form companies, for the average manufacturing firm remained indifferent to the company form. Ploughed-back profits still provided a majority of capital requirements, and the sober firm could always borrow from the bank. Many of the limited companies formed in the 1870s were for such organisations as political clubs and temperance halls, but it was also in that decade that manufacturers in general came to lose their former suspicions. Towards the end of the century there was a great increase in the formation of limited liability companies (partly due to the ageing of the pioneer industrialists, who wanted their firms to continue); and by the end of the century, with the exception of retail trade, joint-stock companies had become the characteristic type of business undertaking.

It was from Scotland that the movement for joint-stock banking came. The Bank of Scotland originally had a monopoly of joint-stock banking in that country, as the Bank of England continued to have in England and Wales, but that privilege was lost in 1716. Private banks did not cease to exist, but they were not important, and, with the exception of a few old-established houses in Edinburgh, they were gradually bought out by their joint-stock competitors. The effect was that the number of banks was small, but they had many branches, so the community was well served; and Scottish banks plumbed much deeper in the social scale for customers, small depositors and small borrowers being given full facilities. In 1825 Scotland had fewer banks than Devon, and there had not been a single bank failure since 1816.

The contrast between the stable Scottish banks and the unstable banks of England was brought out in the financial crisis of 1825. In that panic, the result of over-speculation in South America and at home, 73 English and Welsh banks suspended payment, and about 50 failed altogether. In Scotland there were two or three failures, yet none amongst the older or fully developed joint-stock banks, and not one in Edinburgh or Glasgow. As Clapham put it, 'The country seemed almost immune to the virus.' Thomas Joplin, a Newcastle merchant and banker, thereupon successfully challenged the Bank of England's monopoly. Joint-stock banks were authorised outside a 65-mile radius from London in 1826, and the Bank of England was obliged to open branches in the provinces. Although at first the growth of joint-stock banks was not rapid, there were 32 in England and Wales by 1833, and 115 by 1841. Meanwhile, private banks were either slowly turning themselves into joint-stock or being absorbed, while many disappeared. From a total of 321 in England and Wales in 1841, the number fell to 251 by 1886. In 1833 the Bank of England's charter was renewed for 21 years, but its privileges were further limited, and the 65-mile limit was waived, joint-stock banks henceforward being allowed in London so long as they did not issue notes. Crises in 1836 and 1839 led to increased concern, but both Parliament and the City were completely fogged as to the real nature of the problems involved and the remedies possible. Two committees, in 1836-8 and 1840-1, produced masses of detailed evidence, 'from which the conscientious student of banking reforms could have deduced any remedy he cared, but which the Committees themselves found it impossible to digest'.

There were two schools of thought. The *Currency School* held that a fixed relation was necessary between the amount of gold in the country and the size of the note issues; as gold flowed out the volume of notes should be decreased, while more notes should be issued as gold came in to the country. They believed that by controlling the issue of notes (and over-issue of notes by country bankers had been blamed for the crises of the 1830s), booms and depressions in the value of money would be eliminated. They suggested, therefore, that the issue of notes should be gradually concentrated in the Bank of England, and that note issues should be separated from the business of commercial banking. Curiously enough, the Currency School attached no importance to the circulating bill of exchange (a form of near money) nor to the cheque, which was rapidly becoming a means of payment. The *Banking School* held that the state's duty was simply to see that banknotes were convertible into gold; if that were ensured, the size of the note issue might safely be left to the experience of bankers, and their knowledge of the needs of industry and commerce.

The Bank Charter Act of 1844 marked a triumph for the Currency School. The Bank of England was divided into two departments; a Banking Department and an Issue Department. The note issue was to correspond exactly with the amount of gold coins and bullion held in the reserves, with the exception that there was to be a fiduciary issue of notes, backed by government securities, of £14 million. This compromise was included to relieve the Bank from having to acquire an amount of gold bullion to match existing note issues which it would probably have been unable to acquire at that time. Other provisions applied to the note issue of the country banks. No new privilege of note issue would be granted, although banks which already possessed the right would not lose it unless they amalgamated or let it lapse. In the event of any bank forfeiting its issue, the Bank of England could increase its fiduciary issue by two-thirds of the lapsed issue. The number of note-issuing banks thereafter declined, the last being Fox, Fowler & Co. of Wellington, Somerset, who lost the right when they amalgamated with Lloyds' in 1921.

The rigidity imposed by the Act would have been serious had it not been for the development of the credit system and the discovery of fresh sources of gold in the late 1840s and the 1850s, while the failure of the Act to control financial crises is evidenced by its suspension on three subsequent occasions, one occurring only three years after the Act was passed. In 1847, 1857 and 1866, the Bank was permitted to lend beyond its legal limits; but the crisis of 1866 proved to be the last of its kind, and in the course of time the Bank of England acquired experience and a sense of responsibility which enabled it to regulate the money market with increasing effect.

Meanwhile the development of branch banking and the amalgamation movement went hand in hand. Private banks did not much favour branch banking because of the supervision involved, and hence business was transferred to the joint-stock banks. By 1864 there were over 1000 bank branches, and 2500-2700 in 1886-7. From this period on the five main joint-stock banks, Barclays, Lloyds, Midland, District and Martins, pushed on to establish a national system of branches, sweeping up the private banks into their vast organisations.

7 High farming The repeal of the Corn Laws did not lead to the immediate fall in prices which the Anti-Corn Law League had promised and which the protectionists had feared. During the 30 years after repeal the price of wheat remained fairly stable, and, at an average of 53s a quarter, was only 5s a quarter less than the average price achieved in the last 26 years of protection. Farmers' profits rose, and the landlords' rents increased by a quarter between 1851-3 and 1878-9. Instead of ruin, the repeal of the Corn Laws appeared to usher in a 'Golden Age' of prosperity for British farmers.

The reasons why prices remained relatively stable are not too difficult to see. On the demand side, population was growing, while rising living standards increased per capita consumption. Imports certainly increased—by 1872-4 nearly half the consumption of wheat was imported—yet supplies did not increase fast enough to swamp the demand and break prices. In 1850 four-fifths of British corn imports came from Europe (France, Russia, and the Baltic) while most of the remaining fifth came from the United States. These foreign suppliers were in no position to undercut the home price; their own population was growing rapidly, and what grain surplus they might produce had to bear insurance and freight costs to this country. International dislocation further favoured the British farmer, the Crimean War interfering with Russian exports, and giving home producers their most agreeable years. The potential threat came from the United States. Here again, war intervened in favour of the British farmer, although the main factor insulating him from the full impact of growing American resources was the relatively backward state of transport. The cold wind began to blow over British agriculture with the development of both the American railroad and the British steamship.

There had been earlier portents of that progressive farming which came to fruition in the 'high farming' of the third quarter of the century. In 1838 the Royal Agricultural Society of England was founded, with the motto 'Practice with Science', while the Royal Agricultural College, Circencester, was founded seven years later. Agricultural science was furthered by the publication in 1840 of Justus von Liebig's *Organic Chemistry in its Applications to Agriculutre and Physiology*, and by the establishment of the agricultural research station at Rothamsted by Sir John Lawes in 1843. There were numerous other agricultural journals of an erudite or popular nature; in addition to which there were a number of substantial text-books—Youatt's *The Complete Grazier* had run through eight editions by 1846, and Low's *Elements of Practical Agriculture* had reached a fourth by 1843. The 1840s also witnessed the appearance of many new implements and machines, including some important ones for pipe-making and drainage. The importance of these early developments needs to be stressed, for looking back over the period since he had first reported on English agriculture in 1850-1, James Caird wrote in 1878 that the change had not been any considerable progress beyond what had then seemed the best, but a general uplifting of the middling and the worst.

While most historians would hold that the Corn Laws were repealed for the accepted political reasons, with certain 'sops' thrown in for the farmers, Professor D. C. Moore has argued that Peel brought in repeal as a deliberate effort to stimulate cost-reducing improvements:

Himself a charter member of the English Agricultural Society, he obviously realised that while many agriculturalists were still complaining of depressed prices others were not only exulting in their high yields but proclaiming to the world that because of their heavy investments, especially in drainage and fertiliser, because of their emphasis upon pastoral and dairy farming, and because of their new rotations, they could sell wheat at a profit at almost half the going price. In proposing to repeal the Corn Laws Peel was trying to spike the guns of the Anti-Corn Law League. At the same time he was trying to encourage the adoption of high farming techniques by those agriculturalists who either still resisted the blandishments of science or could not afford to hear them. In his appeal to these men Peel used both the carrot and the stick. Yet because the stick was the same shape as the bludgeon with which the Leaguers hoped to beat their rural opponents, the existence of the carrots has been almost totally ignored and the purpose of the stick seriously distorted. (D. C. Moore, 1965, pages 553-4.)

Admittedly the original £2 million drainage loan which the government offered was small, but Moore argues that it primed the pump. Private companies certainly followed—the General Land Drainage and Improvement Company in 1849, for example, and the Lands Improvement Company in 1853—with the result that by 1864 an estimated £8 million from the Treasury and public companies had been invested in land improvement, rising to £12 million by 1878 and over £18 million by 1912.

Drainage was a fundamental improvement. If properly executed, it enabled farmers of heavy and ill-drained soils to cut their costs of cultivation, speed up their operations, and follow the trend towards mixed farming by introducing root 'breaks' into their rotations; it enabled machinery to be used, and better advantage taken of the new fertilisers whose effectiveness and quality was being improved by scientific experiment. Yet much remained to be done, Caird estimating in 1873 that barely one-fifth of the land in England and Wales which ought to be drained had received that benefit.

There was a great interest in agricultural machinery; McCormick's reaper aroused considerable interest at the Great Exhibition, and a growing number of implements came to be shown at the agricultural shows. At Chester in 1858, the judges of the Royal Agricultural Society had no fewer than 89 threshers on test, and there was an 'avenue of steam engines neatly arranged at equal distances, their fly wheels in perpetual motion'. Unfortunately three of them blew up. However, while the number of implements grew, the major machines became more uniform in principle, and reveal a standardisation arising naturally from the elimination of weaker types and emulation of the more efficient. As an example of the way in which machines could cut costs, it was estimated in the 1860s that the cost of corn harvesting could be reduced by 30-40 per cent with existing machines, but that full benefits could only be obtained on well-drained and levelled land from which water-cuts and furrows had been eliminated and large stones removed.

There were many such hindrances to high farming; a lot of farmers were too small, too poor, too ignorant, or too closely wedded to ancient practices. In Gloucestershire, for example, teams of oxen driven by labourers of 'legendary lethargy' took a seven-hour day to plough three-quarters of an acre, and moved so slowly that an observer claimed that many times he had to look at some tree in the distance to make sure that the plough-teams were moving at all. More important were the size of the farm and the size of the fields. The farms really suited to high farming were those of more than 300 acres, yet in the 1850s they numbered fewer than 17,000 and occupied only about one-third of the acreage. Most important of all was insecurity of tenure. Not until the last quarter of the century was there any statutory control of the relations between landlord and tenant, whose dealings before then were governed entirely by custom and personal agreement. A farmer who leased his farm had some measure of protection, but the many farmers whose farms were let from year to year had virtually none. Improvements which the farmer made to his land might lead to his rent being raised, while the loss of his farm could result in the loss of the capital which he had invested in it. Even a tenant with a long lease had no certainty that it would be renewed. A noted farmer at mid-century was George Hope, who farmed over 600 acres at Fenton Barnes in East Lothian, which his father and grandfather had farmed before him; yet in 1873 his lease was not renewed because eight years before he had stood as a Liberal candidate against Lord Elcho, who was a friend of his landlord.

While high farming undoubtedly produced results in the third quarter of the century, it has been argued that in the longer run it proved to be a strategic miscalculation. High farming meant intensive farming through the application of the most recent techniques, yet its advocates failed to see that technical efficiency is not necessarily the same as economic efficiency. Its success depended on growing markets and high prices, and no amount of technical efficiency could protect the arable farmer from the flood of cheap imported corn after the 1870s. Arable farming became over-capitalised, and much heavy investment was sunk for ever when the 'Great Depression' put an end to all hope of satisfactory returns in the arable districts where so much of the effort had been concentrated. E. L. Jones sums it up:

It is said that the Duke of Bedford inspected his farms after a thorough replanning and observed gravely to a tenant named Jonathan Bodger, 'great improvements, Jonathan', to which Jonathan replied, 'great alterations, your Grace'. Although he nearly lost his farm for it, the tenant had shrewdly summed up much of contemporary landowner investment. (E. L. Jones, 1968, page 30.)

8 Trade unions It is not to be supposed that the economic changes which characterised the mid-Victorian period would leave the labour movement unaffected, nor is it surprising that the year of the Great Exhibition also witnessed, in the formation of the Amalgamated Society of Engineers, the first of what later came to be called the 'New Model Unions'. Although they were in many ways characteristic of the age, however, their prominence should not lead us to accept uncritically the idea of a peaceful trade union movement, under conservative leadership, in the third quarter of the century. There were reactionary as well as forward-looking aspects of the New Model Unions, while at the same time there were other prominent organisations—of miners and cotton operatives, for example—whose different economic position led them to adopt different attitudes and policies.

The essential characteristics of the New Model Unions were the same, and consisted of a close combination of trade and friendly activities. A wide range of unemployment, dispute, sickness and superannuation benefits were provided, to pay for which a high contribution (around a shilling a week) had to be raised. The effect of this was that these unions were confined to the more highly paid and thriftier skilled artisans, while the protection of their large benefit funds encouraged the leaders to avoid strike action as far as possible. 'Never surrender the right to strike', said Robert Applegarth, the secretary of the Amalgamated Society of Carpenters, 'but be careful how you use a double-edged weapon.' George Odger, secretary of the Ladies Shoemakers' Society, put the point more strongly still: 'Strikes in the social world', he said, 'are like wars in the political world; both are crimes unless justified by absolute necessity.' Instead of militant action, the New Model Unions looked towards self-help and education as means of improving the lot of their members. The spread of literacy led to the growth of a trade union press, with well-produced journals such as the *Potters' Examiner* and the *Flint Glass Makers' Magazine*, which once advised its readers to 'get knowledge, and in getting knowledge you get power . . . get intelligence instead of alcohol—it is sweeter and more lasting'. The crafts attempted to keep up the scarcity value of their skill, either by attempting to restrict apprenticeship, by encouraging the unemployed artisan still to 'tramp' for work or to emigrate, or by regulating the supply of labour in some other way. Above all, their aim was to make themselves respectable, but strong. A Manchester foundry owner felt that the engineers in 1868 were 'very nice people if they have their own way, but if they have not they will fight, and they can fight anything and anybody, they are so strong'.

The formation of the Amalgamated Society of Engineers was immediately countered by the establishment of the Central Association of Employers of Operative Engineers, and within months the two were locked in combat. In January 1852 the employers locked out their men when they refused to accept an increase in the number of unskilled men in the workshops, and systematic overtime. The struggle lasted for three months, but in spite of generous financial help from other unions and from the general public, the union was defeated. The men were forced to sign the 'document' before getting their jobs back, but they rightly took the view that this was not binding, having been signed under duress, and retained their membership. The union benefited greatly from the publicity and soon built up its financial and numerical strength.

Whereas the New Model Unions found much of their support in London and the Midlands, the unions of the north and of Scotland displayed a greater militancy. The strength of the New Model Unions lay in the scarcity value of their members' labour; less skilled workers had no such advantage, and were therefore led to more aggressive action, and to the demand for legislative redress of their grievances. The cotton workers pressed for improvement of factory conditions and the limitation of hours of work; while the miners, under their able leader, Alexander McDonald, succeeded in 1860 in gaining the passage of the Coal Mines Regulation Act, which, besides improving pit safety measures, enforced the practice of appointing check-weighmen, chosen by the men, to ensure that the miners were not cheated in their piece-work wages.

Although trade unions had ceased to be illegal in 1824, they laboured under many difficulties, and in the 1860s concerted action was taken to improve the worker's legal position. The body of law which governed the relations between an employer and his employees was grossly unfair to the latter. An employer could give evidence against a worker or on his own behalf, but a worker could not give evidence against his employer, or in his own defence. If an employee broke a contract of employment he could be sent to prison, whereas his employer was only liable to civil proceedings. Furthermore, magistrates had developed the habit of threatening strikers with imprisonment for breach of contract under this law if they did not immediately return to work. It was claimed in the early 1860s that over 10,000 cases came before the courts each year, and as the law pressed most heavily in Scotland (for various legal and industrial reasons) it was there that the agitation for reform began. The lead was taken by the Glasgow Trades Council, which in 1864 convened a national trade union conference in London. Never before had so many prominent unionists from throughout the country met together, and the meeting deserves to be regarded as the first of the modern Trade Union Congresses. Success was not secured, however, until 1867, when the Master and Servant Act remedied most of the worst aspects of the law, although imprisonment (with or without hard labour) for up to three months was still permitted in cases of breach of contract 'of an aggravated character'.

Eighteen-sixty-seven was an eventful year for the labour movement, for events conspired to put the unions under extreme pressure. In contrast to the national and powerful New Model Unions, very small and narrow unions predominated in the Sheffield cutlery trades. The industry was composed of many small firms, making it difficult for unions to organise. In consequence, arbitrary methods of discipline had long been imposed against non-unionists and backsliding union members. The workman's tools or wheel-bands were removed, and if this 'rattening' did not bring about the desired results, more violent action was taken—a can of gunpowder might be placed in the trough of his grinding wheel. In 1865-6 there were numerous incidents, culminating in an outrage in October 1866 when a workman's house was blown up, and the crime was attributed to agents of the Saw Grinders' Union. There was an immediate outcry, and a demand for an investigation of the 'Sheffield Outrages', as they became known in the press. A narrow investigation would have provided bad publicity for the trade union movement, and the London Trades Council successfully demanded an enquiry into trade unionism as a whole.

Just when the agitation against the unions was at its height, the High Court delivered its fateful verdict in the case of *Hornby v. Close*. Since the passage of the Friendly Societies Act of 1855, trade unions had felt that their funds were protected (so long as they had deposited their rules with the Registrar of Friendly Societies) and that they could secure redress from the courts against defaulting officers and members. However, in this case in which the Boilermakers' Society sued the treasurer of their Bradford branch to recover money owed, the Court declared that a trade union could not come within the scope of the Friendly Societies Act. Furthermore, it declared that unions were so far 'in restraint of trade' as to be by nature illegal at common law. Thus, although no one could be indicted under the common law merely for forming or joining a trade union, the taint of illegality was held to exist, to the extent that the courts could neither sanction nor protect trade unions or their funds. This decision not only put trade union funds in imminent danger—anyone could make off with them and the courts would do nothing—but threw the whole legal position of unions into doubt.

All this made of vital significance the outcome of the Royal Commission set up to examine trade unions. The 'Junta' (as the Webbs called it) consisting of Applegarth, Allan of the Engineers, Coulson of the Bricklayers, Odger, and Guile of the Iron Founders, began to emerge as a group seeking to lead the trade union movement. They did not go unchallenged, for a rival group led by George Potter, with strong support from the provinces, also set up a committee to watch the Commission's proceedings, but without the success which the Junta enjoyed.

The Junta first sought to influence the membership of the Royal Commission, and although the government would not agree to a working-class Commissioner, they accepted the nomination by the Junta of Frederick Harrison, for long a staunch supporter of the New Model Unions and the moderate unionism which they represented. With the appointment of the Christian Socialist, Thomas Hughes (of *Tom Brown's Schooldays* fame) to the Commission, the Junta was assured of at least two friends out of the eleven members. In addition, permission was obtained for trade unionist representatives to be present during the examination of witnesses, and Applegarth was the Junta's choice.

The conduct of the unions' case was left largely to Applegarth, in collaboration with Harrison, and with occasional help from Hughes, who missed many of the hearings. The strategy was to distract attention from the Sheffield Outrages and all forms of militant unionism, and concentrate it on the moderate New Model Unions; and an attempt was made to paint a picture of the unions as sober, businesslike, and utterly respectable. The attempt was entirely successful, and was aided by the poor tactics of the hostile Commissioners, who tried to overcome the effect by bringing in actuarial experts to show that the unions' friendly benefits could not in the long run be maintained. This was the kind of question which Applegarth and his colleagues were only too happy to discuss.

The work of the Commission resulted in a Majority and a Minority Report. The tactics of the trade unionists had been so successful that even the Majority Report recommended that unions should be made legal, under certain conditions. But the majority held that trade union funds should only be protected if the union rules were free from restrictive clauses, such as those prohibiting piece-work, or limiting apprentices and the use of machinery; these struck particularly at the New Model

Unions, whose policies were largely dependent on these restrictions, and opposition was therefore bound to be strong. The Minority Report, signed by Harrison, Hughes and the Earl of Lichfield, proposed, simply, that all legal discriminations against workers or trade unions should be repealed.

It was more than eighteen months before the government introduced legislation. The Bill gave legal recognition to trade unions, whose funds might be protected by registration under the Friendly Societies Act. However, several penal clauses were included against all forms of 'molestation', 'obstruction', and 'intimidation', and even against peaceful picketing, which had been legalised in 1859. The defects of the Junta's strategy were now made apparent, for the government had taken them at their word. If the unions really were as respectable as the Junta had professed them to be, there could be no objection. But even the New Model Unions needed to fight on occasion, so there was bound to be resistance. The only compromise to which the government would agree was to separate the penal clauses into a second Bill. Thus two Acts were passed in 1871—the Trade Union Act and the Criminal Law Amendment Act—enabling the unionists to accept the former, while fighting for the repeal of the latter. It was not long before the severity of the law was seen; in 1872 six gas fitters were sentenced to twelve months imprisonment under the Act, and at Chipping Norton in 1873, sixteen women, the wives of striking farm labourers, were sentenced to hard labour (admittedly only for a few days) for 'intimidating' blackleg workers.

At the 1874 General Election candidates were given 'Test Questions', and in cases where the Conservative gave more favourable replies, unionists were encouraged to give him the vote; the working class undoubtedly helped in the defeat of the Liberals and the return of the Conservatives. In addition, two trade unionist candidates secured election to Parliament, where they joined the ranks of the Liberals; Alexander McDonald, the miners' leader, was returned for Stafford, and Thomas Burt, another miner, was returned for Morpeth, a constituency containing a number of mining villages.

One of the first acts of the new government was to appoint a Royal Commission on the Labour Laws. This brought howls of protest from the unions, who saw a danger of the whole question being opened again, and the Trade Union Act of 1871 put in jeopardy. The Parliamentary Committee of the Trade Union Congress decided to boycott the Commission, which therefore proved ineffective. The report of the Commission was unsatisfactory to the unions, but when the government introduced its legislation in June 1875, it was seen that the demands of the unionists were substantially met. The Master and Servant Act of 1867 was replaced by the Employers and Workmen Act—a significant change of name—and from henceforth the contract of employment became a purely civil engagement into which both employer and workman entered as equal parties. The Criminal Law Amendment Act of 1871 was replaced by the Conspiracy and Protection of Property Act, 1875, which ruled out the law of conspiracy as applied to trade disputes unless the actions complained of were criminal in themselves. Peaceful picketing was expressly legalised, and questions of intimidation and violence were left to the ordinary criminal law. Thus the trade unions secured a charter which appeared, until the Taff Vale judgment of 1901, to give them adequate legal status and legal indemnity in trade disputes.

Chapter IV

Britain and the World

1 The opening up of the world Britain entered the nineteenth century as the most industrialised nation in the world, for although her industrial revolution was by no means completed, that of other nations had hardly begun. This initial lead at first increased so that, for a while, as was seen in the last chapter, Britain could truly be called *the* industrial nation—the 'workshop of the world'. It was inevitable that the position would alter, that competitors would arise, and that the industrial monopoly of Britain would be threatened, and by the last quarter of the century these signs of change were clearly to be seen.

But the world was changing also, for in a sense it both grew and shrank; it grew in that vast areas of the world were opened up to habitation and trade, while it shrank in the sense that improvements in transport and communications greatly speeded up contact between different parts of the globe. The battle of New Orleans had been fought on 8 January 1815, two weeks *after* peace between Britain and America had been signed, for the news had not got through; yet fifty-five years later it proved possible for President Grant in Washington to receive, via London, a message which Lord Mayo, Viceroy of India, had telegraphed from his bedroom in Simla only a few minutes before. By the 1880s the telegraph cables covered the whole world with the exception of the Pacific. Clapham says:

It was not yet possible to telegraph to Honolulu, Iceland, New Guinea, or Tierra del Fuego. Nearly every other place of real importance not in the heart of China could be reached overland or under the sea. The world, on the economist's projection, had shrunk into a single market. The final process of shrinkage had only taken about fifteen years and the greater part of it had been done in less then ten. (Clapham, Vol. 2, page 217.)

News of the world's commodities hummed along the copper wires, while the goods themselves slid along the rails of iron and steel to the ships that were to transport them across the oceans.

It has been estimated that the value of world trade expanded more than twenty-five-fold between 1800 and 1913. Imlah gives figures which suggest that the total value of world trade grew from £320 million in 1800 to £560 million in 1840, a rise of about 75 per cent; from then on the rate of increase became faster, the total reaching £1450 million in 1860, £2890 million in 1872-3, and £8360 million in 1913. The fruits of the earth yielded their increase—from abaca, abietine and agar-agar to ylang-ylang, zaffre and zinc—and much of that increase passed through London. Indeed, Britain played a large part both in the opening up of the world and the development of world trade, and in the industrialisation of her competitors. The spread of railways underlay each development. World railway mileage is estimated to have grown from under 5000 miles in 1840 to 386,000 in 1890, of which more than two-fifths were in the United States. Australia built 2681 miles of railway in the 1870s, thereby quadrupling the length of line open to traffic. New Zealand, which had not a single mile in the 1860s, had 2500 miles by the close of the century. In India the development of railways was first delayed and then hastened by the Mutiny; by 1890 there were 17,000 miles. Canada, with 1800 miles in 1860, increased this to nearly 31,000 miles by 1914. Even where the expansion was slower the economic effects could be great. Argentina had only 450 miles in 1870, and even by 1890 had less than Great Britain possessed 40 years before; but here, as in other countries being opened up, a few pioneering lines across virgin territory might have an influence upon trade out of all proportion to their length.

It was with British capital that much of this mileage was constructed, as well as British enterprise, engineering skill, and brawn. Railways were the greatest field for overseas investment, having the same magnetic attraction for investors in the half-century before 1914 that home railways had exerted in the mid-1840s. By 1913, 41 per cent of all British holdings of overseas securities were in railways, the largest single share (over 16 per cent) being invested in the U.S.A. Much of this investment provided a double bonus for Britain, the funds invested subsequently returning to this country for the purchase of rails and rolling stock.

The giant railway contractors such as Brassey and Peto commanded great armies of men and equipment which had to be kept in employment, so that it is not surprising that they often played a leading part in the promotion of railways overseas. From the time when British navvies started to work on the Paris-Rouen railway in 1841 (drawing from French spectators the startled cry, 'Mon Dieu, ces Anglais, comme ils travaillent'), British contractors were continuously at work, for as the *Railway Times* put it in 1852, they had 'started on a kind of knight-errantry to supply railway deficiencies all over the world'. At one time Brassey had railways and docks under construction in five continents, and with the possible exception of Greece, Albania and Finland, every country in Europe was to possess a specimen of his workmanship. In his 35-year working life he was engaged upon 170 different contracts, involving 8000 miles of railway. The railway and the steamship provided the means for an increased flow of goods to appear amongst the items of world trade, and Britain, once open to free trade, provided a ready market.

2 Britain and the industrialisation of Europe   The position of Britain with regard to her potential competitors contains an element of irony, for she helped to speed up their industrialisation and hence to advance their rivalry; in the words of Jenks, 'Great Britain midwived a half-dozen lusty rivals.' Yet it is difficult to see what else could have been done, for the developing nations needed British skills and machinery, as well as capital, and she was in a supreme position to satisfy the demand. As Clapham points out:

Even had the danger been greater there was nothing to be gained by refusing to do today work which you could do well merely because your children might have to do work of another kind tomorrow. The farsighted policy for an industrial nation and its business leaders was to concentrate on the most elaborate and ingenious work of which it was capable. (Clapham, Vol. 3, page 65.)

This is not to say that in the early stages of industrialisation the British government did not try to maintain the country's lead by prohibiting the export of machinery and the emigration of artisans. A number of Acts passed between 1750 and 1799 attempted to prohibit the export of certain classes of machinery, models and drawings. But the law was easily evaded, often with the connivance of the very manufacturers who clamoured for the prohibition, and although two parliamentary commissions, in 1824 and 1825, revealed the defects of the system, their findings did not lead to abolition. Some machinery, including steam engines and machine tools, was exported legally under Treasury licence, although this privilege was not extended to spinning machinery. The value of machinery exported from Great Britain during the years 1822-9 inclusive was reported at over £1,500,000, of which about half went to the continent of Europe, and in 1840 the official value of machinery exports was given as £600,000; how much in addition was smuggled out of the country will never be known, although the sources on the continental countries are full of evidence of the successful purchase and installation of British machinery. Not until 1843 was this, the last British export prohibition, repealed. There was then nothing to prevent foreign industrialists from taking up British machines and techniques, which they often did with great speed; Nasmyth's steam hammer, for example, was actually in use at the Le Creusot ironworks in France before it was adopted by English engineers.

Skilled artisans were also forbidden to leave the country by Acts passed in 1719 and 1750 which were not repealed until 1824. Again, the law was difficult to enforce, and those workmen who were really determined to leave the country usually managed to do so. The actual number who left is not known, and the contemporary figure of 16,000 English artisans who had gone to France in 1822-3 was disputed even at the time. By 1825 there must have been at least two thousand skilled British workmen on the Continent, of whom most were in France. Germany secured only a relatively small portion of those who went to the Continent, although they played a significant role in the early stages of industrialisation in that country. Germans were more likely to come to this country to learn—Krupp, for example, touring the iron and steel districts in 1838-9.

Those British technicians who did succeed in emigrating to the Continent varied. Some were entrepreneurs in their own right, or developed into industrialists, occasionally becoming the leaders in their fields. In France there was Aaron Manby, who took the first iron steamship up the Seine to Paris, founded ironworks at Charenton and reconstructed those at Le Creusot, and pioneered the gas industry; the Jacksons, who introduced both the Huntsman crucible process and the Bessemer process into that country; and several pioneers of the French textile industry. In Germany there was William Mulvany, a prominent mine-owner; in Holland, Thomas Wilson, a cotton manufacturer; and above all, John Cockerill in Belgium. By 1830 Cockerill was employing 2500 men at his Seraing ironworks, and was making a great variety of iron products, including (an unusual example of his work) the huge cast-iron lion on the field of Waterloo. It was said of Cockerill that he 'believed that he had a mission to extend manufactures everywhere and to fill the whole world with machinery'. The reports of the Select Committee on the Exportation of Machinery (1841) contain evidence of the relatively advanced state of the Belgian machine-building industry at the time of John Cockerill's death, one witness declaring that Belgium was Britain's most serious competitor as far as machine-building was concerned, while another remarked that the Seraing works had been 'a wonderful nursery for machinery'.

A far more typical industrial emigrant to the Continent was the simple foreman or skilled craftsman—the man who made a direct contribution to the industrial development of his host country without making a name for himself. The skills of such workmen were often indispensable, and they were not employed merely because they were more productive. Indeed, they were often costly, insubordinate and otherwise troublesome. A German machine-builder wrote in 1821 that he longed for competent German foremen 'so that the Englishmen might all be kicked out', and when in 1824 the French ironmaster, de Wendel, sent the chief of his English workmen back to Britain to bring back some technical information, two more workers, and the wives of those already employed, he wrote imploringly:

I have received you letter from febr your absence me nuit beaucoup je paye your worckmans (?) and they do not worck the carpenter is an ivrogne, one cannot employe him. I believe it is better for you to kom and to remaine her. . . . (Quoted in Landes, 1969, page 149.)

But, as Landes says; 'Perhaps the greatest contribution of these immigrants was not what they did but what they taught.' The Cockerill works in Belgium, where numerous Englishmen were employed, passed on technical skills not only to Belgians but to Germans and other foreigners as well. The firm marketed its products as far east as Poland, and every machine sold carried with it a mechanic to instal the equipment and instruct the customer in its use.

Of course, it would be senseless to exaggerate the extent to which British men, money and machines contributed to the industrialisation of the Continent, but at least one can agree with Jenks that 'the British contribution meant a quicker process, and in several directions a more intelligent one, reaping the advantage of experiments in England'. Likewise one should not overstress the losses which this industrial development of Europe imposed on this country. It certainly meant loss of trade for some export industries, but for others (such as machinery and coal) there was a growth in her export trade. In addition, as Saul has pointed out, industrialisation in Europe brought a rise of demand for imports from primary producers, who in turn bought more heavily from Britain.

3 The statistics of foreign trade The great majority of goods produced in Britain were consumed at home, just as the majority of goods consumed there were home-produced; yet throughout the nineteenth century, foreign trade remained a major influence on the British economy. The country increasingly moved away from self-sufficiency, particularly after 1840. A larger proportion of necessities, both to the consumer and the industrialist, was imported from abroad, while a wider range of home-produced goods incorporated a certain amount of imported materials. More and more communities came to have an export industry in their midst, whose prosperity was inextricably bound up with their own. Booms and slumps in exports, through their influence on the increasing number of people directly or indirectly engaged in export production, had a 'multiplied' repercussion on the level of economic activity at home; as Ashworth puts it, for example: 'Nothing contributed more to the air of prosperity in mid-Victorian Britain than the expansive condition of so many export markets.' Between 1850 and 1875 British foreign trade remained consistently more than a fifth (and at times more than a quarter) of world trade. In 1870 British overseas trade per capita (excluding 'invisible' items) stood at £17 7s as against comparable figures of £6 4s for France, £5 6s for Germany, and £4 9s for the USA. Amongst the industrial states at this time only Belgium had comparable figures.

With foreign trade the economic historian is again faced with the problem of interpreting the available statistics, the root of the trouble lying in the inadequacy of the information recorded by contemporaries. Before 1854, no record existed of the actual costs of imports based on current prices, while details of current costs of exports had only been collected by the customs officials after 1798. Consequently, the only comparable series of imports and exports available until the second half of the nineteenth century were the old 'official values' based on fixed prices. These fixed prices were those prevailing in England and Wales in 1694, although, to complicate the picture, those for Scottish trade were based on the prices of 1755 and those of Irish trade on the prices of 1801. As time passed the actual price structure became increasingly different, with the result that the official values came to misrepresent completely the real balance of trade position. Modern scholars, in particular Dr Werner Schlote and Professor Albert Imlah, have attempted to recast the statistical evidence and to tackle the complicated reconstruction of the actual current values of British foreign trade. In so doing, some of the main generalisations about the movements of overseas trade, the effects of industrialisation on its structure, and the export of capital have been altered, in some cases considerably.

The story found in the older textbooks, based on the official values, is one of success, where the industrialisation of the textile industry is supposed to have released a flood of cotton goods whose export enabled a steadily mounting surplus to be created on the balance of trade. Exports of British goods (excluding re-exports) were counted at under £40 million per annum in 1816-20, rising to £90 million per annum in 1836-40 and almost £150 million per annum in 1846-50. At the same time, the 'official value' figures for imports rose at a much slower pace, falling more and more behind exports, so that, with re-exports, a comfortably rising surplus on the balance of trade was created— £17 million per annum in 1816-20, over £70 million in 1846-50 and over £230 million in 1870. It was therefore confidently felt that the source of the capital lent abroad in the nineteenth century rose as the natural result of the excess of exports which industrialisation had produced. But this picture based on the official values is erroneous in that it ignored the steep fall in export prices in the first half of the nineteenth century as compared with import prices—there was an adverse movement in the 'terms of trade'—so that more had to be sold abroad to earn the same amount of imports. In fact, Britain had to sell twice as much by quantity to earn the same amount of imports in 1860 as in 1800. This movement in the terms of trade was largely determined by the falling price of cotton goods, the major export, occasioned by a fall in costs due to mechanisation, and a fall in the price of raw cotton; the industry remained both profitable and expanding, so that the trend in prices did not necessarily reflect a worsening of Britain's economic position.

The current view, based upon the reconstruction of the statistics, holds that far from industrialisation producing an accumulating surplus, the trend was a mounting deficit right up to the First World War. The capital invested abroad did not therefore arise directly from the commodity trade, but from the surplus in the balance of payments accruing from the earnings of 'invisible' exports—services of various kinds, rather than goods.

It is also seen now that the Free Trade legislation of the 1840s came not after a period of soaring export values but after almost half a century of virtually stagnant export values, when falling prices robbed manufacturers of the rewards of increasing quantities of goods sold abroad. Export values averaged just on £40 million in 1801-5, and they remained about the same in 1835. Imlah puts the point this way:

By the 'official' method of accounting, British commercial policies in the high protectionist period from 1815 to 1842 . . . seem to have been sound, successfully nursing British industries into increasingly vigorous life. The argument Bismarck used when he turned the German Empire toward protection in 1879 seems to be justified completely. England, 'the mighty athlete', had entered the fray of free competition only after hardening her sinews under high tariffs. But if the declared values of exports are authentic, it may be concluded that Britain adopted her free-trade policy after a period of twenty-five years of relative stagnation in the values of her export trade. By these figures, exports of the United Kingdom in 1836, the best year in the decade before Peel's first free-trade budget, were worth only 3 per cent more than in 1815. Or to take depression years, they were scarcely 14 per cent more in 1842 than in 1816, an interval in which population rose by about 40 per cent and the real value of net imports increased by about 55 per cent. This suggests hardening of the arteries instead of the sinews and it more adequately accounts for the symptoms of rising social blood pressure which were evident at the time. Adoption of a free-trade policy may have been an escape from premature senescence. (Albert Imlah, 1958, page 23.)

4 The coming of free trade The theoretical arguments for free trade were elaborated by Adam Smith in his *Wealth of Nations* of 1776, a book which went into eight editions in English and several other languages within 20 years. But although the theory was formalised by Ricardo and by the Benthamite Radicals, outside the textile districts there was little interest in free trade before the late 1830s. Huskisson had made limited reductions of duties in 1824-6, and had reduced to a simple code the mass of customs regulations (over 500 Acts) which only one man, J. D. Hume of the Board of Trade, was said to understand, but even this slight move towards the freeing of trade aroused strong protests from the commercial interests affected.

In the 1830s Parliament was absorbed in the struggles for parliamentary reform and the reform of local government, and a string of social reforms covering education, the Poor Law, and factory conditions. But there was a further obstacle in the way of substantial tariff reductions, namely the question of finding alternative revenue. In 1830 import duties produced 43 per cent of the government's annual revenue (and as much as 75 per cent when taken together with the excise). In practice there was only one possible alternative source—a revival of the income tax, which, at the time of its abolition in 1816, had produced 22 per cent of the revenue. To take such a step would be highly unpopular, and there was little prospect that the weak Whig government returned after the election of 1837 would be prepared to make the change. Yet at this time the tide of free trade began to run more strongly, for protection was blamed for the stagnation of trade in the 1830s.

As a result of the mounting pressure against protection, Parliament agreed to the setting up of a Select Committee on Import Duties in 1840. The instigator of the move (the radical M.P. and free trader, Joseph Hume) is said to have 'observed exultingly . . . that "the battle for free trade was about to be won" '. His confidence as to the outcome was not entirely misplaced, for Hume had the chief share in the nomination of members of the committee, with the consequence that the free trade opinion was over-represented, while to make it a little more difficult for the representatives of the landed interest to attend, meetings were held in the summer months when they were likely to be on their estates away from London. Its bias extended even further, however, for most of the evidence was given by the dedicated free-traders of the Board of Trade, a non-political and impartial civil service having as yet scarcely emerged. As Lucy Brown, an historian who has made a special study of the role of the Board of Trade in the free trade movement, puts it, 'witnesses . . . were not so much examined as invited to give prepared propaganda lectures'. And as a piece of propaganda the Report was eminently successful, for it was well received by the press and the public, and was re-issued, not only in 1841 and 1842, but as late as 1903, when the issue of Tariff Reform was again raised.

The committee concluded that the chaos of import duties was greatly in need of simplification, and that the abolition of many could be safely carried out without diminishing the revenue. Indeed, it was shown that of a total customs revenue of nearly £23 million in 1839, £21 million was raised on only ten commodities, and the remaining £2 million on 1142 articles, such petty impositions being, in the committee's words, 'merely vexatious'. In spite of the evidence the government still acted with curious indecision.

However, the rise in food prices and the industrial depression after 1838 had provided the background to the Anti-Corn Law League, dedicated ostensibly to the single object of achieving free trade in corn. It was not by chance that the League was founded, and had its headquarters, in Manchester, for cotton was the leading export industry and the one most vitally affected by the free trade issue. The League operated a brilliant propaganda machine of a kind never seen before, but to become familiar henceforward. The printed word was backed up by the spoken word from platform and pulpit—and none of them were minced. Landlords were described as 'a bread-taxing oligarchy, a handful of swindlers, rapacious harpies, labour-plunderers, monsters of impiety, putrid and sensual *banditti*, titled felons, rich robbers, and blood-sucking vampires'. Yet the apparent triumph of the League should not make us exaggerate its influence, for the coming of free trade was caught up in the tide of events, the hazards of politics, and the accident of personalities.

The depression which had seen the rise of the Anti-Corn Law League also gave rise to a shortfall in government revenue and to a large budget deficit which foreshadowed the collapse of the Whig government. In 1841 Peel was returned with a government secure in Parliament, and with the country prepared to see firm measures taken to restore prosperity and avert civil disorder. His first budget, of 1842, was nevertheless cautious, any boldness consisting of the direction in which his thinking took him rather than the magnitude of the changes themselves. There was an all-round reduction of duties, but with imperial preference maintained. Duties on raw materials were not to exceed 5 per cent, on partly manufactured goods 12 per cent, and on manufactured goods 20 per cent; in all the reductions cost the revenue only £1·3 million, a little less than Huskisson's measures of 1824. But income tax, reintroduced at 7d in the pound on incomes over £150, not only made up the loss and wiped out the deficit, but supplied a small surplus.

The next four years saw a revival of prosperity and enabled Peel to go further. In 1845 he felt bold enough to renew the income tax, which permitted the repeal of duties on some 450 articles, and the lowering of many others. The triumph of free trade principles was, however, symbolised by the repeal of the Corn Laws in 1846, for now the food of the masses, as well as the raw materials of the factories, would be untaxed. It was a courageous move which cost him office; in his four years Peel had cut tariffs by 25 per cent and brought the average rate down close to that of 1790.

There was now no question of reversing the trend, and the Whigs carried on the development of the free trade ideal. The Navigation Acts were repealed in 1849, and step by step, as revenue needs permitted, duties on the staples of British life were reduced and abolished. The climax came in 1860, with the Cobden free trade treaty with France, and Gladstone's budget of the same year. The number of articles liable to duty, which had been 1146 in 1840, was reduced to 48, and all but 12 of these were purely for revenue on luxury or near luxury commodities. Yet so great was the growth of trade that the vastly reduced rates of duty brought in almost as much revenue as all the duties in the first half of the century. Customs receipts were about £22 million per annum on average between 1840 and 1870, and dropped only to £20m at their lowest in 1890. As a proportion of public revenue, however, customs revenue fell sharply—from 46 per cent of the total in 1840 to 25 per cent in 1880.

5 The growth of trade and the balance of payments Under the stimulus of the repeal of protection there was an immense leap in the values of overseas trade, the boom running on until 1875, by which time the annual value of exports was £240 million, and of imports, £300 million. The deficit also increased, running at c. £62 million per annum between 1871 and 1875. But then exports ran into difficulties and for twenty years did not continue to rise in value, although quantities continued to rise, albeit at a slower rate than before. From 1896 to 1913 expansion continued at a quickened pace in what has been described as 'the Indian summer of the free trade system'. However, the value of imports forged ahead more rapidly than exports after 1895, with the result that the deficit on the balance of trade reached the vast figure of £175 million after 1900. The course of Britain's balance of payments between 1850 and 1913 is outlined in the following table:

Britain's balance of payments 1850-1913 (in £m)

	1850	1870	1900	1913
Exports	83·4	244·1	354·4	634·8
Imports	103·0	303·3	523·1	768·7
Balance of commodity trade	−19·6	−59·2	−168·7	−133·9
Net invisible earnings	+31·2	+112·1	+212·7	+367·8
Surplus on current account (excluding capital and bullion movements)	11·6	52·9	44·0	233·9

Source: Bagwell & Mingay, page 98.

The invisible items, which reversed the deficit on balance of trade and provided the margin out of which it was possible to increase the consumption of imports even when little more was being earned by exports, consisted of income from services and interest from overseas investments. Of income from services, by far the most important was the earnings of shipping, which provided about two-thirds of the total. In addition there was the income which consisted of profits from financing and insuring much of world trade. Well over half of Britain's total foreign trade was shipped, serviced and financed from Britain, for in the new foreign markets which British merchants were creating, most of the enterprise behind the trade was British.

For the first quarter of the nineteenth century this income from services, without the aid of interest and dividends from investment, more than covered the trading deficit, but between 1825 and 1850 it did not quite do so, and after 1875 it was normally no longer adequate. As the century developed, therefore, the deficit was increasingly made up, and a growing balance of payments surplus produced, by the earnings of overseas investments.

The comfortable balance of payments surpluses masked several potential weaknesses which underlay Britain's economic position. All the constituents of her invisible income depended on the maintenance of a high level of world trade, while the failure of exports to pay for the mounting volume of imports reflected a certain weakness in the export industries. An important disrupting influence was the industrialisation of the USA and Germany, for along with other industrialising countries they erected tariff barriers to protect their 'infant industries' from foreign (mainly British) competition. The American tariff wall was built up higher and higher from the 1860s, while European tariff barriers were erected in the 1870s—for example, in Russia in 1877, France in 1878, and Germany in 1879. Not only did it become more difficult for British exporters to sell in those countries which raised tariff barriers, but they faced increasing competition in remaining markets. The effect of this increased competition is exemplified by the changing composition of Britain's exports. Schlote shows that by 1911-13 manufactured goods formed only 75 per cent of Britain's home-produced exports, as against 90 per cent in the mid-Victorian years, mainly because of the rise in the export of coal—much of it to the new industrial powers—which in the early years of the twentieth century reached about 9 per cent of the total as against 2·5 per cent fifty years before. Textiles remained the most important of the manufactured exports, although they fell to less than 40 per cent of the total, while there was a rise in the export of engineering products (machinery, railway rolling-stock, ships' hulls, etc.) to just under 10 per cent in 1911-13, as against less than 5 per cent in 1857-9.

Ashworth notes that contemporary, and some later, critics tended to stress the shortcomings of British exporters, who are alleged to have paid less attention than their rivals to the need to adapt their goods to the tastes and requirements of particular markets, to have sent out their catalogues in the English language and with English weights, measures and prices, to have employed fewer commercial travellers and to have allowed their customers less time to pay. In 1899, for example, 3828 commercial travellers from Germany, 1176 from France, but only 28 from Britain entered Switzerland, while an unwillingness to adapt the product to satisfy local preferences is exemplified by the export of needles; the Brazilians did not like the black paper in which British needles are traditionally packed, so that when the Germans wrapped inferior needles in bright red paper they captured the whole of the market. Ashworth argues that while some allegations were probably not well founded, some of the shortcomings of exporters may have been real, and would have been particularly costly after 1900, when more of the selling opportunities were for more elaborate tastes (so that design and attention to local idiosyncracies were important), and were in places where English was not the local language of business or government. But, he argues, 'the deficiencies of British foreign trade at this time probably came less from slipshod commercial practices than from the limited range of commodities which were available for export'. To this problem we shall return in the following chapter.

While the rise of protection abroad and the increased competition of new exporting nations put a curb on the rise of British exports, Britain's continuing free trade policies put no restraint on her rising imports. The trend is again revealed in the changing composition of her trade. The proportion of foodstuffs in British imports increased in the 1870s to reach that of raw materials, but even more significant was the rapid growth in the last quarter of the nineteenth century of imported manufactures, which rose from a very small proportion to a fifth of total imports by 1900. The resulting pattern between 1900 and 1913 was therefore one where roughly 40 per cent of her imports consisted of foodstuffs, 40 per cent raw materials (of which considerable quantities, together with some foodstuffs, were re-exported) and 20 per cent manufactures.

With regard to the imported manufactures, most attention was paid to those coming from Germany and the USA. 'Made in Germany' was, in the 1880s, a phrase of contempt, but the steady arrival of good quality German manufactures in Britain and the colonies soon made it a phrase of alarm. The spirit of much that was written at the time is caught by a pamphlet published in 1896:

Roam the house over, and the fateful mark will greet you at every turn, from the piano in your drawing room to the mug on your kitchen dresser, blazoned though it be with the legend, A Present from Margate. Descend to your domestic depths, and you shall find your very drain-pipes German made. You pick out of the grate the paper wrappings from a book consignment, and they also are 'Made in Germany'. You stuff them into the fire, and reflect that the poker in your hand was forged in Germany. As you rise from the hearthrug you knock over an ornament on your mantelpiece; picking up the piece you read, on the bit that formed the base, 'Manufactured in Germany'. And you jot your dismal reflections down with a pencil that was made in Germany . . . (Flinn, *Readings in Economic and Social History* Macmillan, London and Basingstoke 1964, pages 261-2.)

German sailors once had the humour to hang the words 'Made in Germany' over the bows of a new Atlantic liner on her first entering Southampton Water. As Clapham puts it; 'It was a fair retort, but it did not help to silence alarmists.'

What was talked of as 'the American invasion' began a little later. The first effects were felt in 1896 when large numbers of American bicycles were imported, accompanied by imports of machine tools for the manufacture of bicycles in Britain. Furthermore, after 1898 several railways began to buy American locomotives. But the most remarkable expansion was in imports of footwear, which increased from £11,000 in 1896 to over £1 million in 1900. However, Saul points out that the American 'invasion' was a temporary phenomenon not repeated before the outbreak of war, for improvement of internal demand within the USA and stagnation of trade in Britain soon caused all imports to be reduced.

It was not unnatural that in these circumstances the principles of free trade should come to be questioned, and in 1881 a Fair Trade League was formed, whose schemes were not fully worked out at first, and never came to be applied. Its idea of 'fairness' was to demand the imposition of moderate tariffs on foreign manufactures, to be removed from the goods of any country as soon as that country agreed to admit British goods free. An imperial sentiment underlay the League, which also wanted the revival of Imperial Preference to strengthen imperial unity and improve the international position of the Empire. It is not certain that the tariff would have been of help to the British economy. In the view of S. B. Saul:

It is true that a tariff might possibly have helped to bring about the much-needed investment in new industries, but it might equally have led to even more delay in the reorganisation required by the older industries or preserved those parts of our industrial structure which needed scrapping altogether. In any case, the loss from the dislocation of the pattern of world settlements, which rested upon the preservation of free trade in Britain, would have been infinitely greater than the gain. (Saul, 1960, page 41.)

By 1910 the balance of payments with the USA was running at a deficit of £50 million per annum and with continental Europe at £45 million per annum, while in other countries where Britain had heavy import bills, such as Canada, South Africa, New Zealand and Argentina, the balance was also negative. These accounts were cleared on a multilateral basis—through Britain's surplus with those countries, particularly in Asia, whose exports of food and raw materials put *them* in credit with *Britain's* main creditors. The complicated pattern of world settlements is shown diagramatically by Saul (on the opposite page).

The arrows point to the country of each pair having a surplus with the other, and therefore indicate the direction of the flow of settlement. The balance of payments of the United Kingdom in 1910 is given below. The deficit of £27 million probably represents small receipts from a number of other countries, and also indicates an under-estimation of invisible income from some of the countries shown.

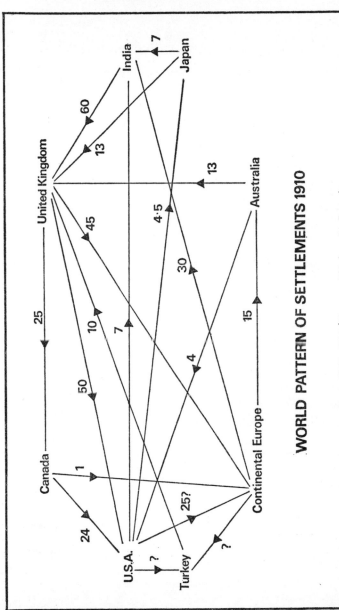

WORLD PATTERN OF SETTLEMENTS 1910

from: Saul, Studies in British Overseas Trade 1870-1914 (Liverpool University Press)

Balance of Payments of the United Kingdom, 1910, (£m.)

Debit		Credit	
USA	50	India	60
Continental Europe	45	Australia	13
Canada	25	Japan	13
Straits Settlements	11	China (inc. Hong Kong)	13
South Africa	8	Turkey	10
New Zealand	4	Uruguay	6
Argentina	2	British West Africa	3
Total	145	Total	118

Source: Saul, 1960, page 58.

Britain's dependence on a high level of multilateral trade is immediately apparent, but it will also be noted that she had become increasingly dependent on the less developed countries. These were the less sophisticated markets of the world which continued to take a traditional style of product in textiles, as well as the capital goods (such as railway rolling-stock and machinery) which they required for their development. More and more, Britain came to be squeezed out of the wealthier markets, which began to be able to make their own cheap textiles and iron and steel, and now demanded new ranges of imports. In other words, the problem of the declining balance of trade with the United States and Europe was not merely one of tariff barriers but revealed a weakness in the structure of the British economy, in particular the failure to innovate and to develop new export lines. It can be argued that the very ease of entry into the markets of the Empire may well have dulled the senses and spirit of many exporters who would otherwise have been forced to compete or fail.

The importance of British trade with India is evident. In 1880, probably one third of Britain's deficits was covered by receipts from India, the proportion rising to nearer one half in 1910. India not only had a large import surplus with Britain (80 per cent of her imports in the 1870s came from Britain) but also paid regular dividends on large past investments, and was the source of remittances made by administrators and soldiers.

The mechanism of international settlements was a delicate one. So long as the world economy was expanding, and Britain was able to balance her trading accounts by a growth of multilateral trade, all was well. Should the mechanism be disrupted, Britain would face unavoidable problems—as the aftermath of the First World War was to show.

6 The export of capital The four decades prior to the First World War witnessed a gigantic explosion in British overseas investment. Recent estimates suppose an even greater increase than earlier writers had allowed, and suggest that from a total of £700 million in 1870, British capital assets abroad increased to £1500 million by 1885, £2400 million by 1900 and £4000 million in 1913. In that year the rate of flow abroad was about 7·5 per cent of the national income, the magnitude of which is illustrated by Mathias, who has remarked upon the difficulty found by the rich industrial nations of the world in the 1960s in investing a mere 1 per cent of their national income in the developing countries during the United Nations 'Development Decade'.

A few foreign loans had been raised during the eighteenth century, but they had been small and Britain remained substantially a net debtor, especially to the Dutch. Organised lending overseas began after the Napoleonic Wars when Barings, who handled the financial arrangements for the armies of occupation in Paris, raised a £10 million loan to provide for the French war indemnity of 1817-19. Thus the allies obtained their reparations because British investors were willing to lend money and become holders of the French government securities or *rentes*. The Barings and the Rothschilds showed their pre-eminence in the issue business, and their successes in raising secure loans for the legitimist régimes of Europe, encouraged by slack trade at home in the early 1820s, led directly into the speculative mania of 1824-5. It was possible for investors to buy stock with an initial 'call', or down payment, of 5 or 10 per cent of the holding they intended to take up. Thus, for a small initial payment, a handsome profit could be made by a rise in price and a quick sale. For example, the £400 shares of the Real del Monte mine, on which investors had only been required to pay an initial call of £50 to acquire the title, stood at a premium of £550 in December 1824. The skill came in knowing just when to sell before the bubble burst.

The struggling republics of South America proved eager borrowers, and British investors proved equally eager lenders, for in the development of Latin America was seen the prospect of permanent markets for British goods independent of the hostile tariffs of the United States and the Continent. Colombia was the first of the republics to gain its independence, and it was also the first to raise a loan, in 1822. It was quickly followed by other states, with the result that between 1822 and 1825, £17 million was invested in Latin America. Most of the loans were for unproductive purposes, so that these countries had no resources out of which to repay interest, let alone the capital sums; loan after loan was made to support governments and armies and 'to secure a ship or so as an appropriate background for their respective admirals'.

In what Mathias describes as 'the rosy glow cast by Lord Byron and a classical education', £3 million was also raised in London to help the struggling Greeks, although in the end all that reached Greece as a result was about £0.5 million in cash and two small ships—which finally appeared off the coast of Greece in 1828. It was half a century before the Greek government showed its gratitude by paying interest on the loans.

After the financial crash of 1825 the flow of funds dried up for some years, and when overseas investment expanded again in the 1830s, South America was out of fashion, and new European loans were rare. The main direction in which funds flowed now became the USA. The states, canal companies and banks borrowed freely, and Britain was the easiest source from which to borrow. By 1836 over $90 million had been invested in canals and railways in the North, of which more than half was guaranteed by public funds; the bulk of this capital was procured from Britain. Unfortunately the United States proved to be hardly more reliable than South America, and by 1841 nine states were defaulting on their loans, with the consequence that it was embarrassing to be an American in London. Confidence in the United States as a borrower did not revive until the 1850s.

In the meantime there was another redirection of the flow of capital, this time towards railway-building. Railways were to be the major field of British investment throughout the remainder of the century, and by 1913 constituted 41 per cent of all capital lent abroad. Railway construction continued in Europe throughout the 1840s and 1850s, with much British money involved, and towards the end of that period the first large Indian railway loans were raised, with interest guaranteed at 5 per cent. Subsequently, American railways came to dominate the market; in 1899 British investors probably held between a fifth and a quarter of the capital of American railways, while by 1914 the aggregate value of American railway securities held in Britain was £620 million, or approximately 16 per cent of British overseas investments.

Lending to South America began again with the establishment of a new and stable government in Argentina in 1865. Within a decade £23 million of British capital had been invested there, rising to £175 million by 1890. But over-confidence led to an over-extension of lending on unsound projects which Barings, the leading brokers in the field, had backed without adequate investigation, and the resulting 'Baring Crisis' of 1890 abruptly stopped all Argentinian loans, and shook the confidence of all investors in overseas lending for over a decade.

The scale of lending in the 1890s was reduced, but was particularly concerned with South Africa and the Rhodesias, where there were mining booms in diamonds, gold, and copper. When the flow revived after 1900, the white Dominions—Canada, Australia and South Africa—were the favourite markets. By 1913 37 per cent of Britain's overseas investment was in the Dominions, with a further 10 per cent in India, making the Empire's share almost one half.

The trend of British overseas investment in the nineteenth century reveals that investors had marked preferences, not only for different types of asset, but for the assets of particular countries. Yet the motives which inspired their choice were many—social, political and sentimental, as well as economic. The prospect of a higher profit was naturally a major element. In the 1870s US government bonds offered an average yield of 7·5 per cent, as compared with under 4 per cent on British government Consols. The average yield on British railway stock was only a little over 4 per cent, while US rails offered 9·3 per cent, South American rails 8·1 per cent, and Indian rails, which were guaranteed, 6·3 per cent. Yet, as Cairncross claims; 'The preferences of investors were to a large extent quite arbitrary, and the price of a security in the London market was by no means a reliable guide to its probable yield.' At times, great ignorance was certainly shown. John Ruskin is reputed once to have asked, 'Who is the Soudan?' But H. S. Ferns has shown that the British investor in Argentina, for example, showed an equal ignorance:

The investors in Argentine bonds did not know and could not know how the money they lent would be spent. Judging from some of their letters addressed to the public press, to the Foreign Office, and to the various committees established to handle the interests of investors, their level of information was extremely low. Some of them confused Argentina with Chile and even Mexico. The distinction between the Province of Buenos Aires and the Argentine Republic was too subtle for most. One dissatisfied investor in Argentine railways appears to have believed that the Buenos Aires Great Southern Railway, of which he owned a small part, was in Brazil. Indeed the name of a banking firm like that of Baring Brothers or Murietta & Company meant more to investors than the names Argentina or Buenos Aires. Their decision to handle Argentine business was a certificate of reliability and a substitute for knowledge, initiative, and enterprise. (Ferns, *Britain and Argentina in the Nineteenth Century* 1960, page 330, by permission of the Clarendon Press, Oxford.)

Initially the bankers made their decisions to market loans on fairly reliable information and sound judgment, although it appears that both judgment and responsibility deteriorated in the 1880s, bringing about the financial crisis of 1890.

Some investment decisions were made with more than just the profit from the bonds in mind. Certain investors, and the organisers and projectors of British overseas investment undoubtedly had commercial and business motives in mind. Thus, the concentration of British investment in Louisiana in the 1820s and 1830s was oriented towards the development of its cotton exports. Similarly, British investment in American railways was heaviest in those lines which tapped the wheat belt and the hog and cattle rearing areas in the Chicago hinterland, while there was very little interest on those trans-continental lines which linked the mid-west with the west coast.

It is not easy, however, to find explicit links between overseas investment and British exports. Certainly, much of the capital invested in railway development must have returned to this country for the purchase of rails and rolling-stock; in India, for example, Jenks has shown that over one third returned to Britain in this way. In the first three-quarters of the nineteenth century the association of capital exports and the export of capital goods was to be expected, for only Britain possessed the necessary low-cost iron industry and modern engineering industry. But from the 1870s such a direct link cannot be taken for granted. Loans were not usually 'tied', and the decisions as to the way they should be spent rested with the borrowers. Sterling might be raised for foreign railway capital, but the locomotives might be purchased from, let us say, Belgium. The relationship between overseas investment and British exports was likely to be mainly indirect, resulting from the stimulus to long-term economic growth. In this context, it must be remembered that much overseas investment, particularly loans to governments, was non-productive of such growth, being spent, in Clapham's words, on 'consumption goods and destruction goods'—more lavish palaces or mightier armies.

It is not easy to draw up a profit and loss account of the effect of overseas investment on the British economy. It must be re-membered that the number of investors was small, and their investment decisions were made in the hope of personal gain, rather than for motives of philanthropy. Cairncross has demon-strated the narrowness of the investing public; in Indian Guaran-teed Railway Securities there were, in 1870, just over 50,000 English investors holding on average nearly £1800, while colonial stocks were never issued in London in denominations of less than £100 before 1909. Although the capitalists were not the only beneficiaries from the export of capital, the working classes gained more by accident than design. They gained chiefly from the fall in the price of imports, particularly foodstuffs, which resulted from the development of overseas sources of supply; while the contribution of interest payments and dividends towards the balance of payments has already been noted. Some of the investments clearly stimulated a demand for exportable goods, but investments at home might have stimulated an equivalent demand. It is exactly this relationship between home and foreign investment which lies at the root of the question.

Cairncross showed that there were cyclical fluctuations between home and foreign investment, the peaks and troughs alternating in each sphere. That this was so is not in dispute, although there is some controversy as to the exact mechanism which operated. The question that is relevant here, however, is how far foreign investment was at the expense of investment in British industry. Two points are immediately apparent. In the first place, fixed capital in industry remained small; the amount of capital in the cotton industry, for example, being only about £100 million in the mid-1870s, although it was the largest manufacturing industry and employed half a million workers. It was transport (especially railways) which consumed large quantities of capital which takes us to the second point—that the great expansion in overseas investment began in the 1870s, just at the time when the British railway network was coming to completion. It can be argued that foreign lending kept interest rates up to some degree, making it more expensive for industrialists to borrow money, but there is little evidence of those who actively went out to get capital finding undue difficulty—the situation was one where *low* interest rates at home drove capital abroad. The problem of lack of innovation and investment in certain industries was more deep-rooted, and will be examined in the following chapter.

It has also been argued that there would have been greater advantage if some of the capital invested abroad had been diverted to social investment at home—in housing, schools, hospitals and city improvements. Against these gains, however, would have to be counted the loss of cheap food which foreign investment brought about. Nor is it certain that had there been no foreign investment, resources would have been diverted in this way. In some degree, the hopes entertained with respect to investment create the resources with which it is sought to realise them. Had the investment opportunities abroad not existed, there is no inherent reason why those with a surplus of income at home should not have used it merely on conspicuous consumption, for example, by building themselves bigger and more comfortable houses or enlarging their estates.

7 Emigration   The last 'export' that we must examine is that of men. Between Waterloo and the outbreak of the First World War, a total of nearly 17 million people emigrated from the United Kingdom, approximately 80 per cent of them going to North America. The total number was almost as great as the country's population in 1815, and well over a third of the population in 1911, which stood at 45 million.

As with many other series of official statistics, those for emigration require careful interpretation. Statistics were first collected under an Act of 1803 passed to cope with the appalling conditions prevalent in the emigrant ships. The regulations proved ineffective, however, for ships could evade inspection by sailing from out-of-the-way parts of the coast, with the effect that the official statistics underestimate the number of persons who actually sailed from the United Kingdom. When the steamship came into its own evasion of the law became more difficult, but another complication appeared. As Britain was the pioneer of this faster and more comfortable form of transport, there was a tendency for emigrants from the continent of Europe to sail from a British port. These emigrants were mainly Germans and Scandinavians, who usually passed along the line from Hull to Liverpool, where they embarked for North America. It is true that from 1853 the published statistics began to distinguish British citizens from aliens, but the port authorities were too seriously understaffed to cope adequately with the flow. In 1850, for example, the staff of emigration officials at Liverpool consisted of one officer, two assistant officers, a clerk and three medical inspectors, yet in that year the staff was called upon to examine as many as 568 ships and superintend the departure of 174,188 passengers. Furthermore, the rapid growth of facilities for international travel after the 1860s encouraged the number of people who travelled abroad on business or pleasure (and who were not, therefore, genuine migrants) to increase considerably, and it was not until 1912 that the authorities collected figures which would enable them to compile a list distinguishing such travellers from the permanent emigrants. The deficiencies of the official statistics therefore suggest that in the first half of the century ending in 1912 the number of British passengers recorded as leaving the United Kingdom is too low, while in the second half it is too high.

Individual motives for emigration naturally differed greatly, but the interest of historians has focused on the comparative strength of those factors which tended to 'push' emigrants out of their country of origin and those which tended to 'pull' immigrants towards them. It is, of course, very difficult to disentangle the two, for elements of each were usually present. Brinley Thomas, however, has attempted this for immigration into the United States, and has suggested that 'push' factors were dominant before the late 1860s, while 'pull' factors governed the flow of immigration thereafter. He bases his conclusion largely on statistical evidence which shows that before the Civil War the trend of railway building *followed* that of immigration, suggesting that the railways were dependent on immigrant labour but did not directly attract it into the country. In the decades after the Civil War, when the American economy evolved into greater maturity, and railway building ceased to be the dominant force, the rate of influx of population was induced by changes in the general level of investment in phase with the alternating cycle of depression and boom.

The strength of the 'push' factors is seen with particular groups of United Kingdom emigrants, especially those from Scotland and Ireland, although our concern with the Highland Clearances and the Irish potato famine should not blind us to the fact that not all emigrants from these countries were destitute. This is particularly evident in the case of emigration from Scotland. A contemporary authority pointed out that one quarter of the Scottish settlers on their way to Canada took out money and other resources, while other estimates place the proportion even higher; similarly, David Macmillan has shown that a considerable number of the Australian settlers came from the 'progressive, aspiring element among the Scottish farming class'.

The Highland Clearances of the first half of the nineteenth century, whereby crofters were replaced by sheep, formed one aspect of the breakdown of the old Highland economy. Philip Gaskell has warned us that we must reject an emotional approach if the clearances are to be understood.

This is difficult because they have attracted popular historians who have been interested chiefly in the propagandist or sensational aspects of the subject; and perhaps because few of us, in our guilt-obsessed century, can look back on the evictions without some feeling of responsibility for them, however mistaken, and a consequent urge to atone for it by coming out on the side of those who suffered. Therefore we must remind ourselves that the Highland clearances were the symptom of the inability of the old Highland economy to adapt to a changing world, and of the breakdown of the old Highland way of life, not their cause. The proprietors who cleared their farms for sheep were acting under severe economic pressure, and the fact that they did not suffer as the people did does not in itself make their actions wrong. (Philip Gaskell, 1968, page 25.)

Right down from 1815 to 1850 the Highlands experienced a period of deflation. The burning of kelp to produce soda had been an important industry, but kelp prices began to drop almost immediately after the Napoleonic Wars, and the removal of the duty on imported barilla in 1827 brought prices so low that kelp manufacture came to an end by 1830. Cattle prices fell at the same time, with the consequence that many small tenants had to make up for poor returns by selling yet more cattle, thus depleting their capital source. The old economy was at best a subsistence economy, and the growth of population in the nineteenth century put strains upon it which it was unable to bear. Some sort of relief was clearly necessary as the problems of over-population and destitution increased, yet in Scotland there was no poor law until 1845. At first the government tried to keep the people in employment through public works schemes, such as the construction of the Crinan and Caledonian Canals and the building of 875 miles of roads and bridges in the Highlands, while large-scale railway building in the 1840s provided some relief.

It was inevitable that emigration would be resorted to as a means of relieving the population pressure, even though it did not meet with the approval of all. Many large landowners assisted their tenants to emigrate, with the result that by 1841 they were sending over 700 people per year, rising to approximately 1000 per year for 1842 and 1843, after which the number dropped markedly until a second exodus took place towards the end of the decade. In 1851, 3466 Scotsmen were aided by their landlords to emigrate to Canada, and in that year Parliamentary approval was given to the lending to landed proprietors of money set aside for land improvements to defray the cost; in Shepperson's words: 'Emigration, as well as draining and ditching, was deemed an improvement for an estate.' The same year saw the establishment of the Skye Emigration Society, which quickly developed into the Highlands and Islands Emigration Society, with an imposing committee of management and offices in London. This society gave more encouragement to emigrants sailing to Australia than to Canada; the sheep-rearing skills of the Scots were welcomed in that country, especially as many sheep-stations had become virtually deserted with the opening of the gold diggings.

Ireland, even more than Scotland, presents a situation where 'push' factors weighed heavily in emigration. The population of Ireland in 1788 is estimated to have been 4,389,000; in 1841 it reached 8,175,000 but by 1911 had fallen to 4,390,000. Between 1853 and 1900 about 3,294,000 Irishmen emigrated from the United Kingdom to places other than Europe, 84 per cent of them going to the United States, 9 per cent to Australia and New Zealand, 6 per cent to Canada, and 1 per cent to other countries. There was, in addition, a considerable migration into England, Scotland and Wales; in 1861 there were 806,000 Irish-born people in Britain as compared with 415,000 in 1841, many of the country's own social problems being aggravated by the influx.

Many of the pressures on the Irish population were similar to those experienced in Scotland, but the potato famine was a major disaster. Between 1841 and 1851 the Irish population declined by one fifth. Other factors were at work as well, however. The barriers of language were being broken down; in 1822 some two million Irishmen spoke only Gaelic, whereas in 1861 fewer than 164,000 were isolated in this way, and as more learned to read more became influenced by the voluminous emigrant press.

When one comes to examine the emigration from England and Wales the situation becomes more complex, for 'push' and 'pull' factors more often worked in combination. Yet here, as in Scotland and Ireland, one can see the growth of emigration in response to changes in the structure of the economy, as well as to expanding opportunities in a rapidly developing world. Both destitution and ambition lay behind the outflow of people.

The rural departures represent an interesting phenomenon, for they usually exceeded those from the urban areas, while many historians have observed a cyclical trend between internal and external migration. John Saville has shown that at some point between 1821 and 1851 a considerable proportion of the villages and rural parishes of England and Wales passed their peak of population and entered upon an almost continuous decline in their total populations. For the remainder, the peak and decline occurred in the second rather than the first half of the century, but few parts of the country failed to conform to the pattern. Between 1861 and 1901 the total of male agricultural labourers declined by just over 40 per cent, and contributed greatly to rural depopulation. Many factors were involved; an increase in farm mechanisation and a shift from arable to pasture farming led to a fall in the demand for labour, while the 'crude wage ratio' (i.e., ignoring non-cash perquisites) between agriculture and industry was about 50 per cent for most of the second half of the nineteenth century. The spread of the railways was a major cause of depopulation, although it was an accelerating rather than an initiating agent, for the flow of population from rural areas was strong even before railways developed. The railways increased mobility and provided a vent for the countryside.

At the same time, the improved communications reinforced the competitiveness of large-scale urban enterprises and brought about the displacement of rural crafts and small country industries. Saville cites the example of the village of Halwell in South Devon, typical of many. In the middle decades of the nineteenth century it possessed a well-balanced group of craftsmen: a thatcher, a carpenter, two tailors, a boot and shoe maker, a baker, a blacksmith, a wheelwright, two masons, two dairymen and a marine store dealer. By the 1920s, following a considerable decline in population, it had lost its thatcher, carpenter, boot and shoe maker, one of its masons, its marine store dealer, both its tailors and one of its two inns. The only craftsmen remaining were a builder, a blacksmith, a wheelwright and a stone-mason.

For part of the time the towns were able to absorb the flow of population from the countryside, but there were periods when the flow was so great that the only escape was through emigration. There was much to lure the rural emigrant, especially the prospect of owning land abroad. The lure of cheap (and after 1862, free) land in the United States encouraged the majority of agricultural emigrants to that country rather than to Canada or Australia, where the land policy was one of charging a 'sufficient price'. The pull was strong, but the dream of owning cheap land more often than not proved illusory. Pioneer farming required skills with which the English farmer or labourer was unfamiliar, while capital was required for a venture to be successful. *The Scientific American* in 1857 declared that every farmer with 100 acres of land needed $400 to $700 worth of farm implements, and although it is certain that very few farms in fact had equipment on anything approaching that scale, the need for such equipment was increasing and its cost high. The mere cost of clearing land might be high; in Australia in the 1830s the cost of 'rapid clearing' varied from 28s to 80s an acre. But even dreams can prove very strong motivation, while opportunities remained higher, whether the emigrant stayed in farming or drifted into industry.

Both the displaced and the enterprising featured amongst the industrial emigrants. Many groups of workers, including some hand-loom weavers, silk workers, and Cornish miners resorted to emigration as a form of relief. Similarly, in the 1890s and 1900s a great many Welsh tin-plate workers flocked to the USA as depression mounted in the Welsh industry while its American counterpart grew apace with the double stimulus of a high protective tariff and an expanding demand.

But throughout the century the prospect of high wages and better conditions abroad encouraged many British craftsmen and industrial workers to leave their mother country. In 1829 Nassau Senior estimated that a labourer's wages in North America were 25 per cent higher than those in England, while an emigrants' guide book of 1830 outlined opportunities available in the USA.

Industrious men need never lack employment in America. Labourers, carpenters, masons, bricklayers, stonecutters, blacksmiths, turners, weavers, farmers, curriers, shoemakers, and tailors, and the useful mechanics generally, are always sure of work and good wages. Stonecutters now receive, in New York, two dollars a day, equal to nine shillings sterling; carpenters, one dollar and 87½ cents; bricklayers, two dollars, labourers, from one dollar to one and a quarter; others in proportion. At this time, house-carpenters, bricklayers, masons, and stonecutters, are paid three dollars per day in Petersburgh (Virginia). The town was recently consumed by fire, but it is now rising from its ashes in more elegance than ever.

Artisans receive better pay in America than in Europe, and can live with less exertion, and more comfort; because they put an additional price on their work, equal to the cost of freight and commission charged by the merchant on importation . . . (Quoted in Handlin, 1959, page 48. From S. M. Collins *The Emigrant's Guide to . . . the United States of America* (Hull, 1830) pages 110-111.)

Even school teachers were encouraged to emigrate, for the same guide book noted that in America 'it does not detract from a man's personal respectability to have been thus employed'. Pottery workers, who in 1882 earned the equivalent of $9·62 in Staffordshire, could earn $16·35 a week in Trenton, New Jersey, while, as one of them wrote; 'We have had as much flesh meat hanging under the porch of our house as any butcher in the Potteries stands market with.' Wage differentials were equally encouraging in the case of Australia, for whereas in 1880 the agricultural labourer in Cornwall or Gloucestershire earned 13s or 14s a week, and the Cornish miner (in prosperous years) £5 a month, the unskilled labourer in New South Wales commanded 7s to

9s a day, farm labourers £30 to £45 a year plus board, and coal miners 10s to 15s a day, while meat was cheaper, bread the same price, and ordinary quality clothing often as cheap, with less of it needed.

Most industrial emigrants, as indeed most emigrants generally, made their way unassisted; in Shepperson's words: 'It was a self-impelled, personally arranged, and individually financed adventure.' One of the main determinants of the destination of emigrants was therefore the cost of the voyage, which made North America remain more popular than Australia in spite of generally decreasing transport costs. Emigrants otherwise tended to go where their skills or labour were in greatest demand, or where they had relatives or friends. Emigrant letters provided information and encouragement to would-be followers, while remittances from emigrants financed much later emigration.

While the mass of emigration was thus individual and un-organised, it remains true that, as Clapham says; 'Official and officious organisations to promote it were always at work, especially in times of gloom.' The 1834 Poor Law Amendment Act granted statutory powers to parish guardians to raise money on the security of the rates to finance the emigration of paupers, the clause being utilised almost totally by rural districts rather than the towns. For the year beginning 1 July, 1835, 5141 persons were sent out, the annual number averaging between 800 and 1000 between 1836 and 1845. Thereafter the number declined to around 200 during the latter 1840s, rising again in the early 1850s, but subsequently falling yet again until in 1860 only 55 persons were assisted under the Act. The only large-scale official operations were those carried out by the Colonial Land and Emigration Commissioners between 1847 and 1872, during which time 340,000 United Kingdom emigrants were given assistance. Three-quarters of the work had been done between November 1847 and the end of 1848, almost all the emigrants being sent to Australia, with a few to the Cape and the Falkland Islands. There was a certain illogicality in government assistance to emigration as a relief for internal distress so long as no assistance was ten-dered to those who wished to remain in Britain. This point was taken up by the Chartists and other radicals, who denounced emigration as the transportation of the innocent and preached instead home-colonisation.

One agency of assisted emigration is of particular interest, although its overall contribution was not, perhaps, very great—the trade union movement. Theoretical support for emigration was given by the acceptance of the wage fund theory, crudely but graphically described by Cobden's dictum; 'Wages rise when two masters run after one workman; wages fall when two men run after one master.' This supply and demand philosophy suggested that benefits were to be obtained from the induced scarcity of labour brought about by the assistance of members to quit the home market by emigrating. The Emigration Fund was a widespread feature of trade unions in the 1850s and 1860s, while Charlotte Erickson has claimed that the efficacy of emigration did not come to be seriously questioned by the English unions until the depression of the 1880s. The established unions, such as the Engineers, the Iron Founders, the Carpenters and the Flint Glass Makers continued to encourage the emigration of their members and to aid them by making grants of money and giving information and advice. One of the most extensively advertised organisations was the Potters' Joint Stock Emigration Society, which had been formed in 1844 and which, for a short period, took over the union itself. A plot of land, christened Pottersville, was purchased in Wisconsin for farming, but the venture proved unsuccessful, and by 1850 the union and the emigration society were dead. Pioneer farming was a risky venture, and Frank Thistlethwaite has shown that most emigrant potters stuck to their wheels, and indeed contributed much to the industry in the United States. Arch's National Agricultural Labourers' Union of 1872 encouraged emigration; he personally visited Canada, and the union assisted the emigration of several thousand men, mostly to Canada but also to Australia and New Zealand.

It is difficult to be precise about the effect of emigration upon the British economy, partly because of the defectiveness of the statistics and partly because the question is concerned with intangibles. In terms of a diminution of the labour force one has to consider *net* migration, i.e. emigration balanced against immigration and the return of former emigrants. In England and Wales there was net immigration of well over a quarter of a million in the 1840s, as Irishmen and Scots moved east and south, adding to the disturbances of the times. In the following decade, however, there was considerable net emigration from England and Wales, almost to the point of labour shortage. In the 1860s Britain probably lost little on balance, but between 1871 and 1911 there was a net loss of 2 million by migration, even though this was a period of increased immigration, especially of Jews fleeing from the revival of anti-semitism on the Continent. But the quality of the population is as important as the quantity, and the people lost were predominantly young adults from the most active sections of the labour force (for it took some courage and determination to leave). Furthermore, more young men than women emigrated, with the consequence that the sex ratio was upset, contributing to the gradual long-term decline in the rate of population growth, and stimulating the employment of women. The rate of population growth still remained high, however, and the effect of the loss of 2 million in the forty years after 1871 was more than offset by the natural increase of some 18 million.

Chapter V

The End of Supremacy

1 The legend of the Great Depression 'Some ages,' says Professor Charles Wilson, 'are born to controversy':

Others have controversy thrust upon them by historians. The debate on the economic situation of late Victorian Britain was begun in the 'seventies by the Victorians themselves. The historians have continued it. Whether the period deserved the name of 'the Great Depression' or not, it was a time 'when people *said* there was a Great Depression'. At any rate *some* people said there was, and the pessimists were vocal in the House of Commons, in the Political Economy Club and in many other places and journals. Their pressure was enough to secure the appointment of two Royal Commissions (in the 70s and the 90s) on agriculture, two (in the 80s) on trade and industry, another on the monetary system (in 1887) and (incidentally) to dominate later thought. With the twentieth century, and the passing of what had first been felt as an acute phase of competition, the fury of controversy abated. But it never quite disappeared, Economists like Marshall continued to echo the disquiet at some of the characteristics of British industry which seemed to them to help to explain the trouble of the preceding decades. And in the 1930s the controversy broke out again in earnest with H. L. Beales' classic article in which he challenged the legend of the Great Depression. There was, he agreed, a *unity* about the period 1873 to 1896. It saw prices and profits fall. There was some demand for protection. There was 'a slight falling off in the rate of industrial progress but the *outstanding* fact was the rapid industrialisation of other countries and the continued industrialisation of this'. For such a phase 'Great Depression' was not, he suggested, an appropriate description. (Wilson, 1965, page 183.)

The legend of the Great Depression was of interest because the period, while clearly one of doubt and self-questioning, was more than the usual trade cycle depression, for it contained within itself the more familiar pattern of boom and slump. The debate took a different turn from the 1950s when, as was outlined in Chapter I, interest increased in the phenomenon of economic growth. A number of historians now began to re-examine the whole of the half-century to 1914 in the belief that it somehow marked a 'climacteric'—a watershed in British economic history. The industrialisation of other countries, in particular Germany and the United States, and growing competition in world trade gave the impression of British economic supremacy coming to an end. In consequence, attention has increasingly turned to the supposed slowing down of the British economy and to an examination of the reasons for this decelerated growth.

The question presents several difficulties. In the first place the problem of deceleration and the question of the Great Depression are not the same, although the two phenomena are likely to have some connection. For the relationship to be a direct one, however, it would have to be shown that the period from 1873 to 1896 was *particularly significant* in terms of the slowing up of the British economy, which in fact is difficult. There is certainly debate as to the dating of the initial turning-point. When the controversy was revived in the 1950s the break was assigned to the 1890s, but since then some writers have claimed that it can be dated to the 1870s, while it has even been suggested that were it not for the distortion introduced by the recovery of the cotton industry after the American Civil War, retardation would be apparent from the 1860s. The apparent slowing down in growth is even more evident in the years after the traditional span of the Great Depression; indeed, in the years 1900-13 the economy was probably growing more slowly than at any time since the great expansion at the end of the eighteenth century.

Secondly, it has to be remembered that what is under examination is a declining *rate* of growth, for there can be no doubt that in absolute terms the economy was growing substantially throughout the period. It is when a comparison is made between the performance of Britain and her overseas competitors that the cause of anxiety is revealed. In 1870 Britain accounted for nearly a third (31·8 per cent) of the world's manufacturing production as against less than a quarter (22·3 per cent) for her nearest rival the United States. Within the next few decades this predominant position was steadily undermined, and by 1913 Britain accounted for only 14·1 per cent of world production while America and Germany had moved to first and second place, with 35·3 per cent and 15·9 per cent respectively. Britain's share in world trade also fell, albeit less sharply. In 1913 she was still the world's greatest trader, although Germany was not far behind, whereas in 1880 Britain had been twice as important as France, her nearest rival.

In spite of the limited amount of comparable data it is apparent that before 1914 Britain's industrial production grew more slowly than that of any other country for which figures are available. The performance of Britain as compared with Germany, France and the USA is outlined in the following table:

Long-term rates of growth, 1870/71-1913 (per cent per annum)				
	Total Output	Output per Man-Hour	Industrial Production	Exports
UK	2·2	1·5	2·1	2·2*
USA	4·3	2·3	4·7	3·2*
Germany	2·9	2·1	4·1	4·3*
France	1·6	1·8	3·1*	2·6*

Source: Aldcroft, 1968, page 13.   (*1880–1913)

The figures leave little room for self-congratulation, and even contemporary commentators were alarmed. Yet some of them, as well as some modern historians, have been guilty of trying to make too much of such international comparisons. It can be argued, for example, that an examination of different *rates* of growth is a statistical illusion when we ignore absolute growth and the different bases from which growth takes place. A. E. Musson has pointed out that 'it is argued that an increase of 10 units in an output of 100 represents the same order of achievement as an increase of 10,000 units in an output of 100,000'.

The absolute difference between Britain's growth and that of her competitors, however, was not so great as to make the argument valid here, nor did Britain and her major competitors start from totally dissimilar positions in the period under investigation.

There is, however, another danger to which Mathias has drawn attention and which

> consists in comparing each facet of British industry with the world's most eminent exemplar, from whatever country, whether Germany in the case of dye-stuffs or cameras, the United States in the case of machine tools and motor cars, and so forth (rather than making the comparison with—say—Germany for motor cars and cotton, France for coal and agricultural efficiency and the United States for ship-building). (Mathias, 1969, page 404.)

There is equally a danger of concentrating on those areas of British 'failure' and ignoring the 'growth areas', of which there were several. In shipbuilding, for example, British power and technological leadership remained unchallenged, while in much light industry and food-processing, together with retail distribution the British record was a fine one. Even the making of industry-wide comparisons can be misleading since the impact of foreign competition often varied considerably between different sectors of the same industry; in fertilisers, soap and heavy inorganic chemicals Britain was often a match for her competitor Germany, while she remained fairly competitive in some of the older branches of the engineering industry such as textile machinery and railway locomotives and rolling-stock.

Finally, the warning about the weakness of statistics needs to be repeated, for while the growing social awareness of contemporaries and the interest of later historians have ensured that this period is better documented statistically than any earlier age, many statistical series give little more than a general indication of direction or quantity involved, so that the historian remains entitled, as Charles Wilson puts it, to use evidence based on 'well-authenticated historical impressions'.

There is less disagreement amongst scholars about the dimensions of Britain's economic growth than about the factors which determined it. The possible causes of retardation fall under three general heads. There are, in the first place, theoretical arguments based on an analysis of economic growth which attempt to show that deceleration is inevitable in a mature economy. Secondly, there is a range of economic causes based on the actual historical situation, which include a lower rate of technical progress, the effects of industrialisation on exports, the character of capital formation, the effects of low profits on industry during the Great Depression, and so on. Thirdly, there are sociological arguments, especially those which, for various reasons, assign responsibility to the entrepreneur or to society as a whole, arguing the loss of 'growthmindedness' after the collapse of mid-Victorian optimism. The arguments are many, and it is unlikely that there was any single cause. However, it is in the nature of historical controversy that different historians have emphasised different factors.

2 British industrial retardation: the arguments   One of the explanations most often put forward to explain Britain's industrial retardation in the late nineteenth century is that she suffered from her *early start* in industrialisation. Theoretically the argument has little to commend it, although in practice things might be a little different. One would expect the early starter to have greater resources to undertake new investment, and old plant and old locations should provide no handicap to progress, for it should pay the older producer, as well as the newcomer, to scrap what he has and invest in the new. Admittedly the latecomer might learn from his predecessors, avoid their mistakes and take short cuts, but while this might give him a faster rate of growth initially, there is no reason why he should overtake the early starter.

In practice, however, other factors come into play. The early starter, for psychological or institutional reasons, may be resistant to change. Yet for all this, difficulties remain in this explanation. The argument can only work when the newcomer is exceptionally backward at the time in question; but we know that by the latter part of the nineteenth century both Germany and America were already powerful industrial nations—in steel, for example, Britain, Germany and the United States were technically on a relatively equal footing around 1870, although Britain was to lose her leading position between 1886 and 1913. Furthermore, if retardation is inevitable in a mature economy, it is presumably inevitable for the followers as well as for the leader. Yet no one has suggested that America incurred these disabilities at any time. This suggests that the handicap applied only to the *first* starter: something which the believers in this argument have not attempted to prove.

Closely related to the early start hypothesis is that of *over-commitment*. This line of argument has been developed most forcefully by H. W. Richardson. It should first be remembered that an expanding economy is a dynamic one, with some sections contracting while newer, more profitable ones expand. The over-commitment argument contends that in Britain too many resources were locked up in the staple industries, with detrimental results to newer growth industries. That a few staple industries did dominate the British economy throughout this period is made clear by the 1907 industrial census, which reveals that coal, textiles, iron and steel, and engineering accounted for about 50 per cent of net industrial output, while the same industries employed one quarter of the occupied population and supplied 70 per cent of Britain's exports. In contrast, the newer industries of potential growth (which included electrical goods, road vehicles, rayon, chemicals, and scientific instruments and apparatus) accounted for only 6·5 per cent of net industrial output, 5·2 per cent of industrial employment, and 7·4 per cent of exports (2·8 per cent without chemicals). The dangers of over-commitment were not fully apparent until after the post-war boom, when heavy unemployment and prolonged depression in those localities relying on the staple industries signified the delay in readjustment. The burden was there even before the First World War, but the danger of relying on a narrow range of old-established industries was masked after 1905 by heavier demands than ever for Britain's staple exports due to development abroad and a capital export boom. Between 1905 and 1907 there was yet further expansion of the cotton industry; for example, 95 new mills were built in Lancashire in these years, but they still made use of the conventional technology. This was a serious indictment of entrepreneurial efficiency, although hindsight must not lead us to condemn management decisions out of hand.

The ways in which over-commitment inhibited a transfer of resources to new industries needs to be considered, for the argument is an important one which, unlike the early start argument (which should be applicable to other advanced industrial economies) probably applies peculiarly to Britain, for there is no other case where so high a proportion of an economy's resources was tied up in so narrow a range of industries.

Richardson argues that over-commitment interfered with the growth of new industries in three main ways:

In the first place, it led to a scarcity of production facilities for these industries. Secondly, the long and unchallenged predominance of Britain's staple industries affected entrepreneurial psychology and lulled businessmen into making decisions and judgements based too much on past experience, which led to a misplaced emphasis on short-run as against long-run benefits. Thirdly, the institutional framework against which decisions are made was so moulded by the lopsided industrial structure that the adoption of new industries was less economic in Britain than abroad. (Aldcroft & Richardson, 1969, page 195.)

He concedes that there was no limitation of the supply of labour to the newer industries. Although the rate of population growth slowed down, the absolute increase was sufficient to meet the demands of industry, largely because the occupied force was becoming a larger proportion of the total population (36·5 per cent in 1881 and 40·6 per cent in 1911). Although the proportion of occupied females to total females fell (from 34·5 per cent to 32·2 per cent between 1881 and 1911) and the incidence of child labour was reduced, the opening up of employment opportunities for women resulted in a relative transfer from over-staffed domestic service to manufacturing industry. At the same time the growth of opportunities for women as office workers must have released some men for employment elsewhere. Admittedly, the transfer of labour resources was chiefly within or between the older staple industries (mining, for example, doubled its labour force between 1881 and 1911) but there is little evidence of newer industries suffering from a labour shortage in the decades before 1914, and the heavy net emigration in the early years of the twentieth century supports the conclusion that there was no general labour shortage.

Nor does Richardson consider that there was a limitation in the supply of efficient entrepreneurs. The decline of the family firm and the development of corporations, together with a spurt in technical education, broadened the base of manager selection, while the progressiveness of many of the newer industries suggests that they were not starved of good managers. He argues that if any factor was in short supply it was capital. General evidence that deficiencies in capital supply were more important than labour shortages before the First World War is to be found in the course of relative factor prices; the price of labour, if real wages are taken as a standard, at best stagnated (the most reliable index indicating a fall from 103 in 1900 to 100 in 1914) while interest rates rose substantially, the yield on Consols, for example, rising from 2·55 per cent to 3·4 per cent. The heavy export of capital probably intensified over-commitment, for it was the staple exports such as railway materials and even cotton goods which gained most from the opening up of markets by overseas investment. The London capital market was preoccupied with foreign investment, which reduced its ability to finance domestic industry, and the self-financing tradition of British industry (by ploughing back profits) made the situation no easier for new industries.

The impact of over-commitment on entrepreneurial psychology will be considered below, but the 'institutional framework against which decisions are made' calls for some comment here. Individual industrial processes are closely interlinked, and advances in one sector are frequently dependent upon changes in others. Extensive power and transport facilities had been constructed in Britain to meet the needs of industrial expansion, with the result that there was a heavy dependence on coal, steam, gas and railways; this was an important factor in Britain's lag in adopting electricity and developing road transport. In turn, this could block the development of other industries—aluminium, for example, was held up by the slow growth of electric power.

The obstacles to progress which the older industries presented were various. The large output of old goods led over the years to substantial cost reductions, so that price competition was fierce while the production of new goods remained at a high cost stage. For this reason, for example, the relative prices of electricity and gas favoured the latter much more in Britain than in other countries. Similarly, the cheapness of cotton textiles inhibited the growth of the market in rayon in this country before the First World War. Vested interests in the older industries also made an obstacle to innovation; both electricity and the motor industry suffered in this way, especially as the vested interests were able to secure restrictive legislation against their competitors.

Other historians have stressed *slow technical growth* in British industry. The argument takes a number of forms. Discontinuity in the flow of major innovations is stressed by some. The high rate of growth of earlier years was maintained, it is alleged, by a series of major innovations—in particular steam power and steel— but by the 1890s the rate of expansion of these innovations had markedly declined. By the same time increasing returns from fuller utilisation of the railway system and from the transition from the domestic to the factory system had also largely ended. Britain, it was argued, had almost literally run out of steam. Unfortunately, the facts do not fit the case well, for the available statistics suggest that there still remained ample opportunities for the extension of steam and steel. The latter had only just begun to take hold in the 1880s—as late as 1885 Britain was producing more puddled iron than steel—and its widespread application only really began in the last decades of the century. Between the early 1880s and 1895 UK steel production more than doubled and it had almost doubled again by 1910. The statistics of steam power are less adequate, but they suggest that the quantity of fixed industrial steam power in use in the UK rose from 500,000 horse power in 1850 to 2 million in 1880 and to over 9 million in 1907. While the latter figure is probably an overestimate, it does suggest that the application of steam power was by no means insignificant during this period.

It remains true that over a wide section of industry Britain lagged behind in her technology. In many branches of the chemical and engineering industries Britain fell behind her competitors technically. Most of the new equipment in dairying came from Denmark, Holland, Sweden and France. In the technology of roller milling Hungary and the United States were twenty years ahead of Britain. The most widely adopted reapers and binders were American, and from that country also came the sewing machine and the typewriter, as well as most of the developments in shoe-making machinery and machine tools.

Why Britain should initially have been the great technological innovator and later have become something of a laggard is an interesting question. Attempts to answer it have emphasised differences in the endowment of factors of production and a greater willingness amongst foreign industrialists to scrap existing equipment in favour of newer techniques. Where a factor of production is in scarce supply attempts will be made to economise it. In America land was abundant while labour was scarce, and it is suggested that this stimulated the installation of labour-saving machinery and capital-intensive techniques. Britain, on the other hand, enjoyed plentiful supplies of all factors of production (with the possible exception of land) so that the same incentive to innovate did not apply. A. J. Taylor, for example, has shown that cheap labour hardly provided an adequate incentive to mechanisation in the coal industry, while the relative abundance of skilled craft labour in Britain compared with America made it less imperative to adopt automatic machinery and mass-production methods. By 1919 half the looms in the American cotton industry were of the automatic type, whereas Britain had only just begun to introduce them.

It is probable that a shortage of labour acts as a more positive incentive to innovation than a shortage of natural resources. Firstly, labour was usually a higher proportion than natural resources of total costs, so that the industrialist might be induced to make the deduction (which does not necessarily follow) that it was the cost most easily reduced. Secondly, the response to a shortage of natural resources was a search for fresh sources of supply rather than an incentive to invent, for scarce materials can be imported from wherever they are in abundant supply much more easily than labour. Finally, it is probable that the available technical knowledge was more capable of solving problems of labour scarcity than of natural resource scarcity, for the former relies on mechanical engineering which, in the nineteenth century, was far in advance of that knowledge of chemistry and electrical engineering required to replace scarce resources. An abundance of labour may therefore explain Britain's lag behind America in technology, although it hardly explains the lag behind our continental competitors, whose labour supply was little worse than ours. Here perhaps, relative fuel scarcity had its effect, for the evidence suggests that ample fuel supplies in this country encouraged wasteful methods (in iron and steel production for example) which continental industrialists could not afford.

The British attitude towards machinery differed greatly from that of the Americans, and induced a greater reluctance to scrap equipment and invest in more up-to-date machines. In Britain machines were usually built to specification, whereas in the USA they were produced for a standardised market. 'Wood machines', wrote an English expert in 1873, 'are made in America at this time like boots and shoes, or shovels and hatchets. You do not, as in most other countries, prepare a specification of what you need. . . . but must take what is made for the general market.' In consequence American machines tended to be cheaper; they were also much flimsier. This may have reflected the inability of American engineers to produce high-quality durable machines, but it reflected more the attitude of industrialists. Manufacturers did not expect their machines to remain in service long, for they were generally optimistic that improvements would be made which they would want to adopt. In Britain the rule was 'repair and replace' rather than re-equip. At least six engines in breweries which were installed before 1800 were still working a century later. The durability of such machines is, says Mathias, 'one of the finest tributes to British engineers and one of the worst indictments of British industrialists'.

It might be argued that the *size of the home market* was a crucial factor in determining the readiness of industrialists to adopt the new production techniques, for the bigger the market the greater the scope for mass-production methods. Both Germany and the USA had a higher population than the United Kingdom in 1870 and in both the rate of increase was greater in the ensuing decades. The population of the UK rose from 31·8 millions in 1871 to 45·3 millions in 1911, an increase of 42·4 per cent. Germany went from 41 millions in 1871 to 64·9 millions in 1910, an increase of 58·2 per cent. In the same years the population of the USA rose by no less than 138 per cent, from 38·5 millions to 91·7 millions.

The argument should not be pressed too far, for the nature of the market (or what Professor Saul has called the 'social depth' of demand) was perhaps more important. The Americans, and to a lesser extent the Germans, were more willing to purchase standardised products than the British, who were more insistent that goods should meet their own specifications. In the steel industry, for example, standardisation proceeded more slowly than with competitors; in 1900 British steelmakers were turning out 122 channel and angle sections as a matter of course, while the Germans made 34 and the Americans 33. In the engineering and the motor car industries the same attitudes prevailed. Henry Ford, who produced the first of his famous Model Ts in 1908 (the model remained in production until 1927, by which time 15 million had been sold) declared that customers could have any colour they liked—so long as it was black! On the other hand, the Argyll Company of Glasgow gave the bodywork of their cars thirty to thirty-five coats of paint and varnish and generally manufactured in a completely bespoke manner. American methods were quite different, and a team of automobile mechanics, sent to England in 1906 by Cadillac, caused a sensation when they strewed the jumbled components of three cars on the floor of a shed at Brooklands and assembled the vehicles with wrench, screwdriver, hammer and pliers.

There is, however, a temptation to beat the British industrialist with two opposing sticks: blaming him for not producing a standardised product, while at the same time condemning him for not considering the particular needs of his customers, as was argued in the case of many export producers. One cannot have it both ways, and one must remember the difficulties which the peculiarities of demand presented. Nevertheless, to some extent it was up to the manufacturer to 'educate' the public into accepting articles of a more standardised nature, just as it was up to them to 'educate' their craftsmen, and turn their attention from technical perfection to techniques of production. Again, the motor car industry presents a good example of the issue. F. W. Lanchester, one of the great British innovators in the field of automobile engineering and one of the few to employ modern production techniques, described how reluctant craftsmen were to work to standardised instructions: 'In those days, when a body builder was asked to work to drawings, gauges or templates, he gave a sullen look such as one might expect from a Royal Academician if asked to colour an engineering drawing.'

This leads us to the last of the major explanations put forward of the deceleration of the British economy in late Victorian England, namely that it was rooted in the *inadequacies of enterprise* or the *obstructiveness of labour*. To argue this is to hold that the problem was sociological rather than economic, something which not all economic historians are prepared to accept. Professor Saul feels that the shortcomings of the entrepreneur may provide a 'residual explanation' for Britain's weaknesses, but that this is 'hardly helpful because it tells us nothing about the relative importance of this residual element'. H. R. Richardson is also unconvinced and feels that the 'contrast is too sharp to be convincing' when attempts are made 'to describe industrialisation before 1870 in terms of dynamism and energy . . . but development after 1870 in terms of complacency, relative backwardness and lack of adaptability'. Nevertheless, the argument has its supporters, while businessmen and traders were often the butt of contemporary critics. Derek Aldcroft cites one example from *Industrial Efficiency*, written by A. Shadwell in 1906:

England is like a composite photograph, in which two likenesses are blurred into one. It shows traces of American enterprise and of German order, but the enterprise is faded and the order muddled . . . . The once enterprising manufacturer has grown slack, he has let the business take care of itself, while he is shooting grouse or yachting in the Mediterranean. (Aldcroft, 1968, page 15.)

s of course an element of caricature here, as Landes says:

orary observers emphasised the failures of British entrepreneur-
the imminent dangers of German competition much as a
newspaper cries up the morbid aspects of the news. That was the way
one sold articles or attracted the notice of officials in London. Besides,
there is such a thing as fashion in opinions, and this was clearly one of
the popular dirges of the day. (Landes, 1969, page 338.)

Criticism of British entrepreneurs centres upon four important
areas; there is what might be termed the 'third-generation
argument' (which is closely related to the early start hypothesis);
and there is criticism of business methods, of business decisions,
and of a lack of interest in science and research.

The original captains of industry were obliged to devote their
attention to their businesses in order to survive, but as they became established and their wealth accumulated, it is possible
that the second and third generations ceased to strive to maximise
profits but instead sought advancement for themselves in society
—either by devoting themselves to interests outside the business
or by acquiring a landed estate. There is some evidence that this
happened—to the Boultons in engineering, the Marshalls in linen
and the Strutts in cotton, for example—but one can as easily
find examples where the third generation proved as enterprising
as the first.

Similarly one can find examples of businessmen pursuing
sound business methods just as one can find failures. The attitude
of many of those concerned with the engineering industry has
been particularly criticised. Both in electrical and in automobile
engineering Britain produced first-class engineers who proved
to be poor businessmen. 'Crompton, Ferranti and Parsons all
had world-wide reputations', says I. C. R. Byatt, 'but they,
like many of the British engineers, did not have very much commercial ability.' Henry Royce constantly held up the flow of
production to make trifling improvements to his cars until he
was banished to a research workshop, and his attitude was not
untypical of other motor car manufacturers. There was a reluctance to break with earlier craft traditions. It was American
production techniques which enabled the famous Cadillac
demonstration, mentioned above, to be carried out. It will be

noted that a file was not amongst the tools used on that occasion; by contrast, this was a tool much used in British workshops, and the term 'fitter', used to describe a mechanic, illustrates the individual nature of the product which he made. Labour productivity was in consequence low, and the industry lagged about five years behind American output and methods. Before 1914 no British firm managed to exceed one car per man per annum. Wolseley, the largest, employed 4000 workers to produce 3000 cars in 1913, and Austin with about 1900 workers must have averaged about the same.

With hindsight it is easy to condemn the decisions made by British industrialists and to argue that they were obsessed by short-run interests to the detriment of long-term needs. It is easy to argue that there should have been a greater and more rapid transfer of resources from the old-fashioned industries to the newer growth industries, but as Saul says:

What reason could there be for not investing in cotton mills in 1905 when profits expected and realised up to the war were comparable with any elsewhere? And if Britain was wrong to go on making steel rails because future demand was to be poor, were the countries of South America to go without? Were the world's steel-makers to say 'we will not make them for you; our crystal balls tell us that in twenty years demand will have collapsed'? Was it unwise to reap the advantages of favourable prices and satisfy the avid demand for coal from Europe even though the future problems this raised were acute indeed? Britain was surely right to develop these industries as she did . . . (Saul, 1969, page 46.)

It paid the nation to continue to specialise in exporting the old-established staples and to leave the modest home demand for new products mainly to imports, while the high dependence of the staple industries on exports suggests that an earlier concentration on predominantly home-demand newer industries would have put strain on the balance of payments. Consequently a more intensive transfer of resources to new industries would almost certainly have resulted in lower current real income than was actually achieved.

Viewed from their standpoint, many of the decisions which British industrialists made were less irrational or complacent than we might at first suppose. Much has been made, for example, of the slowness with which British coal-owners introduced mechanical coal-cutters; by 1900 one fifth of the output of 240 million tons produced in the USA was mechanically cut, while less than one fiftieth of the British output of 225 million tons was produced in this way. Yet these figures should not lead us to assume that the vast majority of British coal-owners were unprogressive and unenterprising, for a wide variety of factors combined to discourage the coal owner from adopting machine methods at the face. Unfavourable geological conditions were one inhibiting factor, while the coal-owner required a firm conviction that investment in machinery would bring financial benefits. So long as labour could be attracted into mining at wage rates which did not eat into the margin of profit (and we have already noted that mining doubled its labour force in the thirty years after 1881) the coal-owner had little incentive to resort to mechanical innovations in labour-saving machinery, especially as such a course might require reorganisation throughout the colliery and might lead to considerable labour unrest.

Was the attitude of the worker rather than that of the entrepreneur inimical to progress? This allegation was made more strongly at the time than it is now. In the 1890s workers in the engineering industry attempted to impose conditions on the use of the capstan, turret lathe, miller and borer which rendered the profitability of their introduction uncertain, and the great engineering lock-out of 1897 arose out of difficulties over manning the new types of machinery. In the same decade, when employers extended the use of machines in the manufacture of boots and shoes, the workers attempted to maintain the cost of production by machines on a par with the cost of hand methods. But such difficulties arose partly from the unwillingness of employers to concede to their labour the higher money earnings which the new devices warranted, so used were they to the idea of low money wages. American manufacturers, on the other hand, compelled by the dearness of labour to mechanise from the start, were less concerned with money- than with efficiency-wages, with the result that the American workman was less resistant to change than his British counterpart.

3 The changing structure of British industry   In 1885, with only a few industries as exceptions, most industrial firms were owned and run by individuals or partnerships; by 1914 company ownership was usual, though private companies (which obtained limited liability without making any public issue of shares) were much more numerous than public ones. The number of companies in the United Kingdom increased from 9344 in 1885 to 62,762 in 1914, of which, in the latter year, 77 per cent were private companies. Lacking the power of appealing to the public for funds, these companies were often small, with control still in family hands—in 1915 the average capital per British company was only £41,000. Of course, there were some great family concerns, such as Huntley & Palmer, Crosse & Blackwell, J. & J. Colman, Pilkington Brothers and Harland & Wolff, but they remained exceptions. The size of the business unit often remained much smaller than in competing countries. In Britain in 1900 only one steel firm had a capacity of over 300,000 tons a year, while there were ten such in Germany. In coal mining there was a great variation in size, although the pre-war industry in Britain was characterised by a large number of concerns; in 1913, 3289 collieries were being operated by 1589 separate undertakings, each colliery employing on average 340 men and producing annually 87,000 tons of coal. While the number of pits was in decline in the early years of the twentieth century concentration had not proceeded as far as in the Ruhr, where the industry was coming to be dominated by about a dozen concerns. Nor was it only in the British staple trades that the small firm predominated, for although most firms in the newer industries were organised as companies from an early stage of their existence the unit remained small. This was one of the factors which inhibited the development of cheap motor car production in this country. Before 1913 nearly 200 makes of car had been placed on the market, of which over 100 had disappeared, and there was little attempt to combine in order to adopt more efficient methods of production.

In the long run the transition to company organisation was to have great effect. An increase in scale was facilitated which was not only economically essential in many cases, but enabled reserves to be built up—either to contribute to further expansion or to give increased stability in times of bad trade. More precise and careful accounting was encouraged by growing dealings with the inland revenue authorities and the requirement of compulsory audit, and professional accountants gained an increasing influence in the running of businesses. As ownership came to be more separated from management a greater pool of talent also came to be tapped, as the running of businesses no longer passed automatically from father to son irrespective of interest or ability. But a greater impersonality in industrial affairs came about with unfortunate results for labour relations; Robert Knight, the secretary of the Boilermakers' Society, wrote that 'the gulf between employers and employed was deeper, wider and more impassable than ever it was', while as early as 1879 George Howell complained of the tendency for the great majority of employers to regard their workpeople as little better than 'mere machines for guiding machinery'.

A further feature, and one which needs to be seen against the background of the depression in prices, was an extension of combination amongst producers, almost invariably with the object of agreeing on minimum prices or establishing spheres of influence. There was, in the first place, the trade association, which was usually an informal 'gentlemen's agreement' without formal sanctions. By the 1880s almost every trade possessed such a grouping, but their economic effect was limited by their informality and lack of penalties. If bad prices continued, someone invariably broke the agreement and cut; or if prices were held, and the unit of production was fairly small, then new men were often tempted into the trade. Likewise, when the trade cycle took an upswing the more aggressive members of the association would break loose and free themselves from all restrictions. It might be added that such associations should not be taken as evidence of a limitation of free competition. Rather, they can be interpreted as evidence of the *effectiveness* of such competition, making producers anxious to free themselves from the effects of vicious price wars.

More formal than the trade association was the cartel or trust, in which there were institutional links between the members. These might take the form of an exchange of shares or the creation of a common fund based on contributions from each member calculated on the basis of his share in the total output. The aims of these more formal associations often extended beyond price-fixing, and included production quotas and agreements over profits. In the 1890s and afterwards widespread cartelisation developed in many branches of British industry and was particularly apparent in the cotton industry, which had been severely affected by twenty years of low profits. The Bleachers Association is one example; when formed in 1900 it brought 53 firms into a cartel, many of which had previously been associated in ineffective price agreements. Shipping perhaps witnessed the most widespread and effective attempt at cartelisation through what was known as the 'conference system'—made all the more effective by the huge capital sums required before outsiders could break into the trade. Here, systematic and regular rate agreements were reached, and the loyalty of shippers enforced by granting deferred rebates if goods were shipped exclusively on members' vessels.

The most formal method of limiting competition was the outright amalgamation of separate businesses into combines. There were several ways in which this could be achieved. For example, one company might simply purchase another, or two or more companies might form a 'holding company' to hold the ordinary share capital of each of the constituent companies and thus control them. The combine then became a new legal entity which could not easily be broken up. There are many examples of such combines formed after 1880. In 1888 the Salt Union was formed, combining 64 firms including all those in Cheshire; this combination controlled 90 per cent of the British salt production. The United Alkali Company was formed in 1891 and brought together all 48 firms concerned with the production of bleaching powder by the Leblanc process, at that time coming under challenge from other processes. The English Sewing Cotton Company gained a virtual monopoly over the British market in sewing cotton when J. & P. Coats brought 14 competing firms together in 1897, while in the Imperial Tobacco Company of 1901 thirteen firms combined to hold the British market against the Americans.

Combines took one of two forms. There was in the first place 'horizontal integration' of firms competing with each other in the same line of business, which included most of those combines which came together under the pressure of severe competition and adverse prices and profits. This gave potential economies of scale, with the added possibility of rationalisation, the small, least efficient plants being closed down, and production concentrated in the most modern and efficient units. In too many cases, however, these possibilities did not materialise, although the leaders of the various firms still hoped to gain by cutting competitive advertising, by centralising research and other facilities, and by securing favourable rates from suppliers and railway companies.

The other form of combination—'vertical integration'—was likely to be encouraged not so much in time of depression as in expansion, when competition developed for raw materials, for transport or for outlets for products. This type of integration led backwards from the manufacturing process to earlier stages of production or to the supply of raw materials, and forward to embrace distribution. Vertical integration became important in some sections of the food industry, and in iron and steel, where some major concerns embraced orefields and collieries (and had their own transport fleets), while there was diversification into engineering and shipbuilding.

4 New industries   A brief examination of four new industries will suffice to illustrate some of the new directions which the economy was taking.

The Bicycle Industry. The origins of the British cycle industry can be dated to 1869, when James Starley and his associates reconstructed their Coventry Sewing Machine Company into the Coventry Machinists Co. Ltd., in order to gain the legal powers to carry out an order for 400 cycles for sale in France. However, the Franco-Prussian War broke out before the transaction could come to fruition, so an attempt was made to develop the home market. As the cycle increasingly came before the public eye the industry expanded, and by 1879 there were some sixty firms making cycles, of which the most successful were in Coventry, several established by former employees of the Coventry Machinists Company. It still remained a minor industry, however, and in 1881 only 700 persons were engaged in it in Coventry and Birmingham. The subsequent boom was due to a number of factors. Entrepreneurship was, on the whole, sound and the product was marketed with great enthusiasm through exhibitions, cycle journals, and a great variety of publicity stunts. Design was greatly improved, the great break-through being the introduction of the 'safety' model by John Kemp Starley in 1885, which incorporated the diamond frame and wheels of equal size; the pneumatic tyre followed three years later. As demand increased, makers both of cycles and components felt justified in installing initially expensive mass production machinery (much of it at first imported from America), and British machine tool manufacturers switched their attention to the cycle. Firms engaged in other branches of standardised production moved into the industry, including the Birmingham Small Arms Company, which had trifled with cycle manufacture some years before.

By 1891, 8300 men were employed in cycle manufacture, and by the middle of the decade several firms were employing around 1000 men. The Coventry Machinists (by then the Swift Cycle Company) were turning out 700 cycles a week in 1896, and two years later Humber claimed a production of 1000 a week. By 1900, when Raleigh were marketing a serviceable machine for £10, the cycle at last coming within reach of the working man. Output expanded—Rudge Whitworth increased theirs from 9000 in 1895 to 75,000 in 1906—and exports also expanded, from £666,000 in 1899 to over £2 million in 1911. In 1913 Britain exported 150,000 cycles, Germany 89,000 and the rest of the world hardly any at all.

The cycle industry was therefore one in which Britain achieved notable success, and it was one which had wider implications for British engineering. New techniques of milling and grinding were popularised, and the production of weldless tubes developed. More important was the development of machinery for the manufacture of ball bearings, while it was James Starley, 'Father of the Cycle Industry', who introduced the differential gear, also essential to the motor car. Starley might also claim to be one of the pioneers of ergonomics—at least he set his mind to designing a really comfortable bicycle saddle:

As 'Old Man' Starley weighed about fourteen stone . . . he often suffered considerable discomfort from the early saddles, which were usually fashioned from iron or wood. One morning he arrived at the works bubbling over with excitement and in an inspired tone ordered his foreman to tip a small load of sand in the yard; then, turning his ample back upon it, he planted himself down firmly. Rising ponderously, he pointed in triumph at the deep impression he had made in the yielding sand. 'There!' he cried. 'That's how a saddle should be shaped—to fit the bum! Get a cast of that and make me a saddle of stout leather.' (G. Williamson, *Wheels Within Wheels*, Bles, 1966, pages 92-3.)

The Motor Car Industry. A number of the early British motor car manufacturers entered the industry via the manufacture of cycles, including Humber, Rover, Singer, Star and Swift. Firms with many other kinds of engineering experience also started manufacturing cars. Douglas (now more famous for their motor-cycles) started as makers of boot-making appliances; Wolseleys manufactured sheep-shearing machines; Napiers had manufactured a wide range of engineering products, from cranes to printing-presses, and Rushton-Hornsby, who turned to cars from aeroplanes and aero-engines after the First World War, were amongst the foremost manufacturers of agricultural equipment and steam-rollers.

Many technical features were contributed by British engineers and inventors. Dunlop introduced the pneumatic tyre, Napier the six-cylinder engine, and Lanchester alone introduced the epicyclic gear, accelerator, magneto ignition, pull-on hand brake, worm transmission gear, pre-selector control, cantilever springing and forced lubrication. However, the major developments in the petrol engine were almost all pioneered on the Continent, work in this country being hampered by repressive legislation in force between 1865 and 1896, said to have been passed at the instigation of railway and horse interests fearful of the development of steam-carriages on the roads. After 1900 the British industry began to make good its late start, and by 1913 its total output of 34,000 vehicles was approximately three-quarters of that of the French industry. Yet both were completely overshadowed by the American industry, which had an output of 485,000 cars in 1914.

Some of the factors working to the detriment of the British motor car industry, including the adherence to older traditions in engineering and the excessive number of small firms, have already been alluded to. The speciality of British manufacturers was medium-priced cars costing £300 and more, their cheap cars being undersized and underpowered, with no future at all. Before the First World War, therefore, although the number of cars registered in Britain rose from 17,000 to 265,000, the motor car remained the rich man's toy, and even then, says Professor Sayers, 'the toy not of every rich man, but only of those with a taste for mechanical things and—in early days at least—a streak of rashness'. He cites the example of one country town of 16,000 people which boasted only four motor cars in 1914, of which two were owned by doctors who were thought unusually lively characters. The First World War, when London buses and Paris taxis (to say nothing of purpose-built military vehicles) showed the full potential of motor transport, brought the real change. Thousands of government-surplus vehicles and thousands of newly trained drivers sought employment, and the introduction of such models as the Austin 'Seven' in 1922 for the first time brought motoring within the reach of the marginal motorist.

The Electrical Industry. Britain tended to lag behind in the electricity industry, although this should not necessarily be taken as proof of industrial inefficiency and conservatism. There were sound reasons why the industry developed slowly up to 1914 as compared with Germany and the United States. To a considerable degree electricity provided a new way of satisfying a need for energy which was already being satisfied by steam, gas and horses. We have seen that the growth rate of industrial production in Britain was slow; in consequence electricity could only develop speedily by replacing existing motive power rather than by satisfying a fresh demand as with more rapidly expanding economies. In 1907 a third of the motive power used in mining and manufacturing was in mines, while textiles took up another quarter. Electricity was little used in either, and with some justification, for cheap coal was close at hand and in textile mills before 1914 electrical driving had little advantage—if any at all— over the traditional shafting and belting. However, the cost of electric motors for factory use fell considerably in the early years of the century, and by 1914 perhaps a quarter of the motive power used in mining and manufacturing was electric.

Electric lighting also proceeded more slowly than abroad. There was a false start in the 1880s when it failed to oust the much cheaper gas, and even in 1900 gas probably provided ten times as much light as electricity. Electric power made some headway with tramways; over 2000 miles were built between 1897 and 1906, by which time horse trams had virtually disappeared. But tramway investment also fell off after that date, for by then the big towns were fairly well equipped, and the existence of a comprehensive railway system made the construction of inter-urban tramways unnecessary. The central London underground railway network (the product largely of American initiative) was virtually complete by 1907, but before the First World War steam railway electrification proceeded slowly.

I. C. R. Byatt has claimed that 'in an important sense, the British electrical manufacturing industry was not an industry of its own at all, but one which after 1895 was an offshoot of the American and German industries with an important fringe of domestic producers'. The major American and German manufacturers established their own factories in Britain, and by 1914 three out of the four major British companies were offshoots of foreign firms—British Westinghouse and British Thomson-Houston springing respectively from the American firms of Westinghouse and General Electric, and Siemens deriving from the German firm, Halske-Siemens Schuckertwerke. This fact needs to be borne in mind when considering the favourable balance of trade in electrical goods which Britain enjoyed for much of the time between 1880 and 1913, although this also disguises the fact that much of the more technically advanced and sophisticated electrical machinery was imported, while British exports were often of a less sophisticated nature, and frequently went to the British Empire or Latin America, where tramway and electricity supply companies were often financed from London.

The Chemical Industry. Up to the 1880s Britain was the dominant chemical producer; thereafter she fell behind, and by 1913 was in third place behind the United States and Germany. The industry was a complex one, however, and competitiveness in particular fields varied considerably. In the manufacture of soda ash (sodium carbonate), used in soap and glass-making and for bleaching, Britain still led the field, while Germany led in dye-stuffs, and the United States in the production of sulphuric acid and superphosphates. Such was the nature of the industry that even minor industrial nations could exert a lead in specialised fields—Norway, for example, was the biggest producer of calcium carbide, used in the production of acetylene. The complexity of the industry needs to be remembered, for it is possible to take an unduly pessimistic view of the achievements of the British chemical industry in the late nineteenth century. Britain had marked successes and was in a strong position with regard to soaps, paints, some fertilisers and heavy chemicals, coal tar intermediates and explosives. Nobel's factory in Scotland, for example, was the largest explosives factory in the world, with an annual output of almost 10,000 tons as early as the 1880s, while the major soap manufacturers such as Lever Brothers built up extensive exports.

The competition between the Leblanc and Solvay processes in alkali production was an important development of the period, and has led to assertions that British entrepreneurship failed by clinging to the former process while overseas producers forged ahead with the cheaper Solvay ammonia process. The struggle between the two processes is illustrated by the world production figures. In 1874 production was 525,000 tons, of which no less than 495,000 tons were made by the Leblanc process; by 1902 the world total had risen to 1,800,000 tons, of which the Leblanc process provided a mere 150,000 tons. By that time the world price of soda had fallen to about £4 a ton compared with £13 in 1863. The Solvay process was undoubtedly the superior of the two, yet for a long while they were worked side by side, the once great British Leblanc soda industry not closing down finally until 1920. Two principal factors account for the ability of the Leblanc industry to survive for so long. In the first place numerous technical improvements were made to the original process in the middle decades of the nineteenth century, while the Leblanc process also produced by-products—such as hydrochloric acid, from which bleaching powder could be extracted—which could not be obtained from the ammonia process. Secondly, a series of amalgamations among the Leblanc producers, culminating in the setting up of the United Alkali Company in 1890, produced a measure of rationalisation, and encouraged members to concentrate less on pure soda and more on profitable products such as bleaching powder and caustic soda, as well as to diversify into such products as fertilisers, laundry blue, sulphur and nitric acid.

Their attempts to revive the Leblanc soda industry nevertheless failed, and historians have been led to ask whether the British chemical industry did everything possible to keep ahead in alkali production. That attempts were made to reduce the costs and increase the yield of the Leblanc process cannot be disputed, but the more radical step of scrapping the process altogether was evaded. Producers may have been reluctant to scrap technically efficient if commercially obsolete plant, but the success of Brunner Mond (who introduced the Solvay process into Britain) gave a clear example of its superiority, and other British soda makers cannot be completely absolved from the charges of inertia and indecision. The more drastic surgery might have saved them from a lot of pain in the long run.

When in 1914 British soldiers went into action in France and Belgium they wore uniforms whose khaki colour depended on imports from Germany. The dyestuffs industry never firmly took hold in Britain before the First World War although many of the pioneer advances in the 1850s and 1860s had taken place here—for example, W. H. Perkin (then aged 18) discovered aniline mauve in 1856 and established a factory near Harrow to produce it. Indeed, the position steadily deteriorated; whereas in the 1880s it was estimated that the German industry was around four times the size of Britain's, by 1913 it was twenty to thirty times as large. Nor was Britain's position inherently unfavourable, which would have excused her; unlike Germany, which long depended on imports, she possessed plentiful supplies of raw materials, and her cloth industry gave rise to a large domestic demand. Many advantages would have accrued from developing the industry, including a derived demand for the products of the ailing Leblanc industry, for dyestuff producers required large quantities of soda ash and hydrochloric acid.

The failings of the British dyestuffs industry illustrate one of the main indictments of British industrial enterprise in this period—a lack of interest in science, research and training. The production of dyestuffs was only one of a number of science-based industries which were dependent to a large extent on technical expertise, but, as Michael Sadler observed, 'England, at heart, hates the expert; Germany rejoices in him.' British economic supremacy had been built up by 'practical tinkerers' using 'rule of thumb' methods. This attitude was widespread in other industries than chemicals; there is the story, for example, of the manager of the Dowlais ironworks in the 1880s who 'made the best guess he could as to the strength there should be, then multiplied by four and the things never broke'—although their weight was painful. Britain failed to provide a system of university and technical education (let alone primary and secondary) on the scale of Germany. Just before the First World War Britain had only 9000 full-time students as compared with 58,000 in Germany, a figure not reached in this country until 1938. In 1916 Lord Haldane remarked in the House of Lords that Britain had only 1500 trained chemists while four large German chemical firms, which had 'played havoc with certain departments of our trade', employed 1000 trained chemists between them. Society at large, rather than the British industrialist, was the sinner.

5 Agriculture At one time agriculture was felt to be the sector of the economy most affected by the 'Great Depression', but in recent years the traditional picture has been considerably revised. In the first place there has been a deeper understanding of the variety of forms which agriculture takes, which make it not one industry but a bundle of industries, serving different markets and making use of the soil in a number of different ways. The depression was a time when technical and business changes were re-structuring much of British agriculture, and the farming history of the years 1870-1914 consists largely of the transfer of resources from sectors of agriculture which no longer paid to others which did, in particular from arable to stock farming. For some farmers the period was one of severe hardship, for others it was one of 'quiet prosperity', but for all it was one of unavoidable change.

There has also been a re-examination of the evidence upon which the textbook generalisations have been based. On the one hand there is the statistical evidence, in particular the index of wheat prices, which has been used to demonstrate the fall in farm prices. On the other hand there is the literary evidence such as the writings of contemporary observers and, more important, the proceedings of the two Royal Commissions of 1879-82 and 1894-7. In the case of the first type of evidence it has to be asked how representative it is of agricultural prices as a whole, in other words whether wheat contributed the same proportion of agricultural earnings and output throughout the period. With the second type of evidence we must remember the warning given in an earlier chapter that the voice of the dissatisfied is generally louder than that of the contented. T. W. Fletcher has drawn attention to the biased representation of the two Royal Commissions. The Richmond Commission of 1879-82 was firmly led by the landowning aristocracy and gentry, all with large properties in the south and midlands. Thirty-five farmers, almost all of them tenants, were amongst the witnesses called before the Commission. Of these 35 only one farmed less than 100 acres, while 31 farmed more than 300 acres (25 of them farming more than 500 and ten more than 1000) at a time when the average size of farm in England was perhaps less than 100 acres. Twenty-six of the witnesses came from the 'corn' counties of the east and south, while only nine came from the 'grazing' counties of the north and west; the ten leading wheat-growing counties produced between them 14 witnesses, while the ten leading dairy counties contributed only five. The composition of the witnesses should not be taken as a deliberate attempt to distort the true picture. It was natural that men with large arable (or stock) farms, adequately staffed and with foremen, should be willing and able to give evidence on the depression to the Royal Commission, or to make their voices heard elsewhere. The working dairy farmer had little opportunity to make *his* voice heard—his cows needed to be milked twice a day every day of the year.

The members of the second Royal Commission were a more mixed body, as were the witnesses. The majority of the farmers giving evidence (22) still came from the east and south, but 18 now came from the west and north, while the dairy counties provided 12 witnesses as against 13 from the corn counties. The final report devoted three pages out of nearly 200 to dairy farming, the subject receiving nothing like the attention given to the plight of the arable farmers in some districts.

The discussions of the time must be read with care, for social as well as economic changes underlay the complaints of depression. There was a feeling amongst landowners and farmers that the agricultural interest was losing ground to manufacturing industry, and there certainly was a sharp fall in the position of agricultural incomes relative to those of the nation as a whole after 1870. Economically, politically and socially, consciousness of a relative decline in the national importance of agriculture was brought home to those concerned with farming, all of which contributed to the impression that a golden age was coming to an end.

There is now little disagreement as to the cause of the depression in British agriculture, although contemporary observers often missed the true significance of the changes which were going on around them. There was great difficulty, for example, in distinguishing the short-term causes of distress from those factors which had been coming into play over a longer period and were likely to be permanent. An immediate cause which received great attention was inclement weather. The wet autumn of 1875 was followed by abnormally heavy rainfall in the winter of 1876-7, while the spring of 1878 began a period of two-and-a-half years of exceptional cold and wet. The excess of rainfall over the local average was greatest in the south and east, and progressively diminished to the north and west. Cumberland and South Wales, for example, had rather less than the local average, while rainfall in Bury St Edmunds in 1879 was 50 per cent more than usual. The wet weather not only ruined much arable land, especially on the heavy clays of the eastern counties, it also brought an epidemic of liver rot in sheep, while a severe outbreak of foot and mouth disease raged in 1881-3. The final report of the Richmond Commission also listed an impressive number of burdens on the farmer, including tithe and local rates, the new Education Act, increasing labour costs, high rents, and unequal railway rates.

In addition to all this, however, the farmer was feeling the full impact of foreign competition. The effects which the protectionists of 1846 had feared were now coming into play as transport improvements opened up the great wheat belts of America, Russia and elsewhere. The cost of carrying a quarter of wheat from Chicago to Liverpool averaged 11s in 1868-79, 4s 3d by 1892 and only 2s 10$\frac{1}{2}$d in 1902. Imports of wheat and flour rose from a little over 40 million cwt. in the early 1870s to an average of nearly 70 million cwt. in the later 1890s, and in 1894 wheat reached its lowest price of 22s 10d a quarter. In 1896 a corn grower could look back over twenty years of almost continually falling prices. But the situation was different for the livestock farmer; he would be gradually acclimatising himself to a price level somewhat lower than in the prosperous seventies, but not very different from that of twenty-five or thirty years earlier, and in compensation he could point to his lower feed costs.

Several factors gave the livestock farmer a measure of protection. The demand position was good, for not only was the population growing, but the fall in the price of bread and cereals left a growing fraction of income available for expenditure on protein; as one writer put it in 1899, 'The sort of man who had bread and cheese for his dinner 40 years ago now demands a chop.' Furthermore, livestock farmers were protected from foreign competition until the introduction of the refrigerated ship in the 1880s. Imports then grew rapidly, and by 1895 meat imports reached over 500,000 tons, equal to about a third of the estimated consumption. In the following year it was calculated that a lamb could be killed in New Zealand, frozen, shipped to London and delivered there to a retailer for as little as 2½d a pound. It was at the cheaper end of the price range that competition was most keenly felt, for the discriminating buyer still preferred home-produced meat. On the other hand, many foreign foods had a high reputation for quality, uniformity and good packing. At the hotels in which he stayed during his tour of the agricultural districts in 1901-2, Rider Haggard found that the food was mainly of foreign origin, while even the village shops were stocking French and Danish butter, American bacon and tinned meat, Canadian cheese, and Dutch eggs and margarine.

If the returns to arable farming were falling relative to those in other branches of agriculture, what could the farmer do about it? The policy which farmers often adopted was one of economy in cash outlay, including (where remissions could be obtained) outlay on rent. Repairs were left undone, ditches were neglected, less fertiliser was used, and outlying fields were allowed to fall into rough pasture. There was little satisfaction in this kind of farming, although it no doubt enabled many of the smaller farmers to keep going through the worst of the depression.

Farmers could also diversify, and the period saw the development of fruit farming and market gardening as well as early experiments in the growing of sugar beet. In the East Anglian fens, on farms near large towns, and in north Cambridgeshire, in Bedfordshire and Kent, and round Evesham and Pershore enterprising men turned to fruit, bulbs, vegetables and flowers, using the readily available town manure as a basis of fertility. Rider Haggard remarked on the profits which one Herefordshire farmer reported to him:

One gentleman, a large farmer, told me that in 1900 from six and a half acres of strawberries he netted £200 clear profit. Another plot of sixty acres was said to have produced 150 tons, which sold at £25 a ton, the net profit on this parcel amounting to £1500. How often does an ordinary cultivator of the soil clear £1500 profit in these days, even from a farm of, let us say, 1000 acres . . . My question leads to another. How many English farmers can grow a strawberry, or, being ignorant, will take the trouble to learn the craft? (Court, *British Economic History 1870-1914* C.U.P. 1965, page 54.)

Much of this fruit no doubt went into jam, made either at home or in the factories which were growing up. The Chivers family began a factory outside Cambridge about 1873, while a similar industry developed around Tiptree in Essex and round Blair-gowrie in Perthshire.

Farmers who changed over to dairying could profit from the growth of the trade in liquid milk; by 1910 the Great Western Railway was bringing milk to the London market from 130 miles away. Dairy farmers began to be assisted by milking machinery, although until the First World War milking by hand predomin-ated, and it remained one of the most burdensome jobs in the production of milk. Cheese-making became more professional, and the work of dairy bacteriologists in explaining and codifying many of the mysteries of the craft showed that any type of cheese could be made anywhere, so that, for example, by the early years of the twentieth century farmers in North Somerset had largely turned from 'Cheddar' to the more profitable 'Caerphilly'.

The changing structure of British agriculture is revealed by the acreage devoted to different types of husbandry. That under wheat fell from 3·4 million acres in 1871 to 1·7 million acres in 1901, while in the same years the area under permanent grass rose from 11·4 to 15·4 million acres. The adjustment facing farmers in the south and east was a formidable one which many failed to accomplish, involving as it did in some cases the con-version of entire arable farms to pasture. Some historians have criticised the slowness with which the transformation was undertaken, although it might be argued that the figures reveal a great measure of flexibility, even if not as great as in some countries such as Denmark. The wet years at the start of the depression misled farmers as to the need for permanent change as well as diminishing their capital resources, a crucial point since the change to pasture required weed-free fields, a long period of careful management with ample supplies of manure and fertiliser, and capital to stock the fields as well as, in many places, to provide water and fences. No doubt it also required a flexibility of mind which farmers are often accused of lacking. Such conservatism is illustrated by A. D. Hall, who in 1913 found that the resorts along the west coast of Wales were apt to run short of milk, butter, cream, eggs, fruit and vegetables in the holiday season, while farmers within ten miles were still prepared to produce wool and store stock, oats and hay, products which afforded a mere subsistence. In many areas the shift to grass followed the migration into the depressed arable areas of Scottish and west-country farmers who brought with them enterprise and experience of the more profitable lines of production.

6 The condition of the people   In Chapter II the standard of living of the working class was considered up to the middle of the century. The trend after that time has ceased to be a point of great controversy amongst historians. During the prosperous years of the middle decades the lives of most Britons improved (although perhaps not as much as contemporaries thought), while they improved much more strikingly during the years of the Great Depression. Between 1889 and 1900 money wages rose in the order of 15 per cent, while the trend of prices was downward until the outbreak of the South African War, whereupon a sharp increase brought them back to the level of 1889. Between 1889 and 1900, therefore, real wages must have risen by well over 10 per cent. However, between 1900 and 1910 the national income did little more than keep pace with the growing population, and it is estimated that real wages fell by something like ten per cent. This reduction in standard of living would have been felt acutely by those workers who remained in the same job, but as the period was marked by a shift from lower-paid to higher-paid jobs (there was a great exodus from agriculture, for example) most wage-earners were almost as well off at the end of the decade as at the beginning. Nevertheless, the years before the First World War were marked by acute labour unrest, and part of the explanation must be sought in the trend of real wages.

The depth of poverty in which a great many of the people lived must also be remembered. The revelations of Charles Booth in London and Seebohm Rowntree in York profoundly shocked the nation, while in 1890 General William Booth of the Salvation Army sorrowfully admitted 'that it would be Utopian . . . to dream of obtaining for every honest Englishman a gaol standard of all the necessaries of life'. Social reformers such as Charles Booth, Rowntree, the Webbs and many others looked critically at the social evils which surrounded them, drawing attention to the appalling conditions which still existed in many urban areas. The Rev. Charles Mearns in 1883 published a pamphlet, *The Bitter Cry of Outcast London*, which created a great stir, for most of what he said might easily have been drawn from Chadwick's report of forty years before. He described the filthy state of the hovels in which many wretched people were forced to live, their conditions made worse by the obnoxious nature of the 'sweated' trades which they carried on:

Here you are choked as you enter by the air laden with particles of the superfluous fur pulled from the skins of rabbits, rats, dogs and other animals in their preparation for the furrier. Here the smell of paste and drying match-boxes, mingling with the fragrance of stale fish or vegetables, not sold on the previous day, and kept in the room overnight. Even when it is possible to do so, the people seldom open their windows, but if they did it is questionable whether much would be gained, for the external air is scarcely less heavily charged with poison than the atmosphere within. (Flinn, *Readings in Economic and Social History* Macmillan London and Basingstoke. 1964, page 322.)

The South African War gave the nation a further jolt. Not only did it cost the country £250 million to subdue a Boer male population no greater than that of Brighton, but the deleterious effect of urban conditions on the health of town inhabitants was revealed by the incredibly poor physique of many of the volunteers for the army. Forty per cent of the recruits had to be rejected—in some areas up to 60 per cent—and although the minimum height for infantrymen had been lowered in 1883, it again had to be lowered in 1902. Yet the population of the urban areas continued to expand till by 1914 41 per cent of the population of England and Wales lived in the six conurbations of London, South-east Lancashire, Merseyside, West Midlands, West Yorkshire, and Tyneside.

By that time something had begun to be done to improve the social condition of the mass of the population, and the first six years of office of the Liberal government were rich in reform measures. In 1906 the Education (Provision of Meals) Act allowed feeding of school children in cases of distress, and the Workmen's Compensation Act extended the right to compensation for industrial injuries and included certain industrial diseases for the first time. In 1907 the Education Act established school medical inspection. In 1908 came Old-Age Pensions and the granting of the eight-hour day for miners. The following year saw a Housing and Town Planning Act (largely ineffective), the Trade Boards Act, which tried to come to grips with the sweated trades, and a Labour Exchanges Act, providing for the setting up of labour exchanges, which were filling over a million vacant jobs annually by 1914. The year 1910 was taken up with the wrangle with the House of Lords over the Finance Bill, but in 1911 there appeared the Coal Mines Regulation Act, which consolidated previous legislation; the National Insurance Act, incorporating health insurance and, for a few trades, unemployment insurance; and the Shops Act, which at last provided a half-holiday, though the legal maximum working week in 1914 was still 74 hours, and even that limit applied only to young persons.

The years of the Great Depression may have witnessed a certain lack of enterprise on the part of some industrialists, but they certainly saw no such failings on the part of entrepreneurs concerned with the distributive trades, for there took place what almost amounted to a revolution in retail distribution, with the growth of multiple stores and department stores backed up by the producers of new consumer goods. Before the 1870s, except for special cases such as the railway station bookstalls of W. H. Smith, multiple stores were very rare, but in the following twenty years they gained a firm hold, with specialised multiple grocers like Liptons, Home & Colonial and Sainsburys, shoe shops like Lilley & Skinner and Freeman Hardy & Willis, chemists like Boots, and tailors such as Hepworths. In 1880 there were about 1500 multiple stores, which by 1900 had multiplied to over 11,500. Behind the spread of such stores lay the late-nineteenth-century mechanisation of the production of many consumer goods such as footwear, hosiery, suits and overcoats, chocolate and sweets. By 1915 the multiple shoe shops had captured one-third of the total footwear trade, and the more types of consumer goods that could be cheaply and attractively produced by comparable methods, the greater the importance of multiple shops became. And not only the shops themselves were new, for the methods which they employed to sell their goods also reflect new attitudes. Advertising assumed a new importance, advertisements losing much of their former deference and taking on more of the attributes we now regard as familiar. In 1886 Levers, the soap firm, spent only £50 on advertising, although in the following two years they spent £2 million. Publicity stunts of the widest variety were devised. At one end of the scale Pears purchased Millais' painting 'Bubbles' to persuade people to buy their soap; at the other end Lipton had his name painted on pigs driven through the streets, hired elephants and brass bands, and used leaflets scattered from balloons to persuade people to patronise a newly opened branch.

Retail trade was one of the most rapidly expanding areas of economic activity—between 1900 and 1915 British retail sales are estimated to have increased by more than 50 per cent—and Charles Wilson has argued that economic historians, obsessed by 'spectacular technological innovation' have ignored the strides that were made. His emphasis on distribution and the consumer goods industries is an interesting one, but great as was their growth, it is difficult to accept that it made up for the slackness elsewhere. Compared with the giants of textiles, coal and engineering these industries were small, and few of them contributed significantly to exports. The simplicity of their technology made them hardly strategic to the growth industries of the twentieth century—as Mathias puts it, 'a major indigenous electrical engineering industry would have proved a greater long-term asset to the economy than a large jam-making or chocolate industry'— and as far as can be measured, these industries contributed only a small percentage to gross domestic product at the time of the first census of production in 1907.

7 The labour movement The intense international economic rivalry which was a feature of the closing decades of the nineteenth century inevitably influenced working-class movements, and in these years the organisation of labour underwent entirely new developments. From the 1840s the employees had, on the whole, tried to work within the framework of capitalism, believing that as Britain grew richer and richer the lot of the working man would improve accordingly. But as the international supremacy of their masters became threatened many workers came to question the system by which production was organised. Real wages tended to increase during the years of the depression, but as it was increased imports and lower prices which allowed conditions to improve, a change was more apparent to the worker's wife than to the worker, who was more aware of the difficulties which faced industry and the threat of unemployment.

At the same time the doctrines of socialism were beginning to take on their modern form, with Marxist movements developing in several countries. The new doctrines were brought back to Britain by a City businessman of some wealth, H. M. Hyndman, who was converted in 1880 after reading Marx's *Capital* (in a French translation, for it was not available in English until 1887). In 1881 he founded the Social Democratic Federation. At first Hyndman planned that the new organisation should support working-class agitation on the old Chartist lines, but by 1883 it had changed front and had become a definite Socialist body, demanding such things as the nationalisation of banks, railways, and land, state-aided schemes for housing, universal free education and school feeding, and the eight-hour day.*

One of the young members of the S.D.F. was Tom Mann, a member of the Amalgamated Society of Engineers who had suffered severe spells of unemployment. In 1886 Mann published a pamphlet advocating the eight-hour day, but going beyond that to convey an entirely new concept of the responsibilities of trade unionism. The established leaders of the British labour movement were severely criticised:

> The true Unionist policy of *aggression* seems entirely lost sight of; in fact the average unionist of today is a man with fossilized intellect, either hopelessly apathetic, or supporting a policy that plays directly into the hands of the capitalist exploiter.

The New Model Unions of the 1850s and 1860s had themselves become the established trade unions, catering for skilled craftsmen and urging restraint in industrial relations for fear of endangering their extensive friendly benefit funds. In the 1880s and 1890s the unskilled workers more and more showed themselves both willing and able to be organised, and these decades were a time of division within the working class movement. The 'New Unionism', as it is called, is often said to have its origins in the London Dock Strike of 1889, but the organisation of unskilled workers dates back beyond this. Before we consider these antecedents, however, it is as well to consider a little more fully the nature of the New Unionism.

Clegg, Fox and Thompson list some of the characteristics which contemporaries and historians have put forward as the distinguishing features of the New Unions:

> There are a membership of unskilled, low-paid labourers; a militant outlook; a readiness to employ coercion against non-unionists and black-legs; low contributions allowing for the payment only of 'fighting' benefits; an acceptance of socialism; and a tendency to look to parliamentary and municipal action to solve labour's problems. (Clegg, Fox and Thompson, 1964, page 92.)

---

*For an account of socialist movements in Britain at this time, and a discussion of the political situation, *see* K. W. W. Aikin, *The Last Years of Liberal England 1900-1914*, in this series.

Yet they take pains to show some of the difficulties involved in accepting this list as a guide to definition. The meaning of the word 'labourer', for example, varied from industry to industry, and would seem to exclude such groups as seamen, gas stokers, carters and tramwaymen, who, although neither labourers, nor unskilled, were swept up in the New Unionist fervour.

The question of 'skill' and the idea of the 'labourer' have been examined most interestingly by Dr Hobsbawm, who demonstrates that while contemporary belief pointed to a sharp division between the 'skilled' and the 'unskilled' and between the 'artisan' and the 'labourer', the facts suggest the gradually ascending scale indicated by our own division of 'unskilled', 'semi-skilled' and 'skilled'. The division between 'artisan' and 'labourer' emphasised the traditional difference between the genuine maker of things and the man who merely fetched and carried for him. 'Builders and engineers', says Dr Hobsbawm, 'boilermakers and tailors might still reasonably imagine that they were capable of making houses, machines, ships and clothes without the convenient, but not indispensable, help of the labourer; as a hotel chef could, at a pinch, produce a dinner without the help of the potato-peeler and bottle-washer'. But every technical and industrial change tended to increase the unreality of this conventional picture. Furthermore, with labour on the defensive during the great depression, the leaders of the established unions became more and more inclined to reinforce the old restrictive barriers against intruders rather than to spread unionism, so that by the late 1880s the ranks of the excluded 'labourers' contained an increasing number of men who were capable of orthodox unionism and who often possessed great bargaining strength. In addition, the spread of mechanisation and modern factory methods made a stable labour force desirable, so that employers even came to doubt that the 'general labourer' lacked all 'special value'. When it came to be felt that such men could make themselves scarce and could cause loss to their employers if their labour were withdrawn, then the New Unions came to have an increasingly large pool for recruitment.

Attempts had been made before the London Dock Strike of 1889 to spread trade unionism to those workers who remained unprovided for by the predominantly craft unions which had developed in the middle decades of the century. Much of this activity took place in the early 1870s. A National Agricultural Labourers' Union was formed by Joseph Arch in 1872, which, with other local unions established at the same time, enjoyed a membership of something like 150,000 at its peak. The 'Revolt of the Field', as the agricultural labourers' movement of the 1870s was called, was an interesting phenomenon, for while in its outward form it conformed to modern trade unionism, its concern went far beyond the material conditions of labour, and it contained a strong streak of Nonconformist idealism. This was the first great outburst of agrarian discontent since the riots of 1830, and although in some respects there were similarities, in the main the movements were very different. The leaders were known men and no longer went under sinister pseudonyms such as 'Captain Swing', and the labourers' discontent was expressed in strikes rather than the destruction of property. The new movement was more widespread than the Swing Riots, and there was better communication between the areas of discontent; the National Union possessed its own weekly journal, the *Labourers' Union Chronicle*, which claimed a circulation of 35,000 in 1873, while the railway and the penny post also helped the leaders to attempt tighter control. Initially the labourers were strong enough to gain an almost general rise in wages and a widespread reduction in working hours, but the farmers and gentry soon recovered. Victimisation was widespread, the most notorious case being that of the sixteen labourers' wives sentenced to prison at Chipping Norton in 1873 for intimidating blacklegs. A lock-out in 1874 broke the power of the union. The unionists had counted on being indispensable, at least during the harvest, but found out that they were not; few of them could afford the loss of harvest money, with which clothing and other expensive items were bought, and after the harvest the prospect of eviction from tied cottages loomed up for many. What the employers failed to accomplish was largely achieved by the onset of the agricultural depression. The conversion of land from arable to pasture greatly reduced the demand for agricultural labour, while many farmers who had been farming too high were forced to abandon labour-intensive methods. Nor did the unions always pursue the most sensible policies; the Kentish union was broken up, for example, because its leader was incompetent enough to bring his men out on strike in the autumn, when agricultural labour is least required. Trade union membership among the labourers dwindled, many of the smaller unions disappeared altogether, and by 1881 Arch's union had shrunk to a membership of only 15,000. In Norfolk alone did the National Union retain its vitality, being sufficiently strong in that county to enable the newly enfranchised labourers to return Joseph Arch to Parliament in 1885.

Other unions with 'new' characteristics grew up alongside the agricultural labourers' unions. Many of the dockers themselves came to be organised at this time in the Labour Protection League which was founded in the East End of London in 1871. This union, however, while springing from unrest among the dockers, showed greater success in organising other workers such as those in the dock warehouses and the more skilled stevedores. The latter probably constituted the majority of the 1200 members who had enrolled by April 1872. Thereafter the growth was phenomenal, 30,000 being reported in October. Not all the members were port workers, for amongst the membership were accounted builders' and engineers' labourers, dustmen, and scavengers, while an attempt was made to enrol coal porters and carmen. The strength of the League was gradually worn away during the depressed years of the second half of the 1870s, although a secure foothold was retained with some port workers such as the stevedores.

The same fate awaited other new unions formed at this time: the Amalgamated Society of Railway Servants (1871) shrank into a friendly society with small membership and power; the Amalgamated Miners' Association (1869) died out, and the Miners National Union (1863) survived only in Northumberland and Durham. Not until trade rapidly revived in 1887 did favourable conditions arise for another period of major growth for the trade union movement.

The revival of trade was not the only stimulus to growth, however. The role of the socialists was important, for not only was there socialist agitation among the London unemployed in 1885-7, but many direct links existed between the socialists and the new movement—between Eleanor Marx-Aveling (daughter of Karl Marx) and the gasworkers, for example, and between H. H. Champion, one-time secretary of the S.D.F., and the dockers. Champion, an individualistic, self-sufficient ex-army officer, was described by William Collison as 'the brains of the Dock Strike', and it was he who had suggested that Mrs Besant should take up the problems of the match girls, and who first came to the assistance of the gasworkers.

The organisation of the match girls and the gasworkers was the prelude to the London Dock Strike. The strike of the London match girls in 1888 was small but significant. The makers of lucifer matches were poorly paid and worked in appalling conditions, many of them suffering from 'phossy jaw', or gangrene of the jaw, caused by the fumes from the phosphorus used in making the matches. Mrs Annie Besant, a Free Thinker and a member of the socialist Fabian Society, drew attention to their plight in her weekly journal *The Link*. Thus encouraged, nearly 700 girls came out on strike against their employers, and with public opinion on their side forced them to give in after a fortnight.

The gasworkers had organised themselves in the period of brisk activity in the early 1870s, although the movement had swiftly collapsed. Potentially, however, they remained in a strong bargaining position. Stokers and firemen did not lack all scarcity value; the process of gas-making was a continuous one, and teams of men worked twelve-hour shifts (eighteen at the week-end changeover) at work of the most exacting physical nature. Technical progress had been slow in the gas industry, so that it was on the exertions of the stokers and firemen—the key men in the process—that the maintenance of the statutory gas pressure depended. Letting the lighting power of gas fall, or worse still, letting lights go out, was something which the companies could not afford, especially as in the early 1880s they were anxiously watching the advances of electricity, a potential rival, and in London the construction of power stations had seriously begun.

Two factors in the main had kept the gasworkers unorganised. In the first place their work was extremely casual, the winter load being three to five times greater than the summer, and the winter labour force double that of the summer months. Secondly the weight of tradition held them back, for not being apprenticed, and their skill being quickly acquired, the stokers were for long prepared to accept a position in the lower stratum of the 'craftsman/labourer' division.

The step forward came early in 1889 when Will Thorne, a stoker at the Becton gasworks in London, launched the National Union of Gasworkers and General Labourers at a public meeting in Canning Town. The eight-hour day was made a prime objective, and although Thorne was almost completely illiterate, he gained support for this objective from a number of his fellow members of the S.D.F., including Mann, Burns, and Karl Marx's daughter (who helped with clerical work). Within four months the union had 20,000 members and Thorne felt strong enough to put forward his demands. To the general surprise, the gas companies gave way. The gasworkers' union had won their demands without striking a blow; their victory, said Tom Mann, was one which 'put older and larger unions to shame'.

From the gasworks the revolt passed to the docks, and this is not surprising, for the work of the dock labourers was also casual; indeed, many men worked in the gas works in the winter, when the trade of the port was slack, and became dockers in the summer months. The London Dock Strike of 1889 was the symbol of the New Unionism. Almost 700,000 working days were lost and the dispute was the biggest of the year, although this is to be accounted for by the fact that in 1889, as in other years of expanding trade, there were no really large and protracted strikes. The next nine years saw eleven more substantial stoppages, the greatest of which was the miners' lock-out of 1893, which lasted nearly four times as long as the London Dock Strike and cost thirty times as many working days.

Just at the moment of the gasworkers' victory a small strike had broken out at the West India Dock which quickly spread until the whole of the port was at a standstill. The men demanded a rise from 5d to 6d an hour, special payment for overtime, and a minimum period of employment of a half-shift of four hours. With the exception of the stevedores (whose main skill was that they loaded the ships) the vast majority of the dock workers were outside any union. Only the small Tea Porters' and General Labourers' Union, founded in 1887 by Ben Tillett, catered for them. However, during the dispute the strikers flocked into the unions, and Tillett, together with Mann, Burns, and Tom McCarthy of the Stevedores, set out to organise the struggle. The strikers set about publicising their cause by holding processions and open-air meetings, greatly aided by the warm, dry weather of that summer. The strike received wider publicity throughout the world than any previous dispute, and the orderliness of the strikers, supported by the appalling revelations of Booth's survey of the *Life and Labour of the People of London* (the first results of which had recently been published) secured immense public sympathy—as well as much-needed cash.

However, a crisis was reached after two weeks, for blackleg labour was being introduced on a large scale and the strikers' fund was running low. The leaders were divided over a decision to issue a 'No-Work Manifesto' calling for a general strike in London, but on the very day that such a manifesto was drawn up news arrived from Australia that the dockers of Brisbane were sending £150 to the London strike fund. The amount was small, yet it persuaded the strike leaders to withdraw their manifesto (which might seriously have affected public sympathy) and to concentrate henceforth on the picket lines. Altogether over £30,000 in aid came from Australia, a sum which represented more than half of the total strike fund. These donations enabled the strikers to hold on until, after a month's stoppage, a Mansion House Committee, including amongst its members Cardinal Manning and Sydney Bixton, M.P., was able to secure a settlement. All the major demands of the strikers, including the 'dockers' tanner', were granted. Tillett's little union was reorganised s the Dock, Wharf, Riverside, and General Labourers' Union, nd by the end of November it claimed a total of 30,000 members.

The success of the gasworkers and the dockers in London produced an effect all over the country, and led to a great revival of trade unionism. From about 750,000 at the end of 1888, trade union membership rose to 2,025,000 in 1901; growth was spectacular up to 1892, and from 1896 there was a further steady increase. The initial enthusiasm was great. Gasworkers everywhere sought the eight-hour day, and there were fierce battles in Leeds, which at the height of the dispute was like an armed camp, hussars with drawn swords patrolling the streets. Tillett's union was less successful outside London, although a National Union of Dock Labourers developed on Merseyside and soon spread to Scotland and Ireland. A National Amalgamated Union of Labour was started on Tyneside, enrolling dockers and general labourers, as well as spreading to the mining districts. The seamen were organised, there was a revival of agricultural labourers' unions, and a General Railway Workers Union was formed to cater for those railwaymen who were left out of the more exclusive and conservative Amalgamated Society of Railway Servants.

It was to be expected that the employers would launch a counter-attack, which they did in the early 1890s. This, more than the recurrence of depression in 1892, accounts for the subsequent slackening of growth. The employers began to enjoy successes even before the end of 1889. George Livesey, chairman of the South Metropolitan Gas Company, determined to make the gasworkers' victory a short-lived one. They were intent on enforcing a 'closed shop', and Livesey prepared for a strike. Advertisements for substitute labour were drafted and distributed to the press, ready for insertion on the receipt of a telegram, and beds and temporary housing were ordered to accommodate the strike-breakers. A strike eventually broke out in December, and 2000 stokers came out. But 4000 strike-breakers had already been engaged; the company reverted to the twelve-hour shift, and as the new men picked up the necessary skills output rose and the unions' chances of success diminished. A settlement was finally reached in February, but the attempt to win a closed shop failed, as it did at other gasworks. At Hull, described as 'the best organised port' in the country, a well-organised counter-attack by the employers resulted in the sound defeat of the sea-men's unions. At the end of a violent, seven-week strike in 1893 *The Times* wrote; 'At Hull, as elsewhere, the New Unionism has been defeated. But nowhere has the defeat been so decisive, or the surrender so abject.'

In fact, the New Unionism was not defeated, and that it managed to survive was largely due to the factors outlined at the beginning of this section—the real degree of skill which many so-called labourers possessed. On the other hand it has to be admitted that the aspiration of many of the new unions to be 'general' unions of workers in different trades had to be abandoned, for such unions came to depend on their foothold in certain industries or large works rather than on an ability to recruit indiscriminately. This, it would seem, led them to recruit a more stable and regular type of worker than had originally been envisaged, which was another factor in the ability of the new unions to remain in existence.

Although the New Unionism thus came to take on character-istics of the existing types of organisation, there were still impor-tant differences. The leaders were often a generation younger than those of the old unions, and they remained more militant and aggressive. They even looked different, as John Burns noted:

Physically, the 'old' unionists were much bigger than the new. . . . A great number of them looked like respectable city gentlemen; wore very good coats, large watch chains, and high hats and in many cases were of such a splendid build and proportions that they presented an aldermanic, not to say a magisterial form and dignity. Amongst the new delegates [to the 1890 T.U.C.] not a single one wore a tall hat. They looked work-men; they were workmen. They were not such sticklers for formality or court procedure, but were guided more by common sense. (Quoted in Pelling, *A History of British Trade Unionism* Penguin, 1963, page 104.)

Cole describes how the new leaders set out

to build up Unions which would be able to appeal to the entire working class, and to follow a fighting policy based on class solidarity and directed, by implication at any rate, against the capitalist system itself. In short, the 'New' Unions were in intention Socialist, in the sense that the leaders, while they concentrated on immediate 'bread and butter' issues, had as their further objective a definitely Socialist policy of class organisation and action. (Cole, 1948, page 246.)

The idea of solidarity led to a great extension of local Trades Councils through which information and ideas could be exchanged and municipal politics influenced. According to the Webbs, some sixty new trades councils were established in the years 1889-91, which must have more than doubled the previous total.

The old unions did not remain entirely unaffected by the new spirit. Their membership increased considerably in these years, partly because the temporary prosperity favoured their growth just as much as it did that of the new unions, but also because the success of the new unions encouraged non-union craftsmen to join the societies for which they were eligible. The fortunes of the Amalgamated Society of Engineers give an idea of the progress of recruitment. It had grown from 5000 at its foundation in 1851 to 45,000 in 1880 and 54,000 in 1888; by 1891 the membership had increased to over 71,000. The unions in some industries opened their ranks to less skilled workers. The entrance requirements of the Engineers, for example, were reduced in 1892, and the Amalgamated Society of Railway Servants launched its first 'All-Grades Programme' in 1897, actually doubling its membership during that year.

One consequence of the spread of trade unionism to less skilled workers was the increased importance of picketing in industrial disputes. Where strikes were conducted by skilled craftsmen, the scarcity value of their labour made them difficult to replace, but where strikes involved unskilled labour, especially in times of trade depression and unemployment, their effectiveness often depended on the ability of the strikers to exclude blacklegs. Strikes tended to become more violent, for not only was more vigorous picketing necessary, but employers (being less used to trade unions) showed a determination to smash them. For example, the shipowners in 1890 formed a Shipping Federation with its own register of seamen, men being offered jobs only if they undertook not to refuse to work with non-union men. In the following years the Federation supplied blackleg labour for ships and dockside work at ports throughout the country, and initially at least, gave the main support to William Collison's National Free Labour Association, an organisation with the specific object of supplying strike-breakers in industrial disputes. The employers had the support of public opinion, which turned against the new unions after the period of great sympathy at the time of the London Dock Strike. *The Times* was in the van of those who attacked the New Unionism, the leaders of which were described by the conservative *Quarterly Review* as 'our national Mafia'.

In the 1890s the courts followed the changes in public opinion quickly, and the unionists' belief that the legislation of the 1870s had given immunity from prosecution for damages, and had upheld the right to picket, was undermined in a series of hostile court decisions. In a picketing case of 1899 one of the judges of the Court of Appeal declared, 'You cannot make a strike effective without doing more than what is lawful.' Perhaps the most serious point for the trade unions was the way in which the law, which had once appeared to be clear, became less and less so, until in 1902 Asquith declared to the House of Commons that it was 'in an unsatisfactory, confused, and I think I might say, chaotic state'.

The case which brought matters to a head was the Taff Vale Judgment of 1901. The case arose from a strike in August 1900 on the Taff Vale Railway in South Wales. The South African War was approaching its climax, coal prices were running high, and demand for coal was still rising. The railwaymen in South Wales therefore decided to seize the moment both to improve their position and to win recognition for the union. Their attention was focused on the Taff Vale line, which was the essential link between the steam-coal collieries upon which the fleet and merchant marine depended, and the ports. Relations on that line were in any case bad, allegations having been made of the victimisation of a signalman who had previously led a movement for a pay rise. The general manager of the company, Ammon Beasley, described as one who 'loved litigation for its own sake', refused to meet the union and prepared for battle. He advertised for strike-breakers and called in the National Free Labour

Association. He was also determined to make full use of the law, and offered £100 for information against anyone damaging railway property; two men were in fact imprisoned for this offence. He also issued 400 summonses against those who had come out without giving proper notice, and secured a fine of £4 against each of 60 men who were dealt with before the close of the strike. Finally he appealed for an injunction, not only against the leaders of the union as individuals, but also against the union itself. The injunction was granted, but the Court of Appeal reversed the decision. Beasley then took the case to the House of Lords, which restored the initial decision. This made it possible for Beasley to bring an action for damages against the union, and in a subsequent case in December 1902 the two sides agreed to settle for a payment by the union of £23,000 to cover damages and the company's costs. Together with its own legal costs, this must have brought the total cost to the Amalgamated Society of Railway Servants to around £42,000.

The judgment struck at the very existence of trade unions, and the leaders became convinced that a change in the law was essential to make the position of unions secure. Neither the Liberal Party nor the Conservative Party was in a great hurry to introduce legislation, however, so many unionists were won over to the idea of independent representation. Before 1900 those trade unionists who sat in Parliament had almost invariably been sponsored by the Liberal Party, thus earning the title 'Lib-Labs'. A Labour Representation Committee had been formed by the T.U.C. in 1900, but when trade unions were invited to affiliate, the response was meagre. The Taff Vale decision changed this, and by 1903-4 a total of 165 trade unions with a combined membership of nearly a million had affiliated. In the general election of 1906 the Labour Representation Committee succeeded in returning 29 of its members to Parliament, and in the same year changed its name to the Labour Party.

In 1903 the Conservatives had appointed a Royal Commission to consider what action should be taken in the face of the Taff Vale decision. No trade unionist was given a seat, and the unions refused to give evidence. By accident or design the Report was not published until after the election of 1906, so it fell to the Liberal government to deal with the situation. The recommendations of the Royal Commission fell far short of the demands of the trade unions, and when the government introduced legislation on the lines of the Report the entire trade union movement was quickly up in arms. The Labour Party, with full backing from the trade unions, pressed strongly for its own alternative Bill and such was the new climate of opinion that the government dropped both the Royal Commission's report and its own Bill capitulating almost entirely to the unions. The resulting Trade Disputes Act of 1906 gave the unions almost all that they wanted the most important section of the Act being the fourth, which laid down that:

An action against a trade union, whether of workmen or masters, or against any members or officials thereof on behalf of themselves and all other members of the trade union, in respect of any tortious act alleged to have been committed by or on behalf of the trade union, shall not be entertained by any court.

A tortious act is any civil wrong (as distinct from a criminal act) other than a breach of contract; this section therefore placed the trade unions in a privileged position, for their funds appeared to be protected from all civil proceedings.

The trade union movement had not yet suffered all its blows from the courts, however, for in 1909 was delivered the Osborne Judgment, which ranks second only to the Taff Vale Judgment for its effect on the unions. In one respect the two cases are related, for just as the Taff Vale case convinced the trade unions of the value of an independent Labour Party in Parliament, so the Osborne Judgment convinced the Socialists of the financial value of trade union affiliation. By a coincidence both cases involved the Amalgamated Society of Railway Servants.

W. V. Osborne was Walthamstow branch secretary of the A.S.R.S., and as a member of the Liberal Party objected to the financial support which his union gave to the Labour Party. The action which he took to restrain the A.S.R.S. from taking a political levy went to the House of Lords. There it was decided that the support of a political party was beyond the powers granted by the Acts of 1871 and 1876. The decision immediately cut off the subsistence allowances from the unions which were the principal source of income for Labour M.P.s. Agitation quickly arose to reverse the decision, and at the 1910 T.U.C. a resolution to that effect was carried by 1,717,000 votes to 13,000. In the following year a House of Commons resolution authorised the state payment of M.Ps., and in 1913 the Trade Union Act laid down that where a majority of members approved a trade union's political objects, it could spend money on political pur- poses provided that a separate fund was kept and individual members were free to 'contract out' of making payments.

Measured in terms of working days lost, the period from 1899 to 1907 was one of industrial peace. This has traditionally been ascribed to the effects of the Taff Vale Judgment. But the period during which this could have affected the strike statistics consisted at most of the four years from 1902 to 1905, for by the election of January 1906 it was highly probable that the law would be altered. Other factors were also at work. The minds of many leaders of the trade union movement were on politics rather than on industrial action, much energy going into the building up of the Labour Representation Committee. Trade conditions were also unfavourable to any sustained advance until about 1910. There is the further possibility that the attitude of employers changed, for the depressed years from 1902 to 1905 were ripe for smashing the unions, yet there are relatively few examples of organised employers taking advantage of the situation. Stoppages in the 1890s had led to the establishment of systematic collective bar- gaining in the engineering, coal-mining and cotton industries, and it could be argued that employers, as well as workers, were anxious for the new methods to work.

The industrial peace was shattered from 1911 on, for the years leading up to the First World War were a period of peculiar malaise, the workers' rebellion being matched by the rebellion of the women. Behind the unrest of the workers lay the spread of syndicalist ideas from France and America. In France, Georges Sorel was shaping the philosophy of the general strike as a political weapon, while the belief that 'the working class and the employing class have nothing in common' led to the setting up in America in 1905 of the Industrial Workers of the World, pledged to the idea of 'One Big Union' of workers and direct action to bring about social revolution. Tom Mann brought the syndicalist ideas to Britain, but the 'amalgamation' movement which he launched did not get far. In 1910 he formed the National Transport Workers Federation, which included dockers and seamen, but not railway workers. The dockers and the seamen were in the van of strike action in 1911, although these years also witnessed the first national railway strike.

The pre-war record of working days lost was set in 1912 when 41 million working days were lost (an average of four days for every worker in the country) as against an average of 7 million working days over the previous twenty years. The miners' strike of that year was by far the largest that had ever occurred in Great Britain, for it involved over a million workers (850,000 of whom were directly parties to the dispute) whereas all the strikes of 1911 put together had directly involved only 830,000 workers.

An attempt by the National Transport Workers Federation to call a national strike of transport workers in 1912 proved a failure, but the formation of the Triple Alliance of miners, railwaymen and transport workers (1913-15) brought the threat of something approaching a general strike appreciably nearer. This particular spectre was to haunt the country after the First World War.

Further Reading

General

E. J. Hobsbawm, *Industry and Empire* (Penguin 1969)

Peter Mathias, *The First Industrial Nation* (Methuen 1969)

David Landes, *The Unbound Prometheus, Technological Change and Industrial Development in Western Europe from 1750 to the Present* (C.U.P. 1969)

T. K. Derry and Trevor Williams, *A Short History of Technology* (O.U.P. 1960)

Phyllis Deane and W. A. Cole, *British Economic Growth, 1688–1959* (C.U.P. 1969)

J. H. Clapham, *Economic History of Modern Britain* (C.U.P. three vols. 1926–1938)

S. G. Checkland, *The Rise of Industrial Society in England, 1815–1885* (Longmans 1964)

W. Ashworth, *An Economic History of England, 1870–1939* (Methuen 1960)

R. S. Sayers, *A History of Economic Change in England, 1880–1939* (O.U.P. 1967)

Philip S. Bagwell and G. E. Mingay, *Britain and America 1850–1939. A Study of Economic Change* (Routledge 1970)

J. F. C. Harrison, *The Early Victorians, 1832–1851* (Weidenfeld 1971)

Geoffrey Best, *Mid-Victorian Britain* (Weidenfeld 1971)

Chapter I

W. O. Henderson, *Industrial Britain Under the Regency* (Cass 1968)

T. S. Ashton, *An Economic History of England. The Eighteenth Century* (Methuen 1955)

T. S. Ashton, *Economic Fluctuations in England, 1700–1800* (O.U.P. 1959)

T. S. Ashton, *The Industrial Revolution, 1760–1830* (O.U.P. 1948)

Phyllis Deane, *The First Industrial Revolution* (C.U.P. 1965)

Paul Mantoux, *The Industrial Revolution in the Eighteenth Century* (English translation, 1928. Cape 1961)

M. W. Flinn, *Origins of the Industrial Revolution* (Longmans 1966)

R. M. Hartwell, *The Causes of the Industrial Revolution in England* (Methuen 1967)

R. M. Hartwell, *The Industrial Revolution in England* (Historical Association 1965)

D. V. Glass and D. E. C. Eversley, *Population in History* (Arnold 1965)

M. W. Flinn, *British Population Growth, 1700–1850* (Macmillan 1970)

M. Drake, *Population in Industrialisation* (Methuen 1969)

A. E. Musson and Eric Robinson, *Science and Technology in the Industrial Revolution* (Manchester U.P. 1969)

Chapter II

J. D. Chambers and G. E. Mingay, *The Agricultural Revolution, 1750–1880* (Batsford 1966)

Lord Ernle, *English Farming Past and Present* (1912. Reissued with new introduction, Heinemann 1961)

G. E. Mingay, *Enclosure and the Small Farmer in the Age of the Industrial Revolution* (Macmillan 1968)

E. L. Jones, *The Development of English Agriculture, 1815–1873* (Macmillan 1968)

J. D. Chambers, 'Enclosure and Labour Supply in the Industrial Revolution,' reprinted in E. L. Jones, *Agriculture and Economic Growth 1650–1815* (Methuen 1967)

E. L. Jones, 'The Agricultural Labour Market in England, 1793–1872' (*Ec. Hist. Review* 1964)

A. J. Taylor, 'Progress and Poverty in Britain, 1780–1850' (*History* 1960)

R. M. Hartwell, 'The Rising Standard of Living in England, 1800–1850' (*Ec. Hist. Review* 1961)

E. J. Hobsbawm, *Labouring Men* (Weidenfeld, reissued with minor corrections 1968)

E. J. Hobsbawm and R. M. Hartwell, 'The Standard of Living During the Industrial Revolution. A Discussion' (*Ec. Hist. Review* 1963)

J. E. Williams, 'The British Standard of Living, 1750–1850' (*Ec. Hist. Review* 1966)

R. S. Neale, 'The Standard of Living, 1780–1844: A Regional and Class Study' (*Ec. Hist. Review* 1966)

S. Pollard and D. W. Crossley, *The Wealth of Britain* (Batsford 1968)

John Burnett, *Plenty and Want* (Penguin 1968)

John Burnett, *A History of the Cost of Living* (Penguin 1969)

W. H. Chaloner, *The Hungry Forties* (Historical Association 1957)

S. Pollard, *The Genesis of Modern Management* (Penguin 1965)

J. T. Ward, *The Factory Movement, 1830–1855* (Macmillan 1962)

J. T. Ward, *The Factory System* (two vols. David & Charles 1970)

E. P. Thompson, *The Making of the English Working Class* (Gollancz 1963)

G. D. H. Cole, *A Short History of the British Working Class Movement* (Allen & Unwin 1948)

G. D. H. Cole and A. W. Filson, *British Working Class Movements, Select Documents, 1789–1875* (Macmillan 1965)

W. H. Chaloner, *The Skilled Artisan During the Industrial Revolution* (Historical Association 1969)

Duncan Bythell, *The Handloom Weavers* (C.U.P. 1969)

J. L. and Barbara Hammond, *The Skilled Labourer, 1760–1832* (Longmans 1920)

F. O. Darvall, *Popular Disturbances and Public Order in Regency England* (1934, reissued by Oxford 1970)

Malcolm Thomis, *The Luddites* (David & Charles 1970)

L. M. Munby (Ed.), *The Luddites and other Essays* (Katanka 1971)

J. L. and Barbara Hammond, *The Village Labourer* (1911, Guild Books 1948)

E. J. Hobsbawm and George Rudé, *Captain Swing* (Lawrence & Wischart 1969)

E. W. Bovill, *English Country Life, 1780–1830* (O.U.P. 1962)

Barbara Kerr, *Bound to the Soil* (Baker 1968)

A. J. Peacock, *Bread or Blood* (Gollancz 1965)

P. H. J. H. Gosden, *The Friendly Societies in England, 1815–1875* (Manchester U.P. 1961)

S. Pollard, 'Nineteenth Century Co-operation. From Community Building to Shopkeeping,' in Asa Briggs and John Saville, *Essays in Labour History* (Macmillan 1967)

Henry Pelling, *A History of British Trade Unionism* (Penguin 1963)

A. Aspinall, *The Early English Trade Unions* (Batchworth Press 1949)

G. D. H. Cole, *Attempts at General Union, 1818–1834* (Macmillan 1955)

W. H. Oliver, 'The Consolidated Trades' Union of 1834' (*Ec. Hist. Review* 1964)

J. F. C. Harrison, *Robert Owen and the Owenites in Britain and America* (Routledge 1969)

E. Royston Pike, *Human Documents of the Industrial Revolution in Britain* (Allen & Unwin 1966)

Chapter III

C. Hobhouse, *1851 and the Crystal Palace* (John Murray 1950)

Asa Briggs, 'The Crystal Palace and the Men of 1851' in *Victorian People* (Penguin 1954)

J. R. T. Hughes, *Fluctuations in Trade, Industry and Finance, 1850–1860* (O.U.P. 1960)

C. P. Kindleburger, *Economic Growth in France and Britain, 1851–1950* (Harvard U.P. 1964)

C. Savage, *An Economic History of Transport* (Hutchinson 1966)

H. J. Dyos and D. H. Aldcroft, *British Transport, An Economic Survey from the Seventeenth Century to the Twentieth* (Leicester U.P. 1969)

Michael Robbins, *The Railway Age* (Penguin 1966)

Jack Simmons, *Railways in Britain* (Macmillan 1968)

Harold Perkin, *The Age of the Railway*, (Panther 1970)

Terry Coleman, *The Railway Navvies* (Penguin 1968)

R. S. Lambert, *The Railway King* (Allen & Unwin 1964)

H. Parris, *Government and the Railways in Nineteenth Century Britain* (Routledge 1965)

J. R. Kellett, *The Impact of Railways on Victorian Cities* (Routledge 1969)

M. C. Reed (Ed.), *Railways in the Victorian Economy* (David & Charles 1969)

Charles Hadfield, *British Canals* (Pan 1971)

John Copeland, *Roads and their Traffic, 1750–1850* (David & Charles 1968)

W. A. Baker, *From Paddle Steamer to Nuclear Ship* (Watts 1965)

Samuel Smiles, *Lives of the Engineers* (three vols. 1862. Reprinted by David & Charles 1968)

W. K. V. Gale, *The British Iron and Steel Industry: A Technical History* (David & Charles 1967)

Charlotte Erickson, *British Industrialists: Steel and Hosiery, 1850–1950* (C.U.P. 1959)

B. C. Hunt, *The Development of the Business Corporation in England, 1800–1867* (O.U.P. 1936)

H. A. Shannon, 'The Coming of General Limited Liability,' and 'The Limited Liability Companies of 1866–1883' both reprinted vol. I of *Essays in Economic History*, edited by E. M. Carus-Wilson (Arnold 1954)

W. V. Morgan and W. A. Thomas, *The Stock Exchange* (Elek 1962)

T. S. Ashton and R. S. Sayers (Eds.), *Papers in English Monetary History* (O.U.P. 1953)

W. F. Crick and J. E. Wadsworth, *100 Years of Joint Stock Banking* (Hodder & Stoughton 1936)

J. H. Clapham, *The Bank of England* (C.U.P. 1944)

C. S. Orwin and E. H. Whetham, *History of British Agriculture, 1846–1914* (Longmans 1964)

D. C. Moore, 'The Corn Laws and High Farming' (*Ec. Hist. Review* 1964)

E. H. Wetham, 'The London Milk Trade, 1860–1900' (*Ec. Hist. Review* 1964)

James Caird, *English Agriculture in 1850–1851* (1852. Cass Reprint 1968)

G. E. Fussell, *The Farmer's Tools* (Melrose 1952)

Chapter IV

W. O. Henderson, *Britain and Industrial Europe, 1750–1870* (Leicester U.P. 1954)

A. J. Youngson, 'The opening up of New Territories' in *Cambridge Economic History of Europe*, Vol. VI part I (C.U.P. 1965)

A. H. Imlah, *Economic Elements in the Pax Britannica* (Harvard U.P. 1958)

Werner Schlote, *British Overseas Trade from 1700 to the 1930s* (English edition, Blackwell 1952)

Lucy Brown, *The Board of Trade and the Free Trade Movement, 1830–1842* (O.U.P. 1958)

Norman McCord, *Free Trade* (David & Charles 1970)

Norman McCord, *The Anti-Corn Law League, 1838–1846* (Allen & Unwin 1958)

Barry Turner, *Free Trade and Protection* (Longmans 1971)

S. B. Saul, *Studies in British Overseas Trade, 1870–1914* (Liverpool U.P. 1960)

L. H. Jenks, *The Migration of British Capital to 1875* (Knopf 1927)

A. K. Cairncross, *Home and Foreign Investment, 1870–1913* (C.U.P. 1953)

A. R. Hall, *The Export of Capital from Britain, 1870–1914* (Methuen 1968)

J. Saville, *Rural Depopulation in England and Wales, 1851–1951* (Routledge 1957)

Brinley Thomas, *Migration and Economic Growth* (C.U.P. 1954)

H. I. Cowan, *British Emigration to British North America* (University of Toronto Press 1961)

W. S. Shepperson, *British Emigration to North America* (Blackwell 1957

E. G. Hartmann, *Americans from Wales* (Christopher Publishing House, U.S.A. 1967)

Oscar Handlin (Ed.), *Immigration as a Factor in American History* (Prentice-Hall, Inc., Eaglewood Cliffs, New Jersey 1959)

W. S. Shepperson, *Emigration and Disenchantment* (Oklahoma U.P. 1965)

Frank Thistlethwaite, 'The Atlantic Migration of the Pottery Industry' (*Ec. Hist. Review* 1958)

Ross Duncan, 'Case Studies in Emigration: Cornwall, Gloucestershire and New South Wales, 1877–1886' (*Ec. Hist. Review* 1963)

David S. Macmillan, *Scotland and Australia, 1788–1850* (O.U.P. 1967)

John Prebble, *The Highland Clearances* (Secker & Warburg 1963)

Philip Gaskell, *Morvern Transformed* (C.U.P. 1968)

Charlotte Erickson, 'The Encouragement of Emigration by British Trade Unions, 1850–1900' (*Population Studies 1949*)

Chapter V

H. L. Beales, 'The "Great Depression" in Industry and Trade,' reprinted in *Essays in Economic History*, Vol. 1 (Arnold 1954)

S. B. Saul, *The Myth of the Great Depression, 1873–1896* (Macmillan 1969)

D. H. Aldcroft (Ed.), *The Development of British Industry and Foreign Competition, 1875–1914* (Allen & Unwin 1968)

D. H. Aldcroft and H. W. Richardson, *The British Economy, 1870–1939* (Macmillan 1969)

A. E. Musson, 'British Industrial Growth during the "Great Depression" (1873-1896): Some Comments' (*Ec. Hist. Review 1963*)

Charles Wilson, 'Economy and Society in Late Victorian Britain' (*Ec. Hist. Review* 1965)

H. J. Habakkuk, *American and British Technology in the Nineteenth Century* (C.U.P. 1962)

S. B. Paul, *Technological Change: The United States and Britain in the Nineteenth Century* (Methuen 1970)

T. W. Fletcher, 'The Great Depression of English Agriculture, 1873–1896' reprinted in W. E. Minchinton (Ed.), *Essays in Agrarian History*, Vol. II (David & Charles 1968)

H. A. Clegg, Alan Fox and A. F. Thompson, *A History of British Trade Unionism since 1889*, Vol. 1 (1889–1910) (O.U.P. 1964)

J. P. D. Dunbabin, 'The Revolt of the Field' (*Past and Present* 1963)

Pamela Horn, *Joseph Arch* (Roundwood 1971)

A. E. P. Duffy, 'New Unionism in Britain, 1889-1890: A Reappraisal' (*Ec. Hist. Review* 1961)

John Lovell, *Stevedores and Dockers* (Macmillan 1969)

John Saville, 'Trade Unions and Free Labour: The Background to the Taff Vale Decision' in *Essays in Labour History*

G. Dangerfield, *The Strange Death of Liberal England* (First published 1935. McGibbon and Kee 1966)

Index